STUDIES IN THE MAKING OF
THE ENGLISH PROTESTANT
TRADITION

STUDIES IN THE MAKING OF
THE ENGLISH PROTESTANT TRADITION

(Mainly in the Reign of Henry VIII)

BY

E. G. RUPP, B.D.

CAMBRIDGE
AT THE UNIVERSITY PRESS
1966

PUBLISHED BY
THE SYNDICS OF THE CAMBRIDGE UNIVERSITY PRESS

Bentley House, 200 Euston Road, London, N.W.1
American Branch: 32 East 57th Street, New York, N.Y. 10022
West African Office: P.M.B. 5181, Ibadan, Nigeria

First printed 1947
Reissued 1966

First printed in Great Britain at the University Press, Cambridge
(Brooke Crutchley, University Printer)
Reprinted by photolithography in the Republic of Ireland
by Browne and Nolan Limited, Dublin

To
CHARLES SMYTH
and
NORMAN SYKES

PREFACE

THE essays in this volume were begun, continued and ended during the sustained air-raids of 1940–1 and 1944–5, when the limitation of duties concerning pastoral care in south-east London provided intervals when reading and writing were possible, albeit under conditions not always ideal for calm reflection. Some of the material in chapters I, II, VI and VII was included in an essay, 'Reformers and Reformation in England in the reigns of Henry VIII and Edward VI', which was awarded the Archbishop Cranmer Prize in 1940. War conditions made it impossible to include the reign of Edward VI with its great liturgical and confessional documents within the present volume, but the hope that it may be possible to resume that period at some future date accounts for the present omission of details concerning the liturgical changes during 1537–47, of a full account of the work of Hugh Latimer, and of the great Eucharistic controversy. I think the last attempt to survey the English Reformation from this point of view was *The Lutheran Movement in England* of H. E. Jacobs (1890). That work is still of value, but many discoveries, and notably the publication in 1905 of the 'Wittenberg Articles of 1536' by Mentz, have made it a book which must now be used with caution. The account I have given in chapter VI of the negotiations between Henry VIII and the German Protestants I believe to be the fullest yet published in English, and some connected account of them was more than overdue.

The recording of acknowledgements is one of the devices by which the undistinguished compound for their own obscurity by making more reputable scholars go bail on their behalf, but decency demands that some be mentioned here, even though the recital of their names does me more honour than my thanks can do them good. Some of those who taught me most are beyond gunshot of my salute: Dr H. Maldwyn Hughes, beloved and honoured by all his students, whom to know was the most inspiring of all lessons; Dr J. P. Whitney and Mr J. G. Sikes who took pains and showed kindness in nursing my studies in Ecclesiastical history; and Sir Edwyn Hoskyns in whose lecture-room I found many lessons and picked up clues which I understood much later; Professor Strohl and my good companions in the Thomas Stift at Stras- bourg, and notably R. F. Aldwinckle, Einar Molland, and Theo Preiss; and Dr Karl Barth in whose lecture-room at Basle the word Protestantism, which had held a dying fall for me, became urgently alive. To Dr R. Newton Flew I owe debts the extent of which he alone understands. With firm and kindly hands he kept me on the course until my studies climbed from duty to vocation. He has given constantly of time and encouragement and made time to read and give advice upon this present volume. Canon Charles Smyth read the essays which gained the Cranmer Prize in 1940 and never did examiner more heartily return good for evil: he has proved his own saying that Academe is the greatest co-operative society in the world by rare and generous friendship to a young student of another communion. Professor Norman Sykes as teacher, tutor and friend is the one from whom largely derive whatever ideals I have of the 'verax historicus', and he has pursued me with practical benison. My wife endured much of the pains of book composition in war-time, and stood up to it as gallantly as to Hitler's bombs which, as I have indicated, were the *sine qua non* of this volume.

THE MANSE
CHISLEHURST

July 1945

CONTENTS

THE following works of reference have been denoted by abbreviations:

Arch.	*Archaeologia.*
H.B.S.	Henry Bradshaw Soc.
Burnet.	*History of the Reformation*, 1829.
Burnet (Pocock)	ed. Pocock, 1865.
C.A.S.	Cambridge Antiquarian Soc.
Camden Soc.	The Camden Soc. Publications.
C.Mod.H.	*Cambridge Modern History.*
C.Q.R.	*Church Quarterly Review.*
C.R.	Corpus Reformatorum edition of the works of the Reformers (ed. Bretschneider).
D.N.B.	*Dictionary of National Biography.*
Dict. Théol. Cath.	*Dictionnaire de théologie catholique* (ed. Vacant).
E.E.T.S.	Early English Text Soc.
E.H.R.	*English Historical Review.*
Foxe, *A. & M.*	*Acts and Monuments* (ed. Pratt).
L. & P. Henry VIII	*Letters and State Papers of Henry VIII* (ed. Brewer and Gairdner).
O.C.M.	*Oxford Companion to Music* (ed. Scholes).
P.S.	Parker Society publications.
R.S.L.	Royal Society of Literature.
Theol. Wort.	*Theologisches Wörterbuch* (ed. Kittel).
V.C.H.	*The Victoria County Histories.*
W.E.	The Weimar edition of the works of Luther.

INTRODUCTION

THE English Reformation is not wholly to be explained in terms of that conspiracy by which a lustful monarch and predatory gentry combined to plunder the Church and rend the unity of Christendom. It had, after all, something to do with the beliefs of Christian men, and that not only in the breaking of an old order, but in the making of the new.

The great political themes have largely occupied the attention of modern historians. The great Acts of the Reformation Parliament, carrying through in a few months a profound political and juridical revolution, forming a National Church under the Royal Supremacy, made deep and impressive impact upon the religious development of the English people. The dissolution of the monasteries, the dispossession of the religious, the destruction of the shrines, these, too, were formative events, not least in the creation of that weight of vested interest which Mary herself was powerless to recoil.

But this is not the whole tale, and there remains that ferment, theological, liturgical and religious, without which the story of the sixteenth century might have been the tale of the destructive virus of human greed and human pride. It has long been the fashion to castigate the greed of the new gentry, even though the reproach of modern writers lacks the verve with which Tyndale and Latimer, Bradford and Lever impeached their generation. Yet vested interest in ecclesiastical property did not begin when the Tudor landlords clung to the lands they had bought at bargain prices. Covetousness is a very horrid thing, but he would be over-bold who should consider it to be a vice peculiar to the laity. Langland attacked 'Lady Meed' and her clerical devotees long before Shakespeare and the Tudor Statutes were complaining of 'Tickling Commodity'. And for both there was some excuse.

The financial embarrassments of the Crown were not the adventitious effects of royal extravagance. The attempt of the monarch to live of his own is a leading theme of the sixteenth as it becomes a central constitutional problem in the seventeenth century. As with the King, so with the landlords. While the merchants were gaining in political influence and social prestige, the gentry were feeling the pinch. It was a time of great social and economic disturbance, the import of which was hardly realized by those who had to cope with the resulting problems. Statesmen, courtiers and clerical moralists spent much of their best energies in a brave attempt to put back the clock to the good old days which never were. The wealth of the Church offered brief respite from urgent problems. To despoil it was short-sighted, altogether apart from the moral issue, and it only aggravated problems by postponing the crisis underlying them. But later generations have not always been wiser, and 'sufficient unto the day' as a political and economic nostrum is painfully modern.

Again, the spirit of individualist secularism did not originate in the sinister Protestant setting of sixteenth-century Germany, England or Holland, but in Italy, in the heart of Catholic Christendom where it had never died, though perhaps it had slumbered, since the ancient world. The Church of Santa Croce in Florence is the Westminster Abbey of modern man. Who views there the monuments which that city has raised to her children, Dante, Michelangelo, Leonardo, Bruni, Galileo, Machiavelli, cannot doubt where lies the watershed between medieval and modern Europe, and in all essentials the secular spirit will be found in the cities and states of medieval Italy. Thomas Cromwell, hobnobbing with Italian prelates, princes and merchant bankers, was meeting men no better and no worse than several generations of their fathers whose portraits fill the art galleries of the world, and which can be labelled 'Portrait of a hard-faced Business Man'. The hands are those of the Courtier of Castiglione, but the eyes and mouth belong to Samuel Smiles.[1]

But our concern is with the Reformers, the men who believed and lived by the doctrines which created the theology, the liturgy, the ecclesiastical disciplines of the Protestant Churches, as well as a certain way of life which the modern world may soon wistfully remember. There is a surprising agreement among historians as to the depth of the English Protestant tradition. Even Mr Belloc admits the intensity of English Protestantism, though in his case the judgement would seem to rest upon a confusion of Protestantism and Original Sin. Anglo-Catholic and liberal historians alike seem willing to admit some value in that tradition, however preferable some alternative 'along Erasmian lines'.

The Reformers themselves are another matter. 'Really I hate the Reformers more and more', wrote Hurrell Froude;[2] this attitude towards the makers of the Reformation received a new impetus with the Oxford Movement. As an antidote to an uncritical acceptance of the tradition of Foxe and Burnet, it was all to the good: the vitriolic essays with which S. R. Maitland castigated the early Reformers must have deflated a good deal of quite unhealthy romanticism. But the rabble of antinomian fanatics, time-serving cowards, and perverted heresiarchs of the modern caricature are farther from the truth. If the Reformers were not the palely idyllic figures of the Victorian Sunday school prize, neither were they the leering, gibbering monsters from a tale by Poe.

The Reformers did not fare much better with the liberal historians. There was after all something plain and homely in Hurrell Froude's denunciation. J. A. Froude seems to look down from another and superior world with disdain: 'We have been led forward unconsciously into a recognition of a

---

[1] See von Martin, *Sociology of the Renaissance*, 1944.
[2] H. Froude, *Remains*, vol. i, pp. 389, 434. London, 1838.

broader Christianity...in this happy change of disposition we have a difficulty in comprehending the intensity with which the different religious parties in England detested each other.'[1] He and his many successors, more at home with a political, social or philosophic yardstick than with the categories of Christian theology, have tended to deplore the sweat and heat of this battle for 'opinions', this preoccupation of the Reformers with what Mr A. L. Rowse, with scant regard for the meaning of words, loves to call 'their idiot controversies'. The Reformers are in a fair way to becoming peripheral annotations to the story of the English Reformation.

There is room for more sympathetic attention to the men whose beliefs and practices were the root of the English Protestant tradition. In the making of that tradition the years 1520–88 were formative years, not in the sense that there was no catastrophic change of content or development afterwards, but because a direction was given to currents in the life of church and nation which still persists.

Within that period, the reign of Henry VIII is the time of ferment rather than of spectacular achievement, but without an appreciation of the labour of that first generation, the work of their successors cannot fairly be assessed. The studies in this volume do not attempt to tell the whole story, since to do so would involve mere text-book repetition of much that has been ably told in recent years. If these pages are little concerned with the great political and ecclesiastical acts carried through by the government it is not that their significance is undervalued. Yet it may be that some account of figures less known and writings half-forgotten will bring more sharply into relief the characteristics of the time.

The Reformers had a strong sense of the unity of Christendom. They were not concerned to avoid or seek to learn from Wittenberg or Geneva or Canterbury, but with the faith once

[1] J. A. Froude, *The Reign of Henry VIII*, p. 1.

for all delivered to the saints. They were wittingly engaged in
a life and death struggle in which they stood nearer to their
contemporary enemies than to those moderns, who until the
advent of the new Wars of (Secular) Religion hardly believed
in truths worth dying for. But with awful sight they were
prepared to pay the cost of their claim to rebuild faith and
order and discipline in accordance with Holy Scripture, the
Primitive Church and the guidance of the Holy Spirit. That it
was Holy Scripture seen through their eyes, and a Primitive
Church viewed from a one-sided interpretation of Christian
origins, and that they were hasty to affirm that what seemed to
them good was also approved of the Holy Ghost is true.
Eppur si muove. Those who value the faith, the liturgies, the
hymns and spiritual songs, the values which have been given
to the world by the English Protestant tradition need not
grudge a homage to the men who made it.

In other days there was a portrait of Edward VI in the
National Portrait Gallery. It was a trick in perspective such
as would delight the Renaissance heart. Stand in front of it,
and all was askew: nose, eyes and ears streaked across the
canvas, hideously distorted. But there was a corner, an angle
from which the disproportion magically vanished and the face
was seen clearly and shapely. To each aspect of history there
is such an angle. If it be true as Dr Maynard Smith has
suggested in a fine study of *Pre-Reformation England* that sym-.
pathy is a truer guide than prejudice, it may be that in these
pages will be found something hidden from splenetic fury or
cold disdain.

Sixteenth-century England was not a quiet place for a man
with a conscience. London during the Six Articles, the West
in the time of Edward VI, all England in the time of Mary,
these were places where men did not prudently noise abroad
their secret thoughts. The underground movement, the secret
police, the agent provocateur, the torture room and execution

squad, the savage penalties exacted by a government which was sore afraid; plague, pestilence and famine, battle, murder, and sudden death. They had not much to learn from us. Yet for most people life went on more normally than the history books might suggest. And for our Reformers life was not all preachments and public trials. There were good years of quiet friendship, family life and sunlit gardens: even our martyrs died not many times before their death. And at the height of the Reformation, Cambridge could find time for its own controversies and Gardiner quarrelled with Cheke about the new pronunciation of Greek, or rated Parker because his students outwent the proprieties in their boisterous performance of *Pammachius*.

Has the story a moral? In these days when the moralists are in disrepute, it would be tempting to abandon the effort to find meaning in the tale: 'Ripeness is all.' But the ecclesiastical historian differs from the secular historian in this, that he sees the life in history of that which intersects it from beyond, a community whose life is hid with Christ in God, even when it seems most clearly part of the world. This makes him more, not less, concerned with the scandal of historical particularity. But it does encourage him to believe that there is a meaning, and that his search for truth will lend discretion to approve the things that are excellent, and to test things that differ. It is this awareness which he shares with the Reformers. They stand and fall, not by the judgement of political expediency or human religiosity, but by the faith they most certainly believed. They knew this, and it was the strength which fed them, and they grasped the hands of fathers and brethren across many centuries because they also confessed: 'Credo in sanctam ecclesiam catholicam, sanctorum communionem.'

Part One

CHAPTER I

'THE SECRET MULTITUDE OF TRUE PROFESSORS'

ANY due assessment of the causes and consequences of the English Reformation must take into account the survival of Lollardy. The new doctrines from the Continent found a ready made and hungry audience among those whom John Foxe named 'the secret multitude of true professors', who prepared for the development of radical and sacramentarian doctrines in the reign of Edward VI and Mary. For the growth of the Anabaptist heresy in those reigns is not wholly to be explained in terms of foreign infiltration. In the high matter of the Sacrament of the Altar new Anabaptist was but old Lollard writ Dutch, and the epithets condemned as irreverent and blasphemous by the government were no transliterated blasphemies of foreign origin, but like 'Jack in a Box' and 'Round Robin' scurrilities homely and hearty, in use among the Lollards for long enough.

In the reign of Henry VIII the Lollards had their own characteristics. The changes and chances of a century of intermittent repression had not left them unmarked. Like other 'underground' movements, both medieval and modern, they could only persist under a mask of subterfuge and evasion, and developed their own tortuous casuistry which engendered abjuration rather than encouraged martyrdom.

In this period, when the name 'Lollard' was fast becoming common speech for 'heretic', it seems best to refer to them by the name by which they were called among their neighbours, as the 'known' or the 'just fast' men.[1]

---

[1] Foxe says that the name 'known men' was first given after the Great Abjuration of the Amersham Lollards in 1506, but a statement by Reginald

The failure of Sir John Oldcastle's rebellion had discredited Lollardy as a popular movement, and losing the support of any influential class it drew its adherents henceforth from among the lower orders. During the Civil Wars it profited from the preoccupations of the secular authorities, while the absence in England of any office of the Inquisition left the destruction of heretical pravity to the more cumbrous machinery of the episcopal courts, where much might depend on the personal disposition of the individual bishop. 'My Lord that is dead was a good man', said the 'known man' Richard Wright, 'and divers known men were called before him, but he sent them home again, bidding them that they should live among their neighbours as good Christian men should do.' But he was misled when he hoped that the successor of Bishop Smith might prove of like accommodation.

The persecutions in Kent in 1499 and in the Amersham district in 1506[1] show that the 'known men' had grown over-bold, or perhaps a little careless. The first persecution might have been such an isolated burst of zeal as was wont to occur at intervals in each century. The second was a more notable scare, but could not seriously have damaged the movement, even though the abjuration and confession of many members must have left a pretty legacy of domestic scandals to a sect which drew much of its strength from certain households. But the leaders escaped if we may accept Thomas Holmes' boast that 'the greatest cobs were behind'. The Bishops of Lincoln and London, Longland and Fitz James, found the movement to be alarming in its size and extent. It was alleged of Thomas Man, one of the four lay teachers of the movement, that he

Pecock attests its use a century before. Pecock attributes it to their claim to 'know' Scripture and to their rendering of 1 Cor. xiv. 8: 'If any man unknoweth he shall be unknown.' R. Pecock, *Repressor of the Clergy* (Rolls Series, 19), vol. 1, p. 53. Also Foxe, *A. & M.* vol. IV, p. 243.

[1] J. Gairdner, *Lollardy and the Reformation*, vol. 1, pp. 274–5. Foxe, *A. & M.* vol. IV, p. 123.

made his circuit between 'Amersham, London, Billericay, Chelmsford, Stratford, and the Forest of Windsor and that he and his wife had turned six or seven hundred people into those opinions that he was abjured of'.

Court proceedings brought to light some of the practices and beliefs of these men. Much of their strength obviously derived from certain families where the Lollard tradition was handed down for generations. This was a great source of strength but also a weakness, since it put a weapon into the hand of any sufferer from domestic discord, the prodigal son-in-law or the jealous kinsman.

Such families were the Durdants, the Bartlets and the Colins. They met with their friends in houses, or barns, or fields. The meetings in country houses had their London counterparts in meetings which ranged from family prayers round the supper table to the organized lectures of the 'night schoole' revealed to Sir Thomas More.[1]

Foxe says that 'in four principal points they stood against the Church of Rome: in pilgrimage, in adoration of saints, in reading of Scripture Books in English and in the carnal presence of Christ's body in the Sacrament'. At the examination of John Pykas at Colchester it was categorically stated that 'none of the "known men" ever sets up lights before images'. There, in antagonism to the ecclesiastical 'good orks' of their day, and with concomitant anti-clericalism to add spleen, was the seed-bed of later iconoclasticism, but in this period it was a more prudent idiosyncrasy which by itself

[1] 'John Barret, Goldsmith of London was heard in his own house before his wife and maid there present to recite the epistle of James which epistle he had perfectly without book.' Strype, *Eccl. Mem.* vol. 1 (i), p. 114.

'A place he named us in London where he said that such heretics were wont to resort to their readings in a chamber at midnight, and when we asked him the names of them that were wont to haunt those midnight lectures he rehearsed us divers.' More, *Dial. Works* (ed. 1557), p. 239; (ed. Campbell, 1931), p. 240.

did little harm. Their Sacramentarianism was their highest heresy, deriving as it did from the teaching of Wyclif albeit in the vulgarized pseudo-Wycliffite tract *The Wicket*, a slender enough tract.

But even this would not arouse public attention unless the 'known men' refused to attend Mass on those occasions when ecclesiastical discipline demanded. For the most part their communities moved within the orbit of accepted orthodoxy, for there is no evidence that they denied Christian baptism or refused Christian burial. It was, as we have said, a way of life which bred abjuration rather than martyrdom, though there is no doubt either that there was a tough core to the movement. It is possible that they supplemented defective religious practice among the orthodox, with customs of their own, and there are two intriguing references to lections at wedding feasts.

'At the marriage of Durdant's daughter they assembled together in a barn, and heard a certain epistle of St Paul read.'[1]

'Being in the house of John Harris, of Upton, at the marriage of Joan, the wife of Robert Burgess, did read in a book called Nicodemus's Gospel who made the cloth which our Lord was buried in (as the register saith).'[2]

The religious life of these people centred in their study of the vernacular scripture.[3] They went to great risks to obtain and circulate the treasured and diminishing portions of the sacred writing. The books were hard to come by and as more and more were confiscated by the authorities, difficult to replace. It is possible that in the records of the various trials we catch glimpses of single copies as they travel by the agency

[1] Foxe, *A. & M.* vol. IV, p. 228.

[2] Ibid. p. 237. This version of the Apocryphal 'Acta Pilati' was well known in the Middle Ages and its account of the 'harrowing of hell' inspired many paintings and statuary. Scarcely a tactful collation for a wedding breakfast.

[3] The earlier Waldenses seem to have used vernacular scripture primarily for a basis of preaching rather than for corporate study. Grundmann, *Religiöse Bewegungen im Mittelalter*, p. 440, Berlin, 1935.

of the lay preachers from the Thames Valley to London and thence to Colchester, while at each stage the most apt to memorize got 'God's Law' by heart. Single Gospels and copies of separate Epistles were easier to circulate, and judging by the trials we should gather that if Wyclif's *Wicket* were, as Dr Maynard Smith suggests, the *vade mecum* of the early Lollards, the Epistle of James with its simple, practical piety and its emphasis on brotherhood was the handbook of the 'known men'.[1]

Apart from the Biblical writings there is evidence of a real lack of theological leadership. Aside from *The Wicket*, *The Examination of William Thorpe* and a few other treatises of an anti-clerical and not very meaty character, they had little on which to feed. Theirs was a simple, practical piety which was wearing more than a little thin, and was badly in need of instruction. The lack of theological leadership and the failure of the movement to produce any living theology marks it off from the later Reformation. Luther's depreciation of the Epistle of St James was a comparative judgement, but between the 'known men' who made so much of it and the Reformers with their focus in the Epistle to the Romans there was a gulf. The 'known men' might not have agreed with Sir Thomas More that 'the Epistle to the Romans containeth such high difficulties as very few learned men can attain unto', but 'Justification by only Faith' was to touch heights and depths unsounded by what we know of later Lollardy. Nor can we say what links there were between the 'known men' and the English Reformers. The probability is that two originally separate strands were drawn together by common need and common persecution. Foxe may have exaggerated the numbers of the sect, and we are not to suppose that they created a powerful 'fifth column' throughout the country. Yet in their

[1] The references to this Epistle are more numerous than to any other. Foxe, *A. & M.* vol. IV, pp. 176, 222, 224, 228, 233, 235, 236. Also *L. & P. Henry VIII*, vol. IV, 4175 (2).

own areas, notably the Thames Valley[1] and parts of Essex, they were a factor to be taken seriously. The eagerness with which they welcomed the new teaching from beyond the sea, the risks they ran to get hold of it, the sacrificial efforts they made to further it, are perhaps the measure of their need.

THE CHRISTIAN BRETHREN

Who were the Christian Brethren, or the Brethren in Christ? Is the name a synonym for the 'known men' or were they, as Froude, J. R. Green and Ranke assumed, a society for the distribution of proscribed books?

The most important evidence that survives is a 'Communication of Sebastian Newdigate to Mr Denny of a Society of Christian Brethren formed for the distribution of Lutheran books' of which the relevant clauses are the following:

'Item yt one Thomas Keyle, Mercer of London shewid me yt there was made for the Augmentacion of Christen brethern of his Sorte: Auditours and Clerks yt in this Citie. And yt every christen brother of their sorte shulde pay a certayn sum of money to the aforesaid Clerks which shulde goo in to all the quarters of this Realme and at certayn tymes, the Auditours to take Accompte of them....

'And then I asked hym how he and his other Felowes wolde do seyng the Kyngs Grace and these greate lordes of the realme were agaynst them: the whiche said yt they had all redy twoo thousande bookes out agaynst the blessid Sacrament in the Commens handes with bookes concernyng dyverse other matters. affirmynge yt if it were once in the Commens heds thei wolde have no farther care.'[2]

Here is evidence of an association operating considerable

[1] The strong colony at Amersham accounts for the great welcome accorded John Knox when he visited the district in the reign of Edward VI. Strype, *Eccl. Mem.* vol. II (ii), p. 73: 'In some places in this circuit, and particularly at Amersham, he took a liking partly for their forwardness to hear him, and partly for their civilities towards him.'

[2] The whole document is printed in Foxe, *A. & M.* vol. v, Appendix XIII. Newdigate was a friend of More and executed as an intransigeant Catholic in 1535. For Thomas Keyle, see *L. & P. Henry VIII* (1529–30), 787 (18), 3008 (9), 4594 (20).

financial ventures whose activities cover 'all quarters of the realme' and which since it aims at the 'Augmentacion of brethren', is a society for the Propagation of the Gospel ('of their sorte') as well as a society for the Promotion of Christian Knowledge (after their kind). It is evident from the feverish attempt of secular and church authorities to stem the traffic in contraband literature that it was being carefully organized and that as well as ordering books to be made, it was subsidizing scholars who continued their work in the comparative safety of distant exile.

'These fellows that nought had here,' said Sir Thomas More, 'and therefore carried naught hence, nor nothing finding there to live upon, be yet sustained and maintained with money sent them by some evil disposed persons out of this realm thither, and that for none other intent but to make them sift and seek out heresies and speedily send them hither.'[1] Of these books he complained that 'though they neither can be there printed without greate cost nor there sold without great adventure and peril, yet they cease not with money sent from thence to print them there and send them hither by the whole fattes full at once, and in some places looking for no lucre, cast them abroad by night'. 'I was by good honest men informed that in Bristow... there were of these pestilent books some thrown in the stretes and left at men's doors by night that where they durst not offer their poison to sell, they would of their charity poison men for nought.'[2]

Or, as one of the exiles more elegantly described it:

> 'How had the Gospel first entrance
> Into England so far of distance?
> Where to read them no man may?
> Good Christian men with pure affect
> Of God singularly thereto elect,
> With cost did him thither convey.'[3]

[1] More, *Works* (ed. 1557), p. 344.   [2] Ibid. p. 727.
[3] Barlow, *Burial of the Mass* (ed. Arber), p. 117.

On the other hand there are depositions in the courts in which the names 'known men' and 'Christian Brethren' are used almost interchangeably. Thus, 'John Gyrlyng has been a "known man" and a "brother in Christ" for three years'— 'Thomas Matthew's wife has been a "known woman" and of the brotherhood for twelve years'—'the said Robert Best has been taken continually for the space of twelve months past as a "known man" and a "brother in Christ" among them that be called "brethren in Christ" and "known men".' It should be noted that all these instances occur in connection with the 'known men' of Essex and Suffolk, in the areas connected with the wool and cloth trade, with its obvious connection with the Continental traffic. It can also be shown that there was a connection between the 'known men' and the trade in forbidden books. Maxwell and Stacey,[1] who were book agents, were cited before Bishop Longland as Lollards and had been workers with Hakker the Lollard agent who travelled continually between the 'known men' of East Anglia and those of the Thames Valley and Chiltern Hills.

On the strength of this connection between the 'known men' and the Christian Brethren, the suggestion has been made that all the first English Reformers who were connected with the Christian Brethren were Lollards, that from them emerged Frith and Tyndale, Barnes and Bilney and that to them we owe Tyndale's New Testament.[2] This is not so. What is likely is that the society of Christian Brethren joined all who shared the cause of the Reform, and especially the making of books.

We ought not to press the term 'Christian Brethren' too hard, for though in many references in the literature of this period, a particular use is intended, the term very quickly became a general reference to the Reformers. Thus Sir Thomas More defends his use of the term in his *Debellacion of Salem*

[1] Foxe, *A. & M.* vol. IV, p. 681. *L. & P. Henry VIII*, vol. IV, 4029.
[2] W. N. Chaplyn, *C.Q.R.* 1938.

and Byzance: 'First as for calling them by the name "brethren",
it is nothing of my bringing up, but a word walking in every
man's mouth and begun by the good blessed brethren themself
as well appeareth in their own letters.'[1] His expressions 'this
blessed new bitched brotherhood', 'this new broached
brotherhood' show that he considered it to be of recent origin.
Even in 1540 Stephen Gardiner could find the allusion not
over-ripe.

'There were ministers and no more fryers. Fye on the name
and the garment. But now they be called by an englyshe name
brethren and go apparelled like other men, amonges which some
be that were fryers...but if the kinges majestie as he hath
banished freres by the French name wolde also banish those
that call themselves brethren in England the devil should be
greatly discomforted.'[2]

While later still, the Homily on Contention and Brawling
spoke of 'Words of contention be now almost in every man's
mouth. He is a Pharisee, he is a gospeller, he is of the new
sort, he is of the old faith, he is a new broached Brother.'

The need for an association which could organize the book
traffic would not emerge until printed books were available
in large numbers. The literature of the 'known men' was not
extensive, as we have seen. It is significant that when William
Roye, as Tyndale said, 'gat him new friends', he was engaged
with Jerome Barlow in an enterprise which included the
reissue of two fragments of Lollard tracts from the preceding
century.

Although the Preface to their *Burial of the Mass* was probably
intended to mask the real authorship, it may contain some
truth, at least with reference to other writings:

'By your laste letter, dere brother in Christ, I perceived that
youre desyre was to have the lytle worke which ye sent well
examened and diligently put into prynt...wherefore dere

[1] More, *Works* (ed. 1557), pp. 940–1.
[2] Muller, *Letters of Stephen Gardiner*, no. 81, p. 170.

brother yf eny mo soche smale stickes come into youre hondes
sende them unto me (yf in englonde they maye not be pub-
lisshed).'[1]

Another tract in which the 'known Men' would have considerable interest was that of John Frith on the Sacrament of
the Altar. In this great mystery their sole illumination had
been Wyclif's *Wicket*, a tract, apart from scriptural quotations,
of only a few pages. There must have been many who doubted
the necessity of participation in this or any sacrament, and the
report of the great controversy opened up between the Continental reformers soon reached England. It is a question not
yet settled how far John Frith, the Melanchthon of the English
Reformers, was a popularizer of the weighty theology of
Oecolampadius[2] in this matter, and how much was his own
original work. But he tells us:

'I chanced, being in these parts to be in company with a
Christian brother, which for his commendable conversation
and sober behaviour might better be made a bishop than many
that wear mitres. This brother after much communication
desired to know my mind as touching the Sacrament of the
body and blood of Christ, which thing I opened unto him
according to the gift which God had given me. When I had
sufficiently published to him my mind he desired me to entitle
the sum of my words and write them for him because they
seemed over long to be well retained in the memory: to say the
truth I wrote it not with the intent that it should have been
published, for the treatise I wrote was not expedient for all
men, albeit it was sufficient for those I took it in hand to
instruct. For they knew the spiritual and necessary eating and
drinking of his body and blood which is not received by the
belly but with the ears of faith and only needed instruction in
the outward eating which thing I therefore declared.'[3]

---

[1] Barlow, *Burial of the Mass* (ed. Arber). Roye, *Rede me and be not wroth*
(ed. Arber), pp. 21–5.

[2] E. Staehelin, *Joh. Oecolampadius* (Basel, 1939).

[3] Tyndale and Frith, *Works* (ed. London, 1831), vol. III, p. 321.

This passage which has been used to prove Frith a Lollard proves if anything the opposite, for their treatment of him in the matter was cavalier. It is possible that this was the tract of which Thomas Keyle boasted that copies were abroad and that the matter of them would soon be in the commons' heads.

How far the Lollard constituency moved Tyndale to work on the New Testament translation, or how much Lollard money went to maintain him and other exiles cannot be known. But it was evident that, once completed, they formed the most important immediate public for reading and for propagating doctrine. The circle of those interested was wider than that of the 'known men' and included a number of merchants, men like Richard Hunne, William Petit, Humphrey Monmouth, Richard Hilles; men of standing in their companies, often of the Livery, who were not above attending an occasional 'night schoole' and who certainly thought it a more godly work to maintain scholars like Tyndale than to subsidize lights and obites; these men though on the verge of orthodoxy should not properly be called 'Lollards'.

Men like these who had many trade contacts with the Continent, who were skilled in their several mysteries whose secrets they had learned to make and keep, were well able to organize the contraband traffic in books, stretching between the English ports, the Low Countries and the great Rhineland cities where were the biggest book fairs and the most skilled printers like the house of Schott in Strasbourg. The merchants of the English house at Antwerp, where Tyndale resided and who included John Lambert and John Rogers among their chaplains, were we may guess one of the headquarters of the society.

Last, there were the scholars at the Universities and at greater religious houses like those of Reading and Bury St Edmunds, who were less interested in vernacular literature than in the Latin volumes (mainly Biblical commentaries) of the Continental Reformers. This threefold constituency, the 'known men', the merchants and the University scholars, was not static, but the persistent centre of missionary propaganda.

They subsidized scholars, like Tyndale and Barlow, Joye and Roye. They ordered books and underwrote the printing of them, when needed for a special purpose, like Frith's tract on the Sacrament. It has been suggested by Mr J. F. Mozley that the first book published by the society, in 1526, was the letter which Bugenhagen (Pomeranus) wrote to the Reformers in England.[1] The work is slight and its guarded references suggest that the author was nearly as much in the dark about the English Reformers as was Sir Thomas More. 'We have heard', said the author, 'that in England and in other countries the joyful message of the glory of God was well taken of diverse', but he expresses concern at the rumour that 'many weaklings have drawn back again because of unknown rumours that there be raised of us by them that withstand the gospel of God'. Yet it is inevitable that scandals and false rumours should arise and the English must learn to prove all things, holding fast to the good. Bugenhagen enumerates some of the matters of current controversy: 'for men dispute of free will, of vows and monastical sects, of satisfaction, of the abuse of the blessed sacrament, of worshipping of saints that be dead'. To the question 'peradventure thou wilt ask what is our opinion?' he disarmingly replies: 'To this I answer that Christ which is our Righteousness is also our Doctor and teacher, whatsoever he hath taught by his word and council are to be observed like as he himself commandeth his disciples.'

Having thus skilfully evaded all the awkward questions, the letter ends with a vague message of goodwill. 'This have I written dear brethren, in few words to testify to you the

---

[1] *A Compendious Letter which John Pomeranus, curate of the Congregation at Wittenberg sent to the faithful Christian congregations in England* (London, 1536). *Ein Sendbrief an die Christen ynn Engeland* (Wittenberg, 1525).

rejoicing that I have of you of the good hope that we have to God against them that with unshamefastliness pervert and overthrow all that we built.' Not, one feels, an apostolic document, but to many of its readers after a century of isolation any sort of greeting from comrades elsewhere must have been heartening. In any case, from this time the contact of the English Reformers with those on the Continent became ever more fruitful.

We should not forget that this was, after all, a trade as well as a missionary adventure: somewhere there were profits as well as risks, and there was a great business in arranging for the sale, transport and distribution of the books when they had been printed, a business attended by risks of wind and water and tide, increased a hundredfold as governmental action was taken to stop the trade. The government might buy up stocks of the books, though they soon discovered the doubtful economics of this stratagem. They might burn the books with solemn pomp and a sermon at Paul's Cross, they might pull in one agent after another and pry open tongues as Tudor governments knew how to do, they might burn some of them like Richard Bayfield, and bully others into recantation like Robert Necton and George Constantine, yet with all these devices it is plain that they were still very much in the dark about the Christian Brethren. Sir Thomas More did not get at the heart of the organization, nor did his successors. One of the last articles against John Nicholson or Lambert, late of the English house, was the inquiry:

'Whether thou hast promised at any time or by any oath or made any confederacy or league with any person or persons that you would always hold and defend certain conclusions and articles seeming to you and to your accomplices right and consonant with the Christian faith?'

But he refused to rat; he did not remember: 'Unless it have chanced me to say—[and did he pause here to make his judges catch their breath?]—that I would never with the aid of God forsake or decline from the truth neither for fear nor yet for the love of man?'[1]

Their mysteries were well kept, and they will likely enough defy the historians. It seems probable, we may conclude, that the Christian brethren were an association which embraced men of different calling, different interest and different theological opinion, yet all joined by common concern for reformation in doctrine and church life, and that it linked the workers for that reform in England with their brethren overseas. Theirs was an organization sufficiently well run to alarm the authorities and to explain the panic severity with which they strove to stamp out the traffic. Those measures cut off in their flower men like Tyndale and Frith who might have been the lasting glory of the English Church, who were yet in their departing not without some savour of it. And in the end, the Word went free.

[1] See Foxe, *A. & M.* vol. v, pp. 183, 224.

CHAPTER II

THE CAMBRIDGE REFORMERS

THE University of Cambridge bore its own coherent part in the making of the English Reformation by providing a series of theological and ecclesiastical leaders such that its contribution, had it been isolated from the context of a wider upheaval, might have become known to historians as 'the Cambridge Movement'.

Nevertheless the year 1517, fateful elsewhere, went peaceably enough in Cambridge and was in fact the only year in the century for which a University annalist could find no remarkable comment. When the rumoured gossip began to circulate of the troubles in which a young professor of divinity in a new and distant German university had become engaged, there can have been few who realized the true import of the news, and many must have regarded the affair as another round in an already mature struggle between the adherents of the New Learning and the obscurantists. For it is in the Universities that the connection between the Renaissance and the Reformation movement becomes most apparent.

'Remember ye not [Tyndale asked More] how within this thirty years and far less, and yet dureth until this day, the old barking curs, Dun's disciples and like draff called Scotists, the children of darkness, raged in every pulpit against Greek, Latin and Hebrew and what sorrow the schoolmasters that taught the true Latin tongue had with them: some beating the pulpits with fists for madness and roaring out with open and foaming mouth, that if there were but one Terence or Virgil in the world, and that same in their sleeves and a fire before them, they would burn them therein though it should cost them their lives.'[1]

[1] Tyndale, *Works*, P.S. vol. III, p. 75. J. F. Mozley, *William Tyndale*, p. 16.

The names of More and Fisher are reminders that the course of true humanism could run smoothly enough with orthodoxy. Yet there were others who must have found the revival of letters the bridge across which they went to concern for doctrinal reform. It was a common argument, though not of the strongest for the orthodox, to protest how unlikely it was that Christendom could have missed truths for a thousand years which might now be unlaid by a few bold and rebellious spirits.

> 'A sect new fangled
> Also none presumed till now a late
> Against the clergye to beare any hate.'[1]

But this was a dangerous gambit with which to approach a generation which had heard how Laurentius Valla had exposed the authorship of the Donation of Constantine and of the 'Celestial Hierarchies' of the Pseudo-Dionysius, or which had seen scholars like Nicholas of Cusa tracking classical manuscripts across Europe, or watched zestfully the effort of Erasmus to find the true base for the text of Scripture. Adventure and discovery were in the air. The sixteenth century made all things new, and probably the word 'new' was used more times between 1450 and 1650 than in the preceding thousand years.

By 1520 a new generation was arriving, which had imbibed the new approach almost uncritically, and was, after the manner of second generations, more self assured in its independence, more impatient in its opposition to obscurantism and bigotry, more ready to note how often wooden opposition to all innovation drew together the opponents of innovation, both in letters and in doctrine.

Of the earlier humanists, John Colet,[2] with his concern for

---

[1] Barlowe, *A proper dialogue between a gentleman and a husbandman* (ed. Arber), p. 149.

[2] R. R. Williams, *Religion and the English Vernacular Literature*, pp. 28–38 (S.P.C.K. 1940).

Biblical studies and for the exposition of the Pauline Epistles, came nearest to the new pattern. We know that Lollards were to be seen, nodding or exchanging patronizing glances during his sermons, while of the orthodox it was said that 'there was no doctor there, either of Divinity or Law, no abbot or other dignitary but came to hear him, and brought his books with him'. Tyndale said 'they would have made the Old Dean Colet of Paul's a heretic for translating the Paternoster into English had not the Archbishop of Canterbury helped the Dean'. It is difficult to estimate the personal influence of Erasmus at Cambridge, but there can be no doubt at all of the impact made there by his new edition of the New Testament, and especially of the Latin edition. This book was to the Cambridge Reformers what the Wycliffite scriptures had been to the Lollards and what the Tyndale Testament was soon to be to the Reformers generally. Bilney tells how eagerly he sought a copy: 'which when I understood to be eloquently done by him, allured rather by the Latin than by the word of God, I bought it.' It played its part in the life of Robert Barnes and of his convert Bayfield, and it was to its pages that the young scholar Dalaber turned for comfort in a perilous hour.

The interest in the New Learning was twofold, a concern for classical literature, and a desire for a more critical study of Holy Scripture. In the University Grace Books for 1517 the names appear of Mr Croke, to win later fame as 'Dr Croke the Grecian', a great setter forth of classical study, and of that Master George Stafford whose sensational readings on the letters of St Paul were to bring the first brush between the Reformers and the University authorities.[1] The first Cambridge Reformers included a number of prominent classical scholars:

[1] George Joye reproaching Gardiner for losing sympathy with the Reformers wrote: 'Ye wrote to Master George Stafford to give him warning when he was complained of to the Cardinal for reading, and declaring truly and faithfully the Epistle to the Romans, and showed him how he should temper his lection.' Foxe, *A. & M.* vol. IV, p. 754.

Dr Robert Barnes with his pupil Parnell had pursued the classics at Louvain and returned to read Terence, Plautus and Cicero to a group of enthusiastic pupils. John Lambert was one who, from his first days at Queens' had 'prospered mightily in the Greek and Latin tongue'. There is the immortal story of how John Frith, a bedraggled refugee on a dangerous visit from exile, was mistaken for a vagabond at Reading, and clapped in the stocks. There he was confronted by the local school-master, Leonard Coxe, and from that grotesque rostrum de-claimed to him, first a Latin lament on his situation, and then in the Greek, 'Homer's verses from the first book of the *Iliad*'. What the gaping yokels made of this strange dialogue between two old Etonians does not appear, but there is an Italianate zest about the tale which was, alas, all too soon overlaid by more sombre happenings.

This concern for letters was the prevailing intellectual fashion among the younger members of a University sus-ceptible to intellectual fashions. 'Ah Master Bradford', chode George Day in 1555, 'you were but a child when this matter began. I was a young man, and then coming from the University I went with the world.'[1] And Stephen Gardiner confessed, in an edition of his salad days too modest to fit the facts, 'because there was not in them malice and they maintained communication having some savour of learning. I was familiar with such sort of men.'[2]

At some time in the 'twenties' those interested in Reform began to meet in the 'White Horse', nicknamed 'Little Ger-many'. It is not quite clear how we should regard those meetings, whether it was a gathering of such a closed company of declared adherents of Reform who, in the reign of Mary, met in the back parlour of a London tavern,

'requesting to have a pig roasted, and half a dozen faggots to be brent, and they were reading...and tarried there about two

[1] Foxe, *A. & M.* vol. VII, p. 176.
[2] Muller, *Letters of Stephen Gardiner*, p. 166.

hours,...how the said multitude called one another "brother" and did every one to his hability cast down upon the table money which was 2d. a piece...to the use and relief of the poor'.[1]

Quite probably it was such an informal and open meeting as could include men like Gardiner and Day, where men might stretch their legs and have their talk out in an all-round debate across which fell no shadows of approaching destiny to warn the bright company that some of them, embracing opinions the opposite of those they now maintained, would sit in judgement upon their friends, among whom nearly every figure of note would come at last to the fire. We could make a list of some fifty or sixty members of the University who might have been of their company. Among them were Nicholas Shaxton, a former President of Physic's Hostel and University Preacher; Dr Crome the evangelical preacher whose series of accommodations to the authorities over the next thirty years was not more remarkable than the fact that he retained the affection of friend and foe. From Queens' the President Dr Forman and John Lambert; from Christ's Mallory and from King's John Frith. Bilney from Trinity Hall and Thomas Arthur and William Paget from St John's, Taverner and Matthew Parker from Corpus.[2] Those at Cambridge during these years make an impressive list: 'the future Archbishops Cranmer, Heath, Parker and May: the future Bishops Latimer, Ridley, Sampson, Shaxton, Bale, Foxe, Day.'[3]

[1] Foxe, *A. & M.* vol. VIII, p. 460. This gathering was largely composed of foreigners however.

[2] Gonville Hall enjoyed great notoriety: Richard Nixe, Bishop of Norwich, to the Archbishop of Canterbury, 14 May 1530: 'ther is a collage in Cambrige called gunwell haule of the foundacion of the Bishoppe of Norwiche. I here of no clerke that hath come ought lately of that collage but savorith of the friainge panne, thoughe he speke never so holely' (A. W. Pollard, *Records of the English Bible*, p. 161).

[3] 'The first edition of the English Prayer Book was almost exclusively the work of Cambridge Divines: of its thirteen compilers all but one was a Cambridge Man'; cf. Bass Mullinger, *History of the University of Cambridge*, p. 101.

Cardinal Wolsey did unwitting service to the Reformers by transplanting some of the best and brightest among them to become junior canons of his new college in Oxford, though the fact that Cromwell had to do with the business arrangements raises the doubt whether the event did not owe more to serpentine guile than to colombine simplicity. The result was that the scenes enacted in Cambridge were repeated there: students were proselytized during supervisions by young dons like Mr Clerk, and in rooms disputations and Bible readings were held behind carefully closed doors. A sudden swoop by the authorities went askew at Cambridge where Dr Forman got a warning round in time. At Oxford, Forman's curate got into more serious trouble: he, one Thomas Garrard, Master of Arts and Fellow of Magdalen, had been an active agent in heretical books, and was apprehended during the search. The narrative in which the young scholar Dalaber describes the subsequent happenings is one of the most vivid of sixteenth-century documents. Garrard managed to escape and went direct to Dalaber to ask assistance from a friend who speedily became more panic stricken than himself. 'He cast off his gown and his hood and desired me to give him a coat with sleeves...then I put on him a sleeved coat of mine of a fine cloth in graine which my mother had given me.' After prayer, they parted amid tears and Garrard made off, leaving Dalaber to seek consolation in the Latin Testament of Erasmus. The refreshed student went to his friends, one Diet and the fateful Nicholas Udall, and finally to Mr Clerk who with Messrs Sumner and Betts were canons of Wolsey's college. Clerk advised them how to behave, but Dalaber, brow-beaten by the authorities, told the truth, but not the whole truth, and added some artistic details culled from a warmed imagination, with a lie direct 'to rid my godly brother out of the trouble and peril of his life'.

Had the commissary, Dr Cottisford, failed to arrest Garrard

it might have been regarded as a crime. But to arrest the man and let him get away again was worse than a crime, it was a mistake, and the official was scared to distraction, or as he put it 'in extreme pensiveness'. Then he did what Somerset was to do when his silver plate was stolen in the next reign, sent for an astronomer to make a cast and tell him where they could find the fugitive. The astronomer's forecast was worthy of a modern newspaper column, almost to the traditional 'tall, dark man' and 'long sea voyage'. Garrard, he confidently affirmed, had fled in a tawny coat south-eastward and was hiding in the middle of London preparatory to taking flight beyond the sea. Of course, and where else should he go? Alas, in truth he had fled north-west and not south-east, and was located not in London but in Bristol. He was taken and upon him was discovered a list of books which revealed among other things, that the Prior of Reading had received upwards of sixty. The commissary and the Warden of New College bombarded the higher authorities with a series of more and more agitated letters, culminating in Dr London's *cri du cœur* to the Bishop of Lincoln: 'Wold godd my lorde is grace hadd never be motyonyd to call hym or any other Cambridge man unto hys most towardly colledge.'[1]

As a result of this investigation a number of arrests were made, and those who did not, as John Frith did, escape over-seas were after penance 'cast into prison into a deep cave under the ground of the college where the salt fish was laid, so that through the filthy stench thereof they were all infected and certain of them taking their death there'. In fact, 'Master Clerk, Master Sumner and Sir Bayly eating nothing but salt fish from February to the midst of August died all three together within the compass of a week'.[2] Wolsey, who left inhumanity to his monarch and to his officials, was deeply shocked and

[1] Foxe, *A. & M.* vol. v, App. vi.
[2] Ibid. p. 5.

gave orders that the rest should be released and confined to
a ten miles' radius of Oxford, while he took Thomas Garrard
into his employ, and set him to work copying manuscripts.
Affairs of more lasting consequence had been afoot during
this time at Cambridge and to them we must return.[1]

Thomas Bilney

When Foxe called Thomas Bilney 'the first framer of that
University in the knowledge of Christ', he intended not so
much to reflect upon the preceding Cambridge piety but to
indicate the pre-eminent place which the little Norfolk parson-
lawyer held among the first generation of Reformers. He was
born about 1495 and went to Cambridge at an early age where
from Trinity Hall he proceeded to the degree of Bachelor in
the civil and in the canon law. In 1519 he was ordained priest
by Bishop West, of Ely, and soon afterwards received licence
to preach within the diocese. But his chief work lay among
his scholars and friends in the University.

Hugh Latimer, that orthodox zealot, chose for his B.D. Act
to attack the *Rhetoric* of Philip Melanchthon,[2] and Bilney determined that something must be done about the young man who
was a self-appointed 'malleus haereticorum'. 'Bilney sought
me out, and he came to me afterwards in my study and desired
me for God's sake to hear his confession: and to say the truth,
by his confession I learned more than afore in many years. So
from this time forward I began to smell the word of God and
forsook the school doctors and all such fooleries.'

---

[1] Skelton's *Replycacyon against certain young scholars abjured of late* adds
nothing but a spate of Rabelaisian invective to our knowledge of the
Cambridge Reformers.

[2] Melanchthon's *Rhetoric* was published in January 1519 while its author
was still mainly occupied with letters. The preface links Luther and
Erasmus as both having been attacked by the Sophists. It says of Erasmus
that he 'primus theologiam ad fontes revocavit'. William Paget of St John's
had been lecturing on the work. (C.R. vol. 1, pp. 32, 39.)

Bilney's confession that afternoon might have been similar to that which he later addressed to Cuthbert Tunstal, and which tells of his spiritual conflict which could not be solaced by the offices of penitence. ' So that there was but small force of strength left in me (who by nature was but weak), small store of money, and very little wit or understanding: for they appointed me fasting, watchings, buying of pardons and money.' But

'at last I heard speak of Jesus even then when the New Testament was first set forth by Erasmus: which when I understood to be eloquently done by him, being allured rather by the Latin than by the word of God for at that time I knew not what it meant, I bought it even by the providence of God (as I do now well understand and perceive): and at the first reading (as I well remember) I chanced upon this sentence of St Paul (O most sweet and comfortable sentence to my soul) in 1 Tim. i: "It is a true saying and worthy of all men to be embraced that Christ Jesus came into the world to save sinners, of whom I am the chief and principal." This one sentence, through God's instruction and inward working, which I did not then perceive, did so exhilarate my heart, being before wounded with the guilt of my sins, and being almost in despair, that even immediately I seemed unto myself inwardly to feel a marvellous comfort and quietness, insomuch that my bruised bones leaped for joy.' [1]

The force of such testimony turns a good deal on the kind of person from whom it comes and of Bilney's high character there is abundant witness, even the somewhat grudging admission of Sir Thomas More. But then More's treatment of Bilney is one of the least satisfactory parts of his far from satisfactory controversial writings. Sir Thomas More was a saint: he was also a great Englishman: he also had a large sense of humour. The three facts make a formidable combination, which makes criticism of him an affair of temerity, especially since at the moment his fame has been attended with

[1] Foxe, *A. & M.* vol. IV, p. 635.

the kind of romanticism which twenty years ago was given to St Francis Assisi. We have no wish to deny facts. Anybody who has regarded More's portraits in the National Portrait Gallery, and passed on from their honest beauty to meet the piggy gaze of Thomas Cromwell will understand something of the case against some of the Reformers, and for some of their opponents. But there is this also to be said.

Miss Deansley has acutely remarked that in the case of Thomas More we must discriminate between the saint and the historian. And it is even more needful to distinguish the saint from the controversialist. Professor Chambers' study of him, fine as it is, has so few shadows because it is too little attentive to his dealings with the heretics. In his controversial writings indeed More was not arguing but fighting, as he says: 'Now as for me, the cause is of my writing not so much to debate and dispute these things with them, which though I trust therein to give them no great place, many men may do much better yet than I, as to give men warning what mischief is in their books.'[1]

In no one of the many hundreds of pages of his controversial works does he find one generous word for his opponents, the enemies of the Church and the poison of society. In these days when it can hardly be said that the Catholic case is going by default, and when even liberal historians are at pains to do justice to the weighty reasons which led to the establishment of the Inquisition and to the prosecution of heretical pravity, it would be easy to succumb before More's honest indictment. Yet these men were heretics and heretics were monsters and he fixed his gaze on them with far less charitable observation than he would accord to the ape at the bottom of his garden, or the poor bewildered savages who had been brought over from the 'New Found Land'.

His belief overrode his charitable temper, and led him again

[1] More, *Works* (ed. 1557), p. 351.

and again to take refuge in the authority of accepted usage. And as that windy and interminable dialogue which is More's 'Confûtation' of Tyndale, Frith and Barnes drags on and on, the jests get fewer and feebler, the style more arid and depressing until in the end we can hardly diagnose the author of *Utopia* or the sparkling and shapely *Dialogue against Tyndale*. On the whole we shall find the saint in his written prayers rather than in his controversial writings.

More says of Bilney that

'he was very fearful and scrupulous and began at the first to fall into such a scrupulous holiness that he reckoned himself bounden so straitly to keep and observe the words of Christ after the very letter, that because our Lord biddeth us when we will pray to enter into our chamber and shut the door, he thought it therefore sin to say his service abroad and always would be sure to have his chamber door shut unto him while he said mattins. which thing indeed I heard him deny in an honourable presence. But I heard again another man more credible than twain of him, and if I had said ten I think I lied not, and one of his best proven friends avow it in his face for truth.'[1]

Even if true it would not amount to much, nor would Bilney be the first or last to cut college prayers for private devotions, or to sport his oak when so engaged. Foxe reports as singular his dislike of music 'when Dr Thirleby then scholar laying in the chamber beneath him would play upon his recorder...he would resort strait to prayer'. Prayer for those who despitefully use us is a virtue which all must admire though few may imitate, and to this day the musical undergraduate is an involuntary penance to most of his neighbours. In effect these are stories about a Don, often repeated and never returning to their authors void.[2]

[1] More, *Works* (ed. Campbell), p. 11; (ed. 1557), p. 208.
[2] Foxe's other story is more important. 'Coming from the Church where singing was he would lament to his scholars the curiosity of their dainty singing which he called rather mockery with God than other-

These light matters raise the weighty affair of Bilney's personal integrity which More impugns. But then for More the charge is axiomatic since all heretics are liars. 'Since they have fallen from God and from the true faith, they have no great care of truth nor be very scrupulous in lending of an oath till they need in like to be paid again.' He makes a serious charge against Bilney which he is careful not to press. 'I have heard it reported right credibly that the man...used among some of that sect to say "Let us preach and set forth our way. And if we be accused let us say we said not so, and yet some of them shall we win alway the while."'[1] Yet More has just complained of Bilney's exaggerated scrupulosity. Can an exaggerated scrupulosity and a carelessness for truth live side by side in one person? They can, and the history of religion abounds with painful instances. But there is abundance of evidence that this was not the case with Thomas Bilney. The evidence shows him to have had a reverence for truth more tender than that of many of his friends. For Bilney, as More himself admits, was later to be granted a most exceptional form of abjuration because of his own obstinate adherence to the truth as he saw it, an adherence which was to bring him to the fire. In truth Bilney might have replied in the very noble words which would come from More at his own trial: 'If I were a man, my lords which did not regard an oath, I needed not, as it is well known, in this place, at this time, nor in this case, to stand here as an accused person.'[2]

wise.' John Wesley had a similar objection. 'There are two things I could never reconcile with common sense: one is singing the same words ten times over, the other singing different words by different persons at the same time, and this is in the most solemn addresses to God' (Wesley, *Journal*, 24 March 1764). See *O.C.M.* art. 'Church Music': 'The Council of Trent recommended bishops to exclude music in which anything impious or lascivious took part. Pius IV appointed a committee of Cardinals and there seems to have been some danger at this time of harmonized music being forbidden altogether, because of the interweaving of voices.'

[1] More, *Works* (ed. Campbell), p. 184; (ed. 1557), p. 208.
[2] R. W. Chambers, *Thomas More*, p. 338 (London, 1935).

Bilney, Barnes, and Latimer were singled out by the authorities as leaders among the Cambridge Reformers, and soon after Barnes had been in trouble, Latimer, Bilney and Arthur were brought before Wolsey. If the traditional account is clear, Latimer had an easy passage, and to Wolsey's amusement succeeded in tying the accusing theologians in knots of their own contriving. Bilney's interview, if not exactly a success, had no such devastating consequence as had attended Robert Barnes who had to face formal trial; but the Cardinal treated the interview as, in our phrase, off the record and dismissed Bilney on an oral promise to refrain from preaching the heresies of Luther, a phrase which begged questions enough.

In 1527 a serious and formal charge was made and Bilney had to face a panel of bishops under the presidency of Cuthbert Tunstal. Mindful of the latter's reputation for humanity and his love of letters, Bilney addressed to him a series of letters to which Tunstal sent guarded replies intended to draw him out on the subject of contemporary preaching, but refusing Bilney's request for a personal and private interview. Tunstal had evidently no intention of becoming another Latimer and he produced these letters in open court 'in exonerationem conscientiae suae'. But this mathematical bishop was not the only one with a conscience to keep. Bilney denied many of the articles laid against him and said that others were garbled misquotations from sermons he had preached round Norwich and London. And in truth most preachers would shiver at the thought of facing trial on the evidence of what their congregations remembered of their sermons. In the case of Bilney the witnesses 'above twenty' according to More, including husbandmen, gentlemen and a number of eminent friars, were all hostile, for under existing law Bilney could bring no witnesses on his own behalf. Some of the articles were of surprising triviality while it is a comment on current orthodoxy that others were brought forward at all, as that Bilney said

'Mary Magdalene was a stewyd hoore: howbeit she afterward turned to grace'. They did not violate Bilney's word to Wolsey for they touched matters of Lollard rather than Lutheran controversy, shrines, images and pilgrimages and the like. But Bilney persisted in his denial even though Tunstal twice postponed sentence to allow his friends to persuade him. At last he yielded so far as to admit a limited submission which deserves careful note. The memory of it annoyed Sir Thomas More as indeed it demolishes his allegations of Bilney's scanty regard for truth.

'His abjuration was such that he therein abjured and foreswore all his heresies, knowledging himself lawfully convict. But whereas they be wont to confess in their own abjuration that they have holden such heresies and be guilty thereof, that he would do in no wise: but as clearly as his fault was proved and by as many, yet he would not to die therefore confess himself faulty but always stood still upon it in virtue of his oath that they all denied him.'[1]

But this limited compromise could not satisfy him. He stood in Paul's and bore his faggot, but in the months that followed, a prisoner in the Tower, he brooded on his submission, haunted by the thought that he had betrayed the cause. When he returned to Cambridge at the end of 1528 he was a broken spirit, and inconsolable. Latimer spoke much later of his distress:

'Little Bilney, that blessed martyr of God, what time he had borne his faggot and was come again to Cambridge had such conflicts within himself beholding this image of death, that his friends were afraid to let him alone. They were fain to be with him day and night and comforted him as they could: but no comforts would serve. As for the comfortable places of scripture, to bring them unto him it was as though a man would run him through the heart with a sword.'[2]

[1] Probably also Bilney had taken note of the consequences of Barnes' submission. See below, p. 37. More, *Works* (ed. Campbell), p. 196.
[2] Latimer, *Sermons* (1824), vol. I, p. 200.

He found peace at last in deliberate action. One evening he left Cambridge telling his friends he was going 'up to Jerusalem'. He preached in Norwich where his enemies were strongest and it is credibly reported that he preached in the open fields. He visited the lady anchoress in Norwich,[1] leaving that successor of the Lady Julian to meditate on Tyndale's New Testament and his *Obedience of a Christian Man*. The rumours of his activity led the aged Bishop Nixe, reluctantly, to order Bilney's arrest. Bilney was tried, condemned as an abjured and relapsed heretic and handed over to the secular arm to be burned.

The trial and execution contain some historical problems which need not detain us.[2] But during the trial the Mayor, Edward Reed, was strongly suspicious of the ecclesiastical authorities and at loggerheads with the Bishop's Commissary, Dr Pellys. After the trial, Pellys complained so strongly to More that Reed had to go to London and face the Chancellor. On the other hand, the spiritual power also slipped, and there seems to have been an appeal to the King, and Pellys himself was convicted of *praemunire* while a later piece of gossip in one of Chapuys' dispatches suggests that Bilney was handed over for execution before the arrival of the Writ *placet*. After Bilney's death the authorities gave out that he had made complete submission and that he read out a complete recantation. The examination of the evidence shows that there is no such clear-cut case as that, and that it is probable that Bilney read out a statement about certain matters of minor scandal, as that he excused the orders of Preachers from conniving his death, and acknowledged that he had done wrong in preaching without licence, that he remitted the question of marriage of

---

[1] Probably Dame Agnes Edrygge, recluse there from 1524. (Blomefield, *Hist. Norfolk*, vol. IV, p. 82.)

[2] See 'The Recantation of Thomas Bilney', E. G. Rupp, *London Quarterly*, April 1942.

clergy to the doctors of the Universities, and that he defended the practice of fasting.

Sir Thomas More, who had a large faculty for believing what he wanted to believe, chose to assert that Bilney had made a complete recantation. Documents printed in an appendix to volume iv of Foxe's *Acts and Monuments* show that Edward Reed had good reason for his suspicions. Nevertheless the authorities had succeeded in blurring the issue. Bilney had been a considerable figure, with a following in the Universities, with a good reputation in Norwich, where his enemies were strongest. And the trumpet had sounded an uncertain note. 'Remember Bilney', Tyndale warned John Frith as he too came near to death, surrounded also by too persuasive friends. The death of Bilney marks a stage. Hitherto in England, the Lollards had provided most of the material for heresy trials. They had built a façade of masquerade and casuistry. There was enough truth in Sir Thomas More's sneer at the perfidy of heretics to make it sting. In Smithfield Mr Standfast and in the Low Countries Mr Valiant for Truth were to set a more inspiring example than Mr Fearing.

It is a pity that in an account of Bilney[1] documents loom large which are of a legal character. Latimer looked back with grateful affection to 'Saint Bilney', the man who changed the current of his life in an afternoon's conversation: the man who gave lavishly to the poor in money and who spent himself in charitable works: the leader of the bright band who comforted those in prison and in lazar house, and for whom the gospel that the 'stewyd hoore' might 'afterward turn to grace' was no abstraction, but the proven fruit of a ministry to penitent Magdalenes and dying thieves. When we consider this man and his friends, their good works, their devotion to the Blessed Sacrament which they were wont to receive every four or five

[1] Foxe, *A. & M.* vol. iv, pp. 619–56, 755–63.

days, their Bible readings, their evangelical zeal for preaching
the mercy of Christ, we may well feel that Bilney merits more
space in the memory of the English Church. After all, what
should we make of the Evangelical Revival and its leaders, if
a few years after the founding in Oxford of the 'Holy Club',
Whitefield had fled overseas, and John Wesley (like Bilney,
a 'little single body in person, but of a good upright coun-
tenance') burned at the stake? In the Lollard's Pit in Norwich
they made an end of Thomas Bilney, on a sunny day in August.
But they could as soon end the cause, as the sunshine.

THE TRAGICAL HISTORY OF DR ROBERT BARNES

The story of Robert Barnes has been told at length in modern
times only by a pen so critically unsympathetic that we make
no excuse for telling it again,[1] not only because its subject
deserves at least the pity of posterity, but because the story is
an illumination of what changes and chances befell the first
generation of Reformers.

He was born at Lynn in Norfolk about the year 1495,[2] and
in due time went to Cambridge. Bale says that he and Barnes
were 'together at Cambridge in 1514, but he far outstripped
me in literary attainments owing to his peculiar genius and
abilities'. At an early age he entered the Austin Friars and
went out to continue his studies at Louvain.[3] He returned
with a fellow student, Thomas Parnell, and became head of the
Cambridge house of his order. He soon made it a circle of
eager classical study and read Terence, Plautus and Cicero to

[1] By James Gairdner in the *D.N.B.*

[2] Foxe, *A. & M.* vol. v, p. 419, says that he was brought up by 'Master
Horne', but this can hardly be Robert Horne, Dean of Durham.

[3] He must surely have come into contact with Erasmus either at Cambridge or at Louvain where Erasmus also spent the years 1517–21. But
there is no direct evidence.

a group of students which included Miles Coverdale. In 1523 he was made D.D. at Cambridge by incorporation.[1]

In the following year he presided at Master George Stafford's Act for the B.D. degree, the ensuing Biblical disputation being, according to Foxe, 'marvellous in the sight of the blind doctors'. He was by now a well-known figure and Gardiner leaves this thumb-nail sketch of him: 'A trim, minion friar Augustine, one of a merry scoffing wit, friarlike, and as a good fellow in company was beloved by many.'

There is no exact reference to the point at which his love of letters turned to concern for the reform. Foxe tells us that he was one of Bilney's two most distinguished converts at the time. The first, Hugh Latimer, was University Chaplain, keeper of the schools and Cross bearer of the University, and he seems to have undertaken care of the University conscience also for as an intransigeant 'spike' he made it his business to interrupt the lectures most favoured by the Reformers. He was in fact, such a nuisance that Bilney sought him out in that memorable interview which left permanent impress on the story of the English Church. Nothing as dramatic seems to have occurred with Barnes.

Bilney, Latimer and Barnes became leaders of the group which finished in its strolls along the 'heretic's hill' the conversation begun in the parlour of the White Horse,[2] and which occupied itself in the good works of prison visitation and relief of the poor. Their activities began to exercise those in authority. If there was any doubt as to what would soon happen the temperament of the three friends made certain: Barnes and Latimer were of that temperament which friends label 'prophetic' and enemies 'fanatic', while Bilney had a conscience

---

[1] It is generally assumed that his was a Louvain doctorate. But the Wittenberg register gives him as D.D. (Oxon.). This may be an unhappy guess by a German registrar.

[2] On its site see Batley, *On a Reformer's Latin Bible*, 1940.

narrow and wiry as his bodily frame. It is possible (the dates are confused and the evidence uncertain) that it was an exchange of pulpits between Latimer and Barnes which was the occasion of open conflict with the University authorities.

On Christmas Eve 1525 Robert Barnes preached at St Edward's Church, belonging to Trinity Hall. He was a friar and it was expected of friars to be more lively, even more scurrilous than the secular clergy. But it was hardly tactful to choose a Church connected with a lawyer's college for an attack on the besetting medieval habit of litigiousness, and if the authorities had been looking for an excuse to attack the Reformers, Barnes presented them one with both hands.

But he had a real excuse, for he was dealing with a particular abuse, the offender sitting impenitently in the congregation.[1] A poor man had died in Cambridge leaving a kettle to the Church, worth 2s. 4d., but his executor in straitened circumstances had withheld the bequest from the churchwarden begging a respite until he could pay. That officer sued him before the commissary and the man was thrown into prison, unable there either to make money to pay his debt or to maintain his wife and child. The wife in great distress came to Barnes and his friends, who promised to do what they could. Barnes sought the churchwarden privately but found him stubborn. 'What mercy will you have at Christ's hands that is so extreme to your poor neighbour whom he bought with his precious blood?' he asked. The man replied that 'all doctors of law did say that they must sue therefore under the pain of deadly sin'. Finding the man in the congregation on Christmas Eve 'because I had not clearly converted him therefore I recited the case in a parable that no man knew what he meant but he and I'. It was a costly digression. This is the basis of the charge made against Barnes at his trial and repeated at a

---

[1] Gairdner makes no mention of all this save to call it a 'puritanical sermon', but it is the clue to the trial and to the events which followed it.

later date by Stephen Gardiner, that Barnes preached the Anabaptist doctrine that lawsuits were unlawful between Christian men: but Barnes correctly replied that he had not condemned all laws and all law-makers but only those who taught that 'they were bound to prosecute to the uttermost of the law under the penalty of sin'.

But the digression, offensive as it must have sounded, did not end matters that day. Barnes could not abandon (what preacher would?) his prepared sermon, and this was to follow Luther's Postill on the Epistle for the Day, 'Gaudete in Domino', which contained some remarks on ecclesiastical pomp and circumstance, in contrast to the simple theme of the Nativity. Barnes found it only too easy to point an English moral to this German tale and concluded his sermon with some racy animadversions on the pride of prelacy and a few witticisms at the expense of Wolsey ('He wears a pair of red gloves—I should have said bloody gloves') which enormously titillated the vulgar, but were hostages to fortune.

His enemies could have desired no more. They got twenty-five offensive articles from the sermon and when Barnes offered to make his meaning clear on the next Sunday the Vice-Chancellor, Dr Natares, inhibited him. Called to face the articles behind the closed doors of the schools, Barnes protested: 'Good Master Tyrell will you present any of these articles as heretical?' He was urged to submit to authority and agreed to submit where it could be proved that he had spoken against 'God's Word and the exposition of the holy doctors', while to those who wished to add 'or offended the law of the Church' he replied that Divinity, not law, was his faculty. He had done better to have considered that before. Then his own friends arrived, a more numerous body than the more audacious Reformers, for there was a good deal of resentment at the action of the Vice-Chancellor and some feeling that the body of the University was being deprived of its rights by its officers. The result was that the meeting was hastily adjourned. At the next session a new tactic was adopted and an attempt made to settle the affair privately as among friends. Barnes shows no trace of arrogance and his only fault seems to be his failure to realize how grave were the matters now arising and that he had already irretrievably ruined a career of promise. The Vice-Chancellor warned him that 'they were all my friends and intended to save my name and fame which they could not do, the law was so dangerous'. His offer to bring witnesses was met with the fact that 'if three witnesses came against me then could not three and twenty help me, that was the law'. Barnes said finally that he would accept the judgement of the Vice-Chancellor so it were not against 'learning and charity'. 'Now they had standing unknown to me a notary which did make an instrument of all my agreements.' Again a deputation of Masters and Bachelors arrived and required to be admitted to the examination. This time the authorities had an answer ready. The matter was now being dealt with informally, and in a private manner they said, and sent off post-haste to London to get the matter cited before Wolsey and away from Cambridge at the earliest moment.

Meanwhile a revocation was prepared in which many of the articles had been sharpened. 'As where I said that after the mind of Jerome all days were of like virtue, they added that certain men did take me that I would have no holy days and that therefore I must revoke that article as heresy.' Barnes consulted his friends who 'concluded that it was neither right or conscience that I should agree with this revocation'. In London Barnes found friends at court, and it was the influence of Stephen Gardiner, secretary to the Cardinal, and Edward Foxe which secured him, first a private interview, and then permission to stay as the guest of his pupil Parnell, rather than in the Tower. Wolsey showed an obvious and real reluctance to set in motion the savage machinery of law. His remarks on

Barnes' sermon were good tempered enough, but the fiery young man was not won over by this incarnation of worldly wisdom. The Cardinal warned him that to persist in declaring his innocence would mean that the law must take its course, while when he offered to bring witnesses Wolsey reminded him that they must be his peers, the hopeless requirement being six or ten doctors of divinity. Then he added words which must have chilled the hearer and which brought into his life a dark shadow which never again lifted until it was fulfilled, 'then you must be burned'.

There followed a formal trial presided over by the Bishop of Bath, over a series of articles no single one of which was within a thousand miles of any central issue of the Christian truth. Barnes insisted that they be read out in public for unless they were 'I cannot tell what I should preach in time to come'. The Bishop acidly and ominously replied that that matter would be taken good care of, and asked him formally and thrice to read the prepared submission. He still insisted that it be read out, and after a whispered consultation among the judges the articles were read by a layman. The Bishop, now annoyed at having to eat his own words, asked sharply: '"whether I would read, or be burned?" Then said I "Jesus have mercy upon me, I will surely not read it".' At this there was confusion,

'and the doctors cried out upon me, the one here and the other there not to cast myself away in this manner for to read the roll they said was but a small thing, and I should see my Lord Cardinal should be good and gracious unto me...so that I supposed that they required no more of me but to have read the roll before the face of the world that I should not seem to have the victory against them, which I did not greatly regard.'[1]

[1] For the foregoing see Barnes' own account in his 'Supplication...to Henry VIII' in his *Works* (ed. Foxe, 1573). Extracts may be found in C. H. Cooper, *Annals of Cambridge*, vol. i, pp. 311–23. Also Muller, *Stephen Gardiner and the Tudor Reaction*, Chap. iii; *Letters*, pp. 164 ff.

But the consequences were as harsh as the law. Public penance at Paul's, where he stood with some Steelyard Lutherans to hear a sermon against Luther, amid all the ceremony that authority could muster, was endurable. 'I had been well content to have suffered these things so that I could have come to a charitable end.' If he had hoped to get back to Cambridge in freedom he was soon disillusioned, for he was ordered what would now be called 'house arrest' in the London Austin Friars. It was the cessation of a developing career, but it was not close confinement and he continued to work and teach there (as did Friar Forrest on the Catholic side at a later date).[1] It was while there that he received the Lollards from Steeple Bumpstead and sold to them some copies of Tyndale's New Testament with its 'more cleaner English' than the old Wycliffite version. At last, two and three-quarter years after his trial in the spring of 1526, a deputation waited on Tunstal and begged that Barnes be released. It included a former Lord Mayor, a sheriff and some merchants of standing. What Tunstal said to them does not appear but it so thoroughly scared them that on their return 'there was one of them durst give me...so much as he durst give his dog'.[2] The only result was that Barnes was soon removed to close confinement at Northampton.

There 'Master Horne who had brought him up and was his special friend having intelligence of the writ which should shortly be sent down to burn him, gave him counsel to feign himself desperate: and that he should write a letter to the Cardinal and leave it on his table where he lay and a paper by to declare whither he was gone to drown himself: and to leave his clothes in the same place: and another letter to be left there to the mayor of the town to search for him in the water because he had a letter written on parchment about his neck, closed in

[1] D.N.B. 'Forrest'.
[2] Barnes, *Works* (ed. Foxe, 1573), p. 225.

wax, for the Cardinal'.[1] For a week they dragged the river, while Barnes 'in a poor man's apparel' got him to London and escaped overseas.

But he had broken penance while an abjured heretic, and the fact was to remain the bar to his later rehabilitation. It mattered not at all that others of his friends were no more discreet than he, over matters more serious than any of the articles objected to Barnes. Barnes knew better than any Joseph Surface how slender a defence is the 'consciousness of one's own innocence' in a naughty world.

The suicide of a heretic was propaganda material highly favoured by the authorities and they had no doubt begun to use it before they discovered they had been deceived. Tunstal swore 'My Lord Cardinal would have me again, an it should cost him a great deal of money'. To which Barnes retorted in words of some nobility:

'I am a simple poor wretch and worth no man's money in the world, saving theirs not the tenth penny that they will give for me. And to burn me or to destroy me cannot so greatly profit them. For when I am dead the sunne and the moone, the starres and the elements, water and fire, yea and also stones shall defend this cause against them rather than the verity should perish.'[2]

He made his way across the Low Countries to Germany, and so to Wittenberg, where he was cordially welcomed and hospitably entertained by the Wittenberg theologians, notably by Bugenhagen who already had contact with the English Reformers, and who was a kind of Foreign Secretary to the German Reformers. There under the name of Antonius Anglus[3] he began to write, and to compose an Apologia which he hoped might placate his King. By the end of 1531 he seems to have composed two works. The first, in Latin, *Sententiae ex*

[1] Foxe, *A. & M.* vol. v, p. 419.
[2] Barnes, *Supplication*, p. 215.
[3] Not Antonius Amerius, a mistake of Gairdner in *D.N.B.*

doctoribus collectae quas papistae valde hodie damnant, was a collection of patristic authorities on behalf of evangelical opinions. It made a useful debating handbook for the Reformers who made their appeal to patristic authority, as well as to the supreme arbitrament of Holy Scripture. The other was a vernacular version of his propositions which Bugenhagen published in German with a commendation towards the end of 1531. They are worth retailing for us to see how very much of what the English Reformers claimed has become a common heritage of English Churchmen.

1. Only Faith justifies.
2. Christ's death has made satisfaction for all sins and not only for original sin.
3. God's Commandments cannot possibly be kept in our own strength.
4. Freewill by its own powers is only able to sin.
5. The just sin in all good works.
6. What is the true Church and how she may be told.
7. God's Word, not men's powers, is the keys of the Church.
8. Councils may err.
9. All should receive the Sacrament in both kinds.
10. Priests may marry.
11. Human ordinances cannot free sinners.
12. Auricular confession is not necessary to salvation.
13. Monks are not more holy than lay folks on account of cowls and monasteries.
14. Christian fasting does not consist in discrimination between foods.
15. For the Christian every day is a Sabbath day and a festal day and not only the seventh day.[1]
16. Unjust banning by the Pope does not disgrace the banned.

[1] Sabbatarianism at this period, as readers of the Tyndale-More controversy will realize, was a Catholic and not a Protestant trait, and is perhaps more easily defensible on Catholic principles.

17. In the Sacrament of the Altar is truly (*wahrhaft*) the Body of Christ.

18. Saints may not be appealed to as mediators.

19. Of the Origin and parts of the Mass.[1]

Barnes' *Supplication* was published at Antwerp towards the end of the year. Stephen Vaughan, Cromwell's agent abroad, was disturbed by it, 'such a piece of work as yet I have not seen one like to it: I think he shall seal it with his blood', but he also pleaded that Barnes be brought into England to speak for himself, for popular support might be given his case if it were thought that the government were afraid to answer him, 'when men be secretly examined, the world murmureth'. It would seem that his advice was taken and that Barnes paid a short visit under a safe conduct which chafed Sir Thomas More greatly, who wrote that 'Barnes but for the King's safe conduct he should have standen in peril to be burned and his books with him which safe conduct because it was granted but for six weeks now more than almost passed...'.[2]

More's agents noted his movements hungrily, 'suppose some good merchant were fallen in with Friar Barnes in the house of his secret hosts at the sign of the Bottell in Botolf's wharf and finding him walking in a merchant's gown with a red bonnet'. He seems to 'have been given a public hearing and to have been given a counsellor to assist him'. According to More he used the opportunity to meet old friends among whom 'he went like a merchant that he might be the less marked...visiting the congregation without whose liberal aid and alms he should never have been able to sustain and bear nor to recover and get again the money that he spent about his

[1] *Furnemlich Artickel, neulich verteuchst von Dr Antonius aus England* (Wittenberg, 1531).

[2] Gairdner's statement that More was only anxious to put into force the law against runaway friars will not stand. More wanted Barnes as a lapsed heretic. More, *Works* (ed. 1557), p. 760.

printing of his book and his coming hither and going over again'.[1] More claimed that these activities violated the safe conduct and that its time limit had expired. But we have the evidence of Frith who had read the safe conduct that it had not, and that Barnes had not been given any date by which he must leave the country, the only requirement being that he arrive in England before Christmas. He left early in the new year.

He took up residence in Hamburg where he lodged with Aepinus its future bishop, and may have shared some of the pastoral work of the Church of St Nicholas. In April 1533 we find him visiting Bugenhagen at Wittenberg, and at the request of the Hamburg authorities taking a sum of money in connection with the expense of Aepinus' doctorate. This apparently was open to misconstruction and Bugenhagen not only swore Barnes to silence about it, but sent a sharp note back to Hamburg protesting about the indiscretion.[2] Barnes stayed at Wittenberg where he matriculated in June and perhaps put in some work at his projected History of the Popes.

During 1533 and 1534 Henry VIII was looking around for allies and making it his business to fish in any waters likely to trouble the Habsburg power. He not only sent Cristopher Mont and Nicholas Heath to make a circular tour of the German courts, beginning with Bavaria, but turned his attention to the neighbour cities of Hamburg and Lübeck. Hamburg had a direct connection with Denmark and Lübeck was the centre of a revolutionary ferment which at this time bade fair to give her the hegemony of the Baltic cities, and a decisive word in determining the fate of Denmark. Henry had already sent Thomas Legh, a merchant banker, to Hamburg as ambassador, and one who was friendly to Barnes. The result was

---

[1] More, Works (ed. 1557), p. 760.
[2] Otto Vogt, Dr Joh. Bugenhagen's Briefwechsel, pp. 127, 205 (Stettin, 1888). Verein für Hamburgischer Geschichte (1886), p. 66.

a sensational embassy from Hamburg and Lübeck to London.
They arrived in two ships, one from Hamburg, the other from
Lübeck, three ambassadors from each city with eighteen
servants who ruffled it before the startled Londoners, the
Lübeckers swaggering about 'bravely dressed in red with
bands of yellow and white satin' and with these words on their
sleeves: 'If God be for us who can be against us?' It may be
significant of the difference between the cities that the Hamburg men wore sober black and the (in comparison) faintly
defeatist: 'Give peace in our time, O Lord.'[1]

The two chief doctors were Adam Paceus who overwhelmed
Henry and his Queen with a two-hour harangue in Latin, and
Henry, who would rather have such a talker for him than
against him, offered him a permanent post if he would remain
in England. The other doctor was Aepinus who arrived later.
It seems that Barnes accompanied them, and lodged with the
Lübeckers at the Steelyard. It is clear that in such a mission
Barnes had some utility value as friend of the Lübeckers and
intimate of the Hamburg doctors. Barnes probably returned
to England with the Hamburg mission. All did not go well.
Henry did not at all want to pay them a large loan: and showed
growing distaste for some debates on doctrine which concerned
sola fide and the doctrine of the Sacrament. Finally the worried
Aepinus wrote to Cromwell that he and his friends were being
accused of spreading heretical doctrine. 'These rumours have
terrified my host who wishes he had never received me.
I request you to obtain my despatch from the King.'[2]

Barnes spent the next months between Hamburg and Antwerp and was very nearly caught in the attempt of the Nether-
land authorities to apprehend Tyndale, Joye and himself.
Meanwhile, foreign affairs continued to make him of use to
the government, and Cromwell gave him cautious favour. In
March he visited Wittenberg to discuss the 'King's matter' of

[1] *L. & P. Henry VIII* (1534), 871.   [2] Ibid. 874.

the divorce with Melanchthon and sound the possibilities of
further discussion which might make the German theologians
give a verdict favourable to the King. As a result he was
allowed to return to England and at last, in July 1535, with
the status of royal chaplain was sent to prepare the way for
a more formal embassy under Foxe and Heath.

The story of those negotiations will be found on another
page. In them Barnes proved himself a loyal servant of his
King as well as zealous for what he called the 'stablishing of
Christendom'. In September 1535 he dedicated his now
finished *History of the Popes* to his royal master. But neither his
literary efforts nor his diplomatic service won the reward he
might have expected. There is a story that Melanchthon said to
Barnes at this time: 'When you are made a Bishop you must
make me your chancellor.' On the fall of Anne in 1536 Barnes
wrote asking if he might be made Master of the Bethlehem
Hospital, which had belonged to the attainted Rochford,
saying he should prefer it to a bishopric. So far from getting
preferment he had not received his diplomatic 'frais de repré-
sentation', through the avaricious hostility of Sir John Gost-
wyke, himself doing well on Church property. In 1538
Cranmer tried to get him the Deanery of Tamworth college:
'Your lordship knoweth full well that hitherto he hath had
very small preferment for such pains and travail as he most
willingly hath sustained in the King's affairs from time to
time.'[1] In the same year he was employed by the King, in
accord with the royal sense of humour, to bait John Lambert
for his Sacramentarian opinions. At last through the good
offices of William Barlow he was rewarded with a miserable
Welsh prebend to the value of £18 a year. The truth seems to
be that Henry greatly disliked him and that Cromwell durst
not advance one whom the King delighted not to honour.
Then, in 1539, it seemed that opportunity had come at last.

[1] Cranmer, *Remains*, P.S. vol. II, p. 380.

His friend Bugenhagen had been called in to reform the Church in Denmark and by all accounts Barnes was the man to go there on behalf of Henry. Accordingly Barnes went with Saint Leger as companion with full diplomatic status, and with full pay. He wrote home enthusiastically from Hamburg, in almost lyrical prospect of the advantage of an alliance to Henry.[1] But in fact nothing came of it and while the ill-fated negotiations with Cleves proceeded, there came news of the Six Articles, so ominous that Barnes did not venture to return at first, and when he did had a cold reception.[2]

Gardiner had now emerged as leader of the party opposed to the Reformers and he had apparently protested in the Privy Council against Barnes, an abjured heretic being sent as ambassador for the King of England: but Cromwell was still in power and the rather startling result was the extrusion of Gardiner from the Privy Council. He was not a man to forget that kind of thing and though not a persecutor and though he did not perhaps intend the death of Barnes he set events going which moved to that grim end. The sermons preached at Paul's Cross during Lent were the sixteenth-century equivalent of the Bishop of London's *Lent Book*, but in 1540 they were more adventurous than edifying. Cranmer did not perhaps show his usual judgement in allowing Barnes, Thomas Garrard and William Jerome, all of them with a past, all of them liable to indiscretion, to be appointed to preach the series of sermons. But, as though to make sure there should be trouble, Gardiner sent his chaplain and had his own name

---

[1] *L. & P. Henry VIII* (1534, wrong date), 970; 1539, vol. I, 1273.

[2] Constantine's narrative (*Arch.* vol. XXIII): 'Barnes...came to court on Sunday. He was very sad and had licence to depart without speaking with the King.' The Dean was very sure the King would not speak with him. 'I know not that, but Dr Barnes told me that my Lord Privy Seal would have had him tarried to have spoken with the King but he prayed licence because of his weariness.' August 1539. For a summary, see *L. & P. Henry VIII* (1539), vol. II, 400.

inserted at the head of the series, and made an open and provocative attack on Barnes. Barnes replied in kind, with something of that eloquence which Cranmer and Melanchthon noted in him. But it was one thing for a bishop to taunt an unfrocked friar with a past, and another for an abjured heretic under a cloud to poke fun at the Lord Bishop of Winchester. Gardiner promptly complained to the King who came down like a wolf on the fold on the unfortunate Barnes to whom the sight of the Royal Supremacy in action was devastating. Once again, Barnes found himself near the line dividing death and life. He broke down and displayed thereafter that blend of truculence and abjectness which Henry most abominated. Gardiner, touched, and perhaps feeling a little guilty, offered Barnes a pension if he would come and live with him and be instructed.[1]

But after a day or so, when the fright had worn off and when he had thought things over Barnes took up his old position. He and Garrard and Jerome were ordered to preach again and to read a retractation of their Lutheran opinions. The recantation was a mild affair and in it Barnes was made to retract no major doctrine.[2] In the sermons that followed the Reformers did their best to satisfy the authorities without jettisoning their own doctrine. This was no new device: others and notably Doctor Crome made this a fine art. But Barnes asked the angry and embarrassed Gardiner to hold up his hand in token of forgiveness: after this the three were arrested. Henry would have no more of this tomfoolery, and Cromwell was no longer able to help had he been willing. They were condemned by Act of Attainder without trial or cause of condemnation being shown, and they were burned at the same time and probably at the same place as three Catholic friars, as a demonstration

[1] Muller, *Letters of Stephen Gardiner*, 'Answer to George Joye'. *Stephen Gardiner and the Tudor Reaction*, chap. XIII.
[2] Foxe, *A. & M.* vol. v, pp. 434-6 and App. 7.

upon the Wittenberg Articles, and that it was not allowed to wait on the return of Foxe and Heath who only arrived shortly before Convocation.

The temper of that assembly can hardly be judged by the vigorous Latin sermon with which it seems that Latimer harangued its opening, still less by the presence in the chair of Thomas Cromwell acting for the King, with the ruling that in his absence the layman Petre might preside as proctor and deputy. Rather should it be gauged by a series of articles condemning irreverent and Sacramentarian expressions and a condemnation of Lutheran opinions. To this assembly Foxe presented a 'book of faith and articles' which may have been the Ten Articles.

When it was all over Heath sent an informative letter to Melanchthon in which it was suggested that things might have gone better, from the German point of view, had their embassy come to England immediately on the return of the English envoys, and while the Parliament and Convocation were in session. He speaks of the 'assembly which among us is called a parliament, one with the bishops, abbots and general clergy . . .for this is our custom that as often as parliament is held, so often and at the same time a synod of bishops and clergy is held'. He describes the attention paid by the parliament to the succession problem and to the legitimacy of the offspring of Katherine and Anne, concluding discreetly 'but to write many things about this matter is not expedient for your sake, nor safe for me'. 'In the synod', he continued, 'they discussed the quietening of tumult and murmuring which had arisen among the people and was filling the minds of the vulgar, owing to the dissension of the preachers. The synod took action by making and publishing certain articles in which a prescribed form is given to the preachers as to how far they may speak of those religious matters which are the subject of controversy.' He promises to send Melanchthon a copy of them in Latin, 'where, however, little care has been taken about their Latinity. For I wished that it should be translated word for word, as far as possible, that you might not only grasp the meaning, but have the words. Yet when they were put forward there were many who assented to the meaning of these articles only with great difficulty. And in the end it was necessary to obtain consent by the intervention of royal authority, and for the sake of concord and the appeasement of causes of tumult. So that if your legation had come in time, some things might have gone better.'[1]

What was the relation between the Wittenberg Articles which had evolved in the course of the earlier negotiations and the 'Ten Articles'? The basis of the Wittenberg Articles had been the Augsburg Confession and its Apology, since these were the doctrinal basis of the Protestant League. But although the Germans had taken their stand on the Confession, they could hardly refuse to discuss the possibility of any alteration, without placing their own tradition above the Word of God. Probably the first draft of the Wittenberg Articles was the work of Melanchthon and they bear evident traces of his theology as adumbrated in his *Loci Communes*.

There was a difference of intention between the Augsburg Confession and the Wittenberg Articles. The first was a confession of faith, the second an attempted *eirenicon*. The Wittenberg Articles are an illumination of the extent to which the Germans would make minor concessions, if only they might add England to the Evangelical Party.

The resultant document was in no way a theological masterpiece and it soon dropped into the background of reformation confessional literature. Pruser points out that in places it contradicted known sentiments of the German theologians. The statement 'est fides ipsa praecipuum opus' in the article concerning Good Works had been explicitly rejected by Luther

[1] Luther, *Letters*, W.E. vol. VIII, pp. 220-3.

where our Reformers set their faces most steadfastly towards
Wittenberg, Strasbourg or Zürich, their caps were tilted after
an English fashion.

William Tyndale was the giant among them, whom More
and Foxe unwontedly agree in styling the 'chief' and 'captain'
of them. It is not our purpose to rehearse facts lately made
accessible through the fourth centenary of the English Bible
or in Mr Mozley's fine biography of the Reformer.[1] Tardy
justice has been done him, his integrity of character which
overwhelmed even his enemies, his unremitting selfless zeal
and apostolic dedication to the task which he believed had
been set him, the depth of his intuitive regard for truth, so
that, even where he borrowed or translated, what he wrote was
coloured by his own rich feeling and expressed in prose which
at times reached limpid purity unsurpassed in English literature, which differs from the cumbrous Latinity of Sir Thomas
More as the prose of Bunyan differs from the conceits of
Donne.

Tyndale was driven abroad by the compulsion of his chief
work: 'I understood...not only that there was no room in
my Lord of London's palace to translate the New Testament,
but also that there was no place to do it in all England.' We
cannot understand the first decade of the English Reformation
unless we recognize that the edition of the English New
Testament was its supreme event, and that it, and the other
Biblical translations following, fell into a more important
category than the theological writings of the Reformers. The
great battle for the vernacular scripture was by no means
settled in 1526, and yet the quality of Tyndale's work made this
the decisive blow. The effect of the burning by the authorities
of the English Testaments was different from that of the
customary burning of heretical literature, and shocked circles
by no means avid of the new opinions. Tyndale's famous

[1] J. F. Mozley, *William Tyndale* (S.P.C.K. 1937).

promise to Stephen Vaughan shows that this was for him the key to the reform of Christendom:

'If it would stand with the king's most gracious pleasure to grant only a bare text of the scripture to be put forth among his people,...be it of the translation of what person soever shall please his majesty. I shall immediately make faithful promise never to write more.'[1]

Next to his Biblical translation, Tyndale was concerned to make known the teaching of Luther in an English dress. He had to walk delicately for the works of Luther were everywhere proscribed, but he succeeded so well that down to our time the full extent of his debt to Luther has not been made apparent.

Westcott's hint has not been explored that 'the extent to which Tyndale silently incorporated free or even verbal translations of passages from Luther's works into his own has escaped the notice of his editors. To define it accurately would be a work of very great labour, but the result as exhibiting the points of contact and divergence in the opinions of the Reformers, would be a most instructive passage in the doctrinal history of the time.'[2] But some facts are indisputable and illuminating.

First, Tyndale took pains to put into English Luther's celebrated Preface to the Epistle to the Romans, and not only included it in his New Testament but issued it in a separate publication. In its way that preface is one of the classics of Protestant theology, to which it is still a brief, clear introduction. To speak of Tyndale's preface as 'founded' on Luther, or as 'Lutheran' greatly understates the debt. The whole of Luther's Preface is translated by Tyndale, with the exception of a few isolated and unimportant words. To this Tyndale has made certain additions which amount in all to about four folio

[1] Greenslade, *William Tyndale*, p. 13.
[2] Westcott, *Hist. English Bible* (1905), p. 146.

was followed in the Bishops' Book), to be distinguished from the rest as being Sacraments of the Gospel, instituted by the Lord and proclaiming the Forgiveness of Sins. On the other hand it is remarkable that no mention is made of the four ecclesiastical abuses which so exercised the Germans. Henry would not meddle with them: whenever they were discussed the debate was broken off: they were the rock on which all future theological discussions were to founder. It is the more striking that Henry himself was to proceed drastically with practical measures which struck at some of them. He would dissolve the monasteries: he would not debate monastic vows. Perhaps it was because anything conceded here might have looked as though the 'Defender of the Faith' was in tutelage to Wittenberg. The result was that the Ten Articles were more garbled even than the Wittenberg Articles. Bishop Foxe's *Book of Articles* bore as little resemblance to the debates in Germany as a novel to its film scenario. 'Confusissime compositi', sighed Melanchthon, as he pondered his copy of them. The verdict may stand, and perhaps it would not be the last English confessional document to deserve it. It sometimes appears that in exalting the Middle Way the English Church has elevated confusion of thought to the level of a theological virtue.

NEGOTIATIONS, 1537–8

There was an interruption of relations between English and German theologians after Heath's letter of 1536. In England the autumn brought the serious open rebellion in the North which moved Henry to walk delicately. Yet he could not ignore the danger of the Papal council and issued a statement which the German reformers approved. There is an anxious note in this inquiry: 'What the States will do, if the Emperor, French King and the Bishop of Rome conclude upon a General council and do anything contrary to the Law of God?'

Once again Cristopher Mont set out for Germany and in February 1538 he attended a meeting of the League at Brunswick, where he asked for the long-awaited delegation. This time it was dispatched. The leader, Francis Burchardt, Vice-Chancellor of Saxony, was a man of parts, and one who could hold his own in theology and in politics. The theologian of the party was Frederick Myconius the Superintendent of Gotha. With them came a Hessian nobleman, George a Boyneburg. The delegates bore a letter from Luther to Edward Foxe, in which Luther tried to put the best interpretation on the silent interval, and hoped that the delegates might now bring back word that the English Church had embraced the Gospel. Luther had established cordial relationship with Foxe on the basis of their common disease, the stone, and had indeed exchanged remedies with him. But a higher authority had sealed the lips of the Bishop, for death had taken him four days before Luther wrote.[1] In the passing of Edward Foxe the Reformers lost a good friend. Though the Germans might find a 'prelatical manner' and a propensity for 'sophistry' in one who, after all had trained in the old diplomatic school of Wolsey, the months following his return to England showed him to have intervened with some learning and growing warmth in the evangelical cause. The difference between the Bishops' and the King's Book might have been mitigated had he been alive, for his was a healing and moderating influence, who was a friend of both Thomas Cranmer and of Stephen Gardiner.

The Germans found that the conduct of debate had been entrusted to three bishops, Stokesley, Sampson and Cranmer the 'archbishop of Kandelberg', and to four doctors, including Barnes and Heath. As a team they could not compare with the giants of Wittenberg, but Burchardt and Myconius far from home were soon hard pressed and so

[1] He died 8 May 1538.

William Roye was Tyndale's garrulous amanuensis, and it is as well that we have Tyndale's own version of their relationship, or Tyndale's New Testament might, like Jerome Barlow's *Burial of the Mass*, have been attracted into the orbit of the fame of William Roye.

'While I abode a faithful companion [wrote Tyndale in the preface to the *Wicked Mammon*], one William Roye, a man somewhat crafty when he cometh unto new acquaintance and before he be thorow known, and namely when all is spent, came unto me and offered his help. As long as he had no money, somewhat I could rule him, but as soon as he had gotten him money, he became like himself again. Nevertheless I suffered all things till that was ended which I could not do alone without one, both to write, and to help me to compare the texts together. When that was ended, I took my leave, and bade him farewell for our two lives, and (as men say) a day longer.'[1]

Roye, or Petit, came from Calais where his father had been a citizen and enemies declared that the family were what would now be called 'Non-Aryan', or as Roye more delicately phrased it, 'would eat no pork'. He may have studied at Cambridge: he may even have transcribed there the Leicester[2] Codex, which would be proof of an early ability for linguistic and textual study. He entered the Franciscan Observants and became a member of their house at Greenwich, and was probably there during the uproar which was created against Wolsey's visitation. In the summer of 1525 we find him matriculating at Wittenberg and soon after, penniless and seeking employment, he came to Tyndale. His own opinion of his abilities was not mean and he seems to have persuaded most people, and perhaps came nearer than we realize to persuading posterity, that he was the real linguistic genius among the exiles and had played Paul to Tyndale's Barnabas. I think

[1] Tyndale, *Wicked Mammon*, P.S. p. 38.
[2] See the conjectures, they are hardly more, in Rendel Harris, *The Leicester Codex*, 1887.

it possible that the well-known tribute of Spalatin to the linguistic ability of one of the exiles was a result of Roye's boasting about himself, for Tyndale was not the kind of man to flaunt such dangerous gifts.[1] In any case we have other examples of Roye's boasting. In his own treatise he refers to Tyndale 'unto whom I was (after the grace given me of the Lord) as healpe felowe and parte taker of his laboures', and claims that events have 'couraged my mynde to go aboute the translacion of holy Scripture. Insomoche that I have allredy translated certayne bokes of the olde Testament, which with the healpe of God yer long shal be brought to light', asking the prayers of his readers 'that I may have both mynde and strengthe wother soche bokes to translate, and the whole olde Testament whereby ye of englonde maye also knowe and heare the voyce of youre true shepherde.'[2] It is very doubtful if the work was ever begun and Tyndale's comment that he had promised more than he was likely to perform was well deserved.[3]

Disowned by Tyndale, Roye proceeded to 'gat him new friends' and it is probable that he made contact with the agents of the Christian Brethren, for he soon had money, not only for himself but to employ Jerome Barlow in 'making rhymes' and in composing a series of dialogues which incorporated long sections of old Lollard works. Roye himself translated from the Latin a *Dialogue between a Christian Father and his stubborn Son*,[4] a catechetical work probably written by one of

[1] Spalatin to Buschius: 'Sex mille exemplaria Novi Testamenti anglice excussa. Id operis versum esse ab Anglo illic cum duobus aliis Britannis divertente, ita septem linguarum perito, Hebraicae, Graecae, Latinae, Italicae, Hispanicae, Britannicae, Gallicae, ut quamcunque loquatur in ea natum putes.' Apud Foxe, *A. & M.* vol. v, p. 812.

[2] Roye, *Dialogue between Father and Son*, ed. Wolf, pp. 34–6.

[3] Tyndale, *Doctrinal Treatises*, P.S. p. 39.

[4] Strasbourg, 1527. Ed. Adolf Wolf, Vienna, 1874. See R. Steele, 'Notes on English Books translated abroad 1525–48', *Trans. Bibliog. Soc.* vol. II. C. H. Herford, *Literary Relations between England and Germany in the Sixteenth Century*. 1886.

Art. 5. *De Ecclesia.* A definition of the Church was a notable omission from the Wittenberg Articles. This long article amplifies but does not contradict the Augsburg Confession and enunciates the distinction between the visible and the invisible church, besides including part of Art. 8 of the Augsburg Confession.

Art. 6. *De Baptismo.* Here the short statement of the Augsburg Confession is abandoned for the fuller statement of the Wittenberg Articles which is reproduced in full.

Art. 7. *De Eucharistia.* The article is that of the Wittenberg Articles but the important addition is made that the sacrament is received 'sive bonis et malis'.

Art. 8. *De Poenitentia.* Here extensive alterations have been made. Yet this is not an entirely new article and there are quotations from the Wittenberg Articles. But it differs from evangelical doctrine by its statement that auricular confession is 'valde utilem ac summe necessariam'.

Art. 9. *De Sacramentorum Usu.* Quoted verbally and in full from the Wittenberg Articles.

Art. 10. *De Ministris Ecclesiae.* Quotes Art. 14 of the Augsburg Confession verbally and in full.

Art. 11. *De Ritibus Ecclesiasticis.* Shows substantial differences from any German document but has traces of the words and more of the ideas of the Wittenberg Articles.

Art. 12. *De Rebus Civilibus.* Does not traverse the Augsburg Confession or the Wittenberg Articles but enlarges them, though most of the article is new. Is by far the longest of these articles.

Art. 13. *De Corporum Resurrectione.* 'De Judicio Extremo' is verbally identical with Art. 17 of the Augsburg Confession.

BREAKDOWN OF NEGOTIATIONS, 1539–40

The last years of the negotiations have less importance from our point of view, for, two long disquisitions on the 'four abuses' apart, they produced no important theological documents. In 1538 the danger to Henry VIII from foreign powers had receded, but the spoliation of the shrines sensationally stirred Catholic opinion. Cardinal Pole went to the imperial court to solicit aid against his schismatic kinsman. In Scotland, Cardinal Beaton received from the Pope a sword and the title 'Defensor Fidei', pointed compliments with their edge towards England. The King of France rudely interrupted the printing of English Bibles at Paris. Rumours reached England of an invasion fleet assembled at German ports, and of a plan to oust Henry and put the Duke of Orleans on the English throne. Once again Henry sought allies, but this time he looked elsewhere than the League, to the King of Denmark and to the nobles of the Palatinate and of the House of Cleves who stood without the League but favoured moderate reform. Once again Cristopher Mont went to Germany where the Reformers too were a little alarmed at the bristling armament of the Catholic powers.

There followed a warning from John Frederick to Henry about the Anabaptist peril, but Henry had his own grim methods and needed little advice on this subject. The question of a wider alliance then arose. Cromwell sought an alliance of anti-Catholic powers which would have a wider basis than that of the Schmalkaldic League and which would offer the advantage of political alliance without the disadvantage of theological entanglements. In 1538 Burchardt had discussed the possibility of a match between the Duke of Cleves and the Princess Mary, a match which John Frederick promised to further as far as in him lay. Cromwell now had a more elevated thought and suggested the match be between Henry and Anne, the sister of the Duke. Mont reported the idea to be so favourably received that Drs Wootton and Bird were sent to Cleves to gain information and to make personal acquaintance with the favoured lady. John Frederick was not so pleased and made the excuse that his painter, Lukas Cranach, was ill, to by which it was known by friend and foe in the sixteenth century.

The treatise is of a complicated structure, a dialogue in rhyme interspersed with a number of 'baletts'. It attempts to combine two themes: the first borrowed from a popular satire, the *Krankheit der Messe*, a rather clumsy if not elephantine satire; the other, and this the more virile part, an all-out attack on the governance of England under Cardinal Wolsey. Wolsey was the most generally hated statesman in English history, and attracted the pens of satirists as diverse as Simon Fish, Skelton, and Alexander Barclay, but none of them excelled the *Burial of the Mass*. Its author has no qualms, and he rushes into places too delicate for fools or angels, the effects of Wolsey's foreign policy, the Cardinal's private life, and even the relations between Henry and Katherine. It is an attack on the executive such as would have got its author into trouble in any century and any country and, reading it, we can understand why Wolsey paid two friars to hunt out the author.

The title-page [1] is an ingenious affair, an escutcheon in which the Cardinal's hat is second to the butcher *cum* cur of Ipswich, the whole printed in blood red, while three verses expound the meaning of this, in case any readers should mistake it. The preface is probably a blind, and pretends that the work has been sent out from England. Then follows a dialogue between the treatise and the author in which the treatise expresses some pardonable indeed inevitable misgivings concerning the fate of such a work. In fact, the intreaty 'Rede me and be not wroth' and the plea that the reader should not 'take this as a thing convicious' are, to say the least, optimistic.

Then follows the work itself, beginning with a lament in which a priest bewails the decease of the Mass, and the main part of it, a 'brief dialogue between two priest's servants

---

[1] Ed. Arber, *English Reprints* (attr. to Roye), *Rede me and be not wroth*, 1871.

Watkyn and Jeffry'. The dialogue is in two parts: the first concerned with the Burial of the Mass, and the attack on Wolsey; the second half may be what Barlow in his recantation referred to as the 'climbing up of friars and religious', and is an attack on the religious and particularly on the Friars Observant. It is an intriguing work; parts of it have dramatic art and are not without merit as verse, as the following, a pat comment on the spirit of the time, will show:

> *Wat.* Fyrst synge a balett, go to,
> And then will we to diner.
> *Jef.* Alas, I am marvelously dry.
> *Wat.* Thou shalt dryncke man, by and by,
> What nedeth the so to lynger?
> *Jef.* Have at it in the best manner.
>
> 'In the joyfull moneth of joly June,
> Walkynge all alone my care to solas
> I herde a voyce with a dolorous tune
> Full pitously cryinge alas, alas,
> The worlde is worsse than evyr it was.
> Never so depe in miserable decaye,
> But it cannot thus endure all waye.'[1]

There are some vivid personal sketches of Cochlaeus, Dr Allen and Standish. The picture of Wolsey in procession has often been quoted, but perhaps even livelier is the attack, *con amore*, on the Franciscan Observants:

> 'peradventure the goode father
> Hath in his sleve a bladder,
> Full of gynger, nutmegges or graynes
> Which to make the drincke myghtye
> He putteth therin a quantite
> to comforte and warme his veynes',[2]

and the unforgettable description of two friars planning their itinerary so that, by a happy coincidence they shall pass near such houses as would be marked three star in *Baedeker*.

---

[1] P. 66.   [2] P. 82.

appearance of Alexander Alesius at Wittenberg. That self-appointed Chorus to the English Reformation, though he felt the new measures dangerous enough to merit his own rapid withdrawal, did his best to exculpate Henry and put the blame on the English Bishops. The news that Barnes had failed in his mission to Denmark, and the arrest of leading English Reformers were other signs that the evangelical cause in England must be gravely imperilled.

Now the Cleves match was the only link between England and Germany. Duke William was still agreeable. Holbein went to take the portraits of sister Anne, and, just in case, of her sister Amelia. Two councillors from Cleves set out for London and John Frederick agreed to send two envoys. Now unexpected support came from the Landgrave Philip and his Strassburger theologians who were always glad of a chance to expend righteous indignation at the expense of Wittenberg. Mont visited Bucer and went on to John Frederick in Saxony. The Elector was adamant that there could be no alliance without theological agreement, and while the sinister Six Articles held law. Bucer plunged into his favourite fuss of peace-making, and in a letter of 16 September 1539 reported to his patron on the English situation, seeing Gardiner's hand at work in it all, and criticizing the Wittenberg theologians for their half-heartedness. Why had Melanchthon refused to visit England, again and again? Written treatises were no substitute for that personal argument which alone could defeat the 'sophistischen Griffe und Scheinargument'. Was it not the special mission of the Christian to seek out the erring?

'Our Lord Jesus left heaven to help us in his pity, and suffered bitter death: he left the ninety and nine sheep and sought the hundredth, he has richly dowered us and bidden us help others as freely as he has given to us: and said that he will repay us an hundred fold with eternal blessedness. That is: "Go into all the world and preach the Gospel to every creature." Yet we think that when somebody comes to us, that we have done and suffered everything for them that is needful. But that in this way we might win some for our Lord, that we do not understand as we should. The Lord help us to a better knowledge of it, and then we shall be better able to act for the salvation of others and of our own selves according to his will.'[1]

With these words he urged Philip of Hesse to secure that an embassy be sent to England, headed by Melanchthon and in a confidential postscript blamed Burchardt for the failure. He and Myconius were no match for the sophisters and had been in too great a hurry to get home. It was all very well for Bucer to talk like this at the eleventh hour, when the theologians of Wittenberg had borne the heat and burden of a long and wearisome day, but there was perhaps something in it.

At the same time Bucer wrote to Luther whose reply fore-shadowed the response of the other Wittenberg theologians. 'About the King of England', Martin wrote, 'I fear your hope is vain. We heard the English themselves complaining about their king when they were here, envying us our liberty.'[2] The fuller and more official reply bears the weight of their growing exasperation. The Germans have been forced to believe that Henry is acting deliberately against his conscience. There they did him an injustice: Henry never acted against his conscience which he had long educated to walk humbly with him. They added the comment upon the Six Articles: 'The King does not seek the honour of God, but wishes to do just as he pleases, as he told our Vice-Chancellor "He would rule his Kingdom himself".' 'We will write an expostulation to the King', they concluded, 'but further we are not bound to go. As for Master Bucer's quotation "Go ye into all the world..." we do that with our writings, and to leave our present calling is not

---

[1] Lenz, *Briefwechsel*, pp. 103–4.
[2] Luther, *Letters*, W.E. vol. VIII, 3394.

have been allowed to retract, for More says that he 'graciously turned to God again'. Either More or Stokesley had the bright idea of making him write another dialogue, this time denouncing the Protestants, and the result was the *Dialogue against the Lutheran factions*. The new dialogue between one Nicholas and William[1] is of poor spirit and adds nothing to the already crystallized anti-Protestant polemic which More and Cochlaeus had devised.

Yet even here Barlow's talent for indiscretion peeps out:

'Ye must consider that God hath not made the people for the sensual pleasure of princes, governors or prelates but hath ordained them to the weal and commodity of the people.'

At other times the evangelical catchwords come a thought too trippingly off his tongue:

'*N*. How should lay men come to this knowledge when the Gospell is locked from them?

W. The Gospell of Christ which is God's word, is free, and cannot be bounde nor kepte from any Christen men.'

There is an interesting description of how the author became a Protestant:

'The very begynnynge was this. I had redde certayn treatyses of Martyn Luther, of the Justifycacion onely by Fayth wythoute good deedes, how man had no free wyl, how oure good workes avayled us nothing to be saved, nother oure yll deedes shoulde cause us to be damned....I dylygentlye noted howe he descrybed the abuses of Popes, Cardinalles, Bysshoppes, priests and relygious personnes declarynge howe the present dekay of the church farre differed from the perfectyon of the apostles and holy fathers, at the fyrst beginnynge: wherin he made no lye, though in other thinges he spared the truthe. Furthermore, gevyng eare to the pleasant rumoures of his reformations highly commended among new fangled

---

[1] Foxe says that John Lambert, alias Nicholson, was betrayed by one Barlow and it may be that they are the Nicholson and William of the dialogue, perhaps based on genuine conversations.

people: it set myne harte so on fyre that I could not rest untyll I had bene with them.'[1]

From the letters of Wolsey's spy Friar West, it seems that Barlow went to Antwerp and lived near Tyndale. But he may have accompanied Roye on his daring visit to his mother, who lived in London. The Greenwich Observants have the reputation of extreme orthodoxy, but it is obvious from the letters of the disgruntled West that they were by no means disposed to betray Roye and may even have given him refuge. West's last despatch shows Roye[2] making for Newcastle with a red-headed companion who, he surmises, may be Barlow. Thereafter the only direct news of either is the gossip that Roye was burned in Portugal in 1531, and the tantalizing letter of submission signed 'Wm Barlo'. So the two shadowy figures melt into the background, a few copies of their tracts, little regarded, as their sole and ineffective monuments.

---

[1] W. Barlow, *Dialogue Against Lutheran Factions* (London, 1553). *Bishop Barlowe's Dialogue* (ed. Lunn), 1897, p. 70.

[2] For W. Roye, see *L. & P. Henry VIII* (1528–30), 2607, 2652, 2721, 2797, 3132, 3960, 4260, 4693, 4810, 4811, 4826, 4827, 5018, 5043, 5462.

CHAPTER IV

THE EARLY CAREER OF BISHOP BARLOW

THEOLOGICAL controversy regarding Anglican orders has brought the career of Bishop William Barlow into a prominence which perhaps outpasses the desert of his episcopal labours, or recorded utterances, or even that supreme, but involuntary achievement, of becoming father-in-law to half the episcopal Bench. Yet the beginning of his career presents an even prettier historical problem than the obscure process whereby he, Prior of Haverfordwest, became Bishop of St Asaph's and St David's. At any rate it can be shown that the dictionary accounts[1] conflate the careers of two, three, and possibly four persons, besides being embellished with details proper to the career of his brothers John and Roger. The result is a picture, not so much as Fuller said, a 'man of much motion and promotion' as of a veritable ecclesiastical corkscrew.

According to the usual story, William Barlow was an Austin Canon who held executive position in a number of houses in Essex and Norfolk, whose house was suppressed by Wolsey and who went off in dudgeon to the Continent, there to write the notorious *Burial of the Mass* and other 'convicious' dialogues, and thereafter signing an abject recantation, to find reward and preferment, not as we might expect from More and Stokesley but from Anne Boleyn and her father, and Thomas Cromwell. Here we shall endeavour to straighten the story and to give a fuller examination than has hitherto been made of the question raised in the dictionary account and made explicit by Professor Koszul:[2] whether Bishop Barlow is to be

[1] Cooper, *Athenae Cantabrigienses*, vol. I, p. 276; and T. F. Tout in the *D.N.B.*
[2] In the *Review of English Studies*, vol. IV, pp. 25 ff.

identified with the Friar Jerome Barlow of the *Burial of the Mass*.

William Barlow, Bishop, with his brothers Roger, John and Thomas, and his sister Elizabeth was a member of the Essex-Hertfordshire branches of the Barlow family.[1] This family was well connected, and owned considerable property in both counties, but one of its members was involved in the rebellion of Perkin Warbeck and in flight to the Continent took refuge in the house of his brother John, the father of the future Bishop. The result was that both brothers lost their possessions and the children had to make their own way in the world. Three of the four sons entered the Church. Elizabeth became friend and lady in waiting to Queen Margaret of Scotland, and later accompanied her mistress to that country where she made a good match and became Lady Elphinstone.[2] Roger shaped an adventurous career. In 1526 we find him as an English merchant in Spain, in the service of that country, and partner with two friends Robert and Nicholas Thorne sharing with them (he risked 550 ducats and his own person) in the perils of an adventure to South America with Sebastian Cabot, of which he has left permanent record in his *Briefe Summe of Geographie*.[3]

The expedition returned to Lisbon in October 1528 and perhaps in view of growing tension between England and Spain, Roger made contact with Sir Thomas Boleyn,[4] and returned to Bristol, hoping that the King might be interested in a daring project to get to the Indies across the North Pole.

[1] Sir M. Barlow, *Barlow Family Records*, 1932. The most fruitful document is the Wotton MS. which is of late date (1739), however, and of proven inaccuracy in some details. See also Morant, *Hist. Essex* (1768), pp. 249, 410; vol. II, p. 570. The pedigree in Thoresby, *Leod. Duc.* is inaccurate (Venn, *Alumni Cant.* App. 'Barlow').

[2] M. Barlow, *Family Records*, p. 6.

[3] R. Barlow, *A Briefe Summe of Geographie* (ed. E. G. R. Taylor), Hakluyt Soc., 2nd ser., vol. LXIX, App. 3, p. 188.

[4] Perhaps through John who was chaplain to Sir Thomas Boleyn.

It seems likely that it was Roger who began the westward migration of the Barlow family, but in any case he was soon joined by brother John who in 1530 became Dean of the college of Westbury-on-Trym, within reach of Bristol. Whether a man in his thirties and forties sees with a shrewder eye the glittering plans of his twenties, or whether he just settled down, and the cares of other things choked the pioneering word, he put off the grand project which might have won him lasting fame in English chronicles, instead of the few faded pages of an old MS. which are its only record.

There is more material for a character sketch of John than for the other members of the family. He may well have been the John Barlow who (from Essex) became fellow of Corpus Christi, Oxford, admitted B.A. 13 November 1517 and M.A. in July 1521.[1] Between 1521 and 1527 he held the Essex livings of South Benfleet, Great Bentley and Hawkswell.[2] At some time between 1525 and 1528 he entered the service of the Boleyn family, as chaplain to Sir Thomas, and was much employed in connection with the Divorce.[3] He was indeed so well known as Anne's servant (he became a member of her household), that he was lucky not to be implicated in her fall, which gave him a thorough scare.[4] A report from Louvain in 1532 shows us John, the diplomat: 'He is of small stature, with red hair, sober in eating and drinking, speaking little and ignorant of music and games.' In 1534 he informed Cromwell that he was now on the side of reform, and since we have

[1] Foster, *Alumni Oxonienses*. If this be so, then the Thomas Barlow who proceeded M.A. 2 July 1521 was probably his brother.

[2] Newcourt, *Repertorium*, vol. II. Thomas Boleyn was patron of Hawkswell.

[3] See the complaint of R. Colyn, *L. & P. Henry VIII*, 1536, 22 June: 'he said Barlow always belonged to her, and had his promotion by her, and had been ambassador for her in diverse places beyond the sea before she was Queen.'

[4] Ibid.: 'on the first knowledge of the treason of Queen Anne, Barlow came with speed into the country.'

accounts of his reporting others for heresy, including the
delation of a troop of tennis-players for playing during morning
service, it is possible that it was John and not William Barlow
who informed against John Nicholson or Lambert.[1] After the
preferment of his brother William, John Barlow became Archdeacon of Westbury, and on the dissolution of his college at
Westbury, became prebendary of Peterborough and Dean of
Worcester.[2] Thomas held the living of Abberton[3] from
1519–41, and was parson of Catfield. He resided with John at
Westbury and shared with Roger in the purchase of church
lands at Slebech and at Haverfordwest. Whether because the
dullest, or the unluckiest, or perhaps the youngest, Thomas
was the least notable of the brothers Barlow.

By 1534 then, they were settled in the west of England.
Roger had bought property, and was fast becoming the
country squire, although his nautical experience led the government to consult him about such matters as the appraisal of a
ballinger, and the gold from a wrecked ship, and was acquiring
that knowledge of the district which made him fit for his office
of Vice-Admiral of the Pembroke coast, which was given him
in 1549.

That is the family background against which we must fit the
career of Bishop Barlow. But just here, to put it mildly,
confusion begins. The two Barlow brothers implicated in the
Warbeck rebellion had each a son named William who entered
the Church. This other William studied law at Cambridge and
became Bachelor of Law.[4] His sister Anne married Lord Gray,

---

[1] Constantine's picture in his vivid narrative (*L. & P. Henry VIII*,
1539, 400; *Arch.* vol. XXIII, pp. 50–78) is convincing though malicious:
'Mr Dean is a man that can make of a piece a whole tale, and if he have
a man down can invent as him lusteth.'

[2] Westbury College had a value of £232 and was probably more valuable
than William's priory at Haverfordwest. If we could say how and why
William outstripped John in preferment, we should have the solution of
the Barlow mystery.   [3] Newcourt, *Repertorium*, vol. II.

[4] *Grace Book*, Beta, 1511. Barlow, B.A. 1512–15. *L. & P. Henry VIII*
(1528–30), 3869.

and his other sister Dorothy became Abbess of Barking. In 1528 he received a pension in the gift of the Abbess for a clerk of the King's nomination 'until he be appointed to a benefice'; in 1530 he held the living of Dagenham also in the gift of his sister. He may have been the William Barlow who in 1529 was made prebendary of Bridgnorth, Salop, and held livings in Bugbroke and in Market Bosworth (Lincolnshire). If he were, as some have suggested, Archdeacon of Northampton, it would be an office suited to his legal training. His will was proved in 1541.[1]

We come next to consider Friar Jerome Barlow, author of the *Burial of the Mass*. In his preface to the *Wicked Mammon* Tyndale explicitly states that 'came one Jerome, a brother of Greenwich also'.[2] But in addition to this we have the added testimony of Herman Rinck who includes Jerome Barlow in a list of apostate Observants (which, however, includes Tyndale who was certainly not an Observant or a Franciscan). We have also the repeated statements of that Friar West who was Wolsey's agent. He names Barlow as 'Jerome Barlow, a friar of our religion'[3] and in one letter describing William Roye's flight to Newcastle he suggests that Roye's red-headed companion may be Barlow, though West's letter does not suggest that he had personal acquaintance with either fugitive. Thus we have three different witnesses to the fact that Jerome Barlow was an Apostate Observant from Greenwich.[4]

Internal evidence from the *Burial of the Mass*, not conclusive, since we cannot be sure that Roye had no share in it, favours

[1] Sir M. Barlow, *Barlow Family Records*, where a pedigree is given, not without difficulties.

[2] Tyndale, *Doctrinal Treatises*, P.S. p. 38. Tyndale says that Jerome went to Roye to 'gat him to hire' (*Harleian Misc.* vol. IX, p. 2) and 'set him a work to make rhymes'.

[3] Arber, *Reprints, Rede me and be not wroth* (1871), Introd. pp. 10–14.

[4] Professor Koszul can only identify the friar and the Bishop by assuming that Tyndale had made a mistake, but the evidence is threefold, as we have seen.

the same conclusion. The satire devotes its liveliest section to the special characteristics of the Observant friars and its author confesses to have lived 'above twelve years continually' in that religion. The attitude to the Divorce is that of the friars who had a great affection for Queen Katherine and for the Princess Mary, not at all the attitude of a friend of the Boleyn family such as we know the Bishop Barlow to have been.

Now comes the rub: there is extant a letter of submission and recantation addressed to the King, acknowledging authorship of the dialogues and a number of other works, admitting great heresy and asking pardon. It is almost certain that the recantation was followed soon by the *Dialogue of Lutheran factions*. But this recantation is signed 'William Barlo'.[1] And it is also to be noted that Foxe includes a William Barlo, priest in a long list of those abjured in the reign of Henry VIII.[2] Meanwhile, there is evidence that Jerome Barlow had recanted. To complicate the problem, the second edition of the *Dialogue of Lutheran Factions*, 1553, had as its author 'William Barlow, Chanon, late Bishop of Bath and Wells'.

Must we then identify Friar Jerome Barlow with the future Bishop Barlow? Professor Koszul suggests it, but we have seen that his assumption that Tyndale was mistaken about Jerome Barlow's antecedents ignores other testimonies. We could only assume it by supposing a deliberate deception on the part of William, at a time when his brother was in the

[1] Wright, *Letters relative to the Suppression of the Monasteries* (Camden Soc.), p. 6. Conditions in 1944 did not admit of inspecting the original autograph.

[2] Foxe, *A. & M.* vol. IV, p. 585. It is noticeable that this is the only name on the list for which no later amplification is given. It may be that Foxe had only seen the letter of submission, but it is more likely that he identified the author with Bishop Barlow and thought it more tactful to pass over this episode in the career of one who, if not among the Fathers, is first of the fathers-in-law of Anglicanism. I have only been able to search one folio of the Stokesley Register.

service of the Boleyns. It is not very likely. There is another objection, which grows weightier the more one ponders it. We know how gravely the career of Robert Barnes was damaged by the fact that he was an abjured heretic: we know how violently Stephen Gardiner objected in the Privy Council against such an one being employed as an ambassador. Yet Bishop William Barlow was sent in 1535–6 as Ambassador to Scotland, and he held his see during the triumph of the Catholic Party in 1539 onwards, and there is no record at all of this past blemish on his career being raised by his enemies. I find this inconceivable.

Now we may return to the point where the dictionary accounts begin, with the East Anglian career of William Barlow, Canon Regular of the order of Augustinian Canons. This William Barlow held a succession of Priories, but an examination of them reveals that this part of his career was not as dazzling as might appear. He was first Canon of Bicknacre (dissolved 1509[1] for lack of numbers) and then (after some months at Blackmore?)[2] Prior of Tiptree, a house of one Canon in addition to himself. From September 1515 to September 1524 he was Prior of Lees Parva and in 1525 moved to Norfolk to become the Prior of Bromehill, a house of three or four Canons.[3] He was there at the Visitation of 1526, but in 1528 the house was dissolved in order to assist the foundation of Wolsey's College at Ipswich, and Prior Barlow received a compensation of 40s.

There follows a gap in the career of Prior Barlow and we next find a Prior Barlow in an altogether different part of the

[1] The 'alias Finch' is the result of a misreading. He may have been a member of the house of St Osyth but it does not seem to be more than a guess of Bale.

[2] He was not Prior of Blackmore, as Dugdale suggests. See V.C.H. Essex and Dugdale, Monasticon, vol. VI.

[3] V.C.H. Norfolk, vol. II, p. 374. He may also have been rector of Great Cressingham.

country, in Queen Anne's lordship of Pembroke, and at her installation as Prior of Haverfordwest.[1] It would seem natural to assume that the two Priors were one and the same. And yet there were in fact two William Barlows, both Canons Regular of the Austin Canons. When the large Augustinian house of St Bartholomew, Smithfield, was dissolved in 1540 a William Barlowe heads the list of Canons and continued to receive a pension of £6. 13s. 4d. from the court of Augmentations.[2]

There are thus two possibilities. One that the Prior Barlow who between 1509 and 1525 had held a number of small houses had entered the great house of St Bartholomew on losing his monastery in 1528. Or we might suggest that Jerome Barlow returned to England, was pardoned and made to enter St Bartholomew's, a favourite place for stowing abjured heretics.[3]

On the other hand, if Prior Barlow of Bromehill were this canon Barlow of Smithfield we might suggest that Bishop William Barlow did not begin as a Canon Regular at all, but entered the Franciscan Observants at Greenwich. The difficulty here is that it is certain that Bishop William Barlow was Prior of the Canons Regular at Haverfordwest and then at Bisham from 1534 onwards.

Probably most readers will think it more likely that the Prior Barlow of the Essex houses was the future Bishop. If so, there is the gap in his career between 1526–8 and 1534. And although there is the tempting fact that the known career of Jerome Barlow fills just this interval, it is difficult to fit the writing of the *Burial of the Mass* (Strasbourg, 1527) into the

---

[1] *L. & P. Henry VIII* (1534), 1024 (19). The site was bought by Thos. and Rog. Barlow, *c.* 1547.

[2] *L. & P. Henry VIII* (1540), p. 547.

[3] Had we only Tyndale's account we should suppose that Jerome was a surname. One has to consider whether Jerome Barlow was the William Jerome who in 1537 was chaplain to Sir Francis Bigod, himself author of an anti-clerical and Lollard tract, and who was made Vicar of Stepney and burned in 1540. But this William Jerome was a black monk of Canterbury and there is evidence of him there and at Oxford.

presence of the Prior of Bromehill in England in 1526 (and presumably until the dissolution in 1528).

There remains a further possibility which seems to leave less facts unexplained than any other. One of the problems to consider is why William outstripped John in the race for preferment, and outwent him even before 1536, when we might expect John to be halted at the fall of Anne. The fact that a Barlow was a seemly ambassador from Henry VIII to Scotland in 1535 is explained by the presence there of their sister Elizabeth, but why should William, rather than John, be sent when John had already considerable diplomatic experience? Moreover, it would be unusual for an ambassador to be sent on so important an embassy who had not been tried out on other minor missions.

There are two possible explanations. First, William may have been older and abler than John. But there is the additional possibility that William Barlow was himself a former diplomatist, and that it was in that service that he spent the years 1528–34. There are numerous references to one 'Barlow' in the State Papers, and these in the first edition were attributed to the future Bishop but were later ascribed to John. It is possible that there has been over-simplification here and that both brothers were concerned.

The first reference dates from January 1528 when 'Barlow' was sent with an important minute from Wolsey to Knight who was seeking an interview with the Pope about the Divorce. This Barlow returned to England bearing letters to Wolsey from Dom Gregory Casale and returned again with letters from Edward Foxe in England to Stephen Gardiner in Italy.[1] In 1528 a William Barlow was given the living of Wotton, Lincs, and is noted as a 'king's chaplain'.[2] It was a common practice to make clerical diplomats chaplains to the King since

[1] L. & P. Henry VIII (1528), 3749, 3784, 3787, 4249.
[2] This might refer to William Barlow, B.L.

it gave them status and allowed them to hold benefices in absence. We know that John Barlow was not appointed king's chaplain until 1530 when he departed on a diplomatic mission. Were there then, two Barlows employed, William an agent in the royal service as courier for the 'King's matter' and John in the personal service of the Boleyns?[1]

There is, moreover, a letter from one Robert Clyffe to Bonner, in 1530 which refers to 'young Barley, lately come from beyond the sea' and the context shows that it refers to John. The 'young' is intelligible if there were two brothers, each engaged in the diplomatic service.[2]

It may be that William Barlow, faced with unemployment on the dissolution of Bromehill (in which Cromwell, Gardiner and Foxe were all concerned), accepted employment in the diplomatic service in the 'King's matter'. This explains his rise to preferment. William Barlow then belongs to the company of Henrician Bishops, Foxe, Gardiner, Bonner, Cranmer, who rose through their diplomatic experience and pains on the King's behalf. It is the kind of background we should expect for a future Bishop who should be sent as the Ambassador of England soon after his preferment.

If this be correct, then Friar Jerome Barlow has no connection with the Bishop. Yet it is easy to see how the confusion arose, especially if Jerome Barlow died soon in obscurity.[3] The

[1] The only difficulty is the request of Thomas Boleyn, August 1528, for the living of Sundridge, Kent, for 'Barlow the bearer', a living made vacant by the promotion of Dr Allen to Dublin. The grant was made of Tonbridge by error and Anne had herself to write on behalf of 'Barlow' asserting her will to reward all 'who have taken pains in the King's matter'. On the other hand Hasted, in his history of Kent, gives William Barlow as Rector of Sundridge which would fit our hypothesis, cf. L. & P. Henry VIII (1528–30), App. 197, 4647.

[2] L. & P. Henry VIII (1530), 6411. It could by a stretch fit Roger, but it is unlikely.

[3] The 1547 edition of the Burial of the Mass assumes the death of the author. The promise in the 'Lutheran factions' to write another dialogue exposing Tyndale was never fulfilled.

signed submission to the King would naturally suggest the Bishop to all who had no knowledge of the Friar Observant. The 1553 edition of the *Dialogue of Lutheran Factions* is explained by the fact that it was put out by the enemies of the Bishop, without his knowledge and while he was either in prison or in exile.

This, like every other solution, leaves some untidy ends. The coincidence that John and Jerome Barlow were both red-headed, the fact that the author of the *Dialogue of Lutheran Factions* like the diplomat Barlow, had visited Rome,[1] the fact that Bishop Barlow gave jobs to Robert Barnes and George Constantine both abjured heretics and book agents: all these are trails which seem to lead nowhere.[2] But at least we have shown that the dictionary narratives can no longer be accepted, and that Bishop Barlow's early career was more normal and less extravagant than has been commonly supposed.

[1] *Dialogue of Lutheran Factions* (1553):
Nicholas. That ye can tell for ye were lately at Rome.
William. I tarried little while there.
[2] See also Koszul's discovery of a bit of unreliable gossip in Bémont, *Bib. de l'école des hautes études*, p. 221 (Paris, 1917). For more gossip, see *L. & P. Henry VIII* (1536), 283.

Part Two

CHAPTER V

OF CHRISTIAN OBEDIENCE

NOT only all history, but all theology is contemporary in the sense that we cannot help asking our own questions of the past. Yet for the historian there is a prior discipline, of patiently listening to events themselves, and to the men who made them, and who in turn were themselves fashioned by them. Only when we have overheard them minding their own business, caught their undertones, realized what themes possessed their minds, may we go on with our proper questions. Neglect this and we make of the past a sounding-board from which we catch only the echo of our own voices.

These considerations apply particularly to what we may call the problem of spiritual and temporal power, or the problem of Church and State, though properly speaking the sixteenth century fits neither category. It is only too easy to read back into that time our modern conceptions of a 'Free Church in a free State' or of a State conceived in terms of a modern notion of sovereignty. It is even more tempting to be pre-occupied with our own immediate problems, of safeguarding the liberty of the Church in a secularized society, or of arming the Church for conflict in a totalitarian state. The problems are urgent enough. It has wisely been suggested that 'where contemporary Anglican theology is defective is not in its doctrine of the Church, but in its doctrine of the State'.[1] That defect holds good outside the Establishment. Those Churches which in the light of hard-won liberty can speak most assuredly of the 'Crown Rights of the Redeemer' need to recover within their own tradition a concern for the whole life of the nation, which is implicit in the Puritan hope of a 'mighty and puissant

[1] C. H. Smyth, *Religion and Politics* (S.P.C.K. 1943).

nation' and in the design of the first Methodist Preachers 'above all, to reform the nation by spreading scriptural holiness over the land'. Thus, while on the continent of Europe the Church has had to call the State to remember the limits of its power, the dire results of trespass, it may be that in England the best bulwark against totalitarianism will be to reaffirm and assuredly also to readjust the Biblical and Christian teaching about earthly authority.

In turning to the thirteenth chapter of Romans for their *locus classicus*, the Reformers were not applying to an isolated text. They found a hierarchic balance of duties and obediences implicit in the social and political structure of Israel in the Old Testament and explicitly enunciated in the New Testament, notably in the Epistles of Saint Paul. It is a view of human life which was maintained throughout the patristic and medieval period, and which until well on into the eighteenth century was the main tradition of Protestant thought.

The noblest expression of it is to be found in a famous passage in the *Homily of Obedience*:

'Almighty God hath created and appointed all things in heaven and earth in a most excellent and perfect order. In heaven he hath appointed distinct and several orders of arch-angels and angels. In earth he hath assigned kings, princes and other governors, under them in all good and necessary order...every degree of people in their vocation, calling and office...hath appointed unto them their duty and order: some are in high degree, some in low, some kings and princes, some inferiors and subjects, priests and laymen, masters and servants, fathers and children, husbands and wives, rich and poor: and every one hath need of other: so that in all things is to be lauded and praised the goodly order of God without which no house, no city, no commonwealth can endure or last.'

In this conception there are perhaps two thoughts inter-locked. The first is what a German thinker in one of the longest of all compound words has called 'Das Sich-selbst-nicht-sogesetzt-haben'. The context of our human existence is not altogether apart from the providence of God for us, and before we can criticize or disturb it we owe a duty of acceptance and reverence to it. Second, this involves a balance of offices and duties to be recognized before we can speak of rights and equalities. Very few would accept either doctrine to-day without much qualification, but it is important to realize that they dominated Christian thought on this subject for many centuries.

In fact, the main principles of Tyndale's exposition in the *Obedience of a Christian Man* will be found in the writings of John Wesley, in his thoughts on education and family life, his Toryism and his deep suspicion of the catchwords of revolutionary idealism. The same sentiments are found in the hymns of his brother Charles.

> 'Sovereign of all! whose will ordains
> The powers on earth that be,
> By whom our rightful monarch reigns,
> Subject to none but Thee....'

The same obedience is due from children to parents, whose office is similarly delegate.

> 'Themselves the slaves of sense and praise,
> Their babes who pamper and admire,
> And make the helpless infants pass
> To murderer Moloch through the fire.
>
> .   .   .   .
>
> 'Him let us tend, severely kind,
> As guardians of his giddy youth,
> As set to form his tender mind,
> By principles of virtuous truth.'

It would be hard to find a doctrine about which the attitude of Christians has been so radically changed as this. It would be interesting, though beyond the scope of our present argument, to discuss how far that change has resulted from an indigenous ferment within the Christian gospel, and how much is due to the liberal doctrines of the Rights of Man which have their roots in ancient Stoicism.

One thing should be remembered. Human life from Biblical times to the sixteenth century lived closer to the edge of things, to the elemental struggle for bare existence than our own recent, though perhaps not too recent, past. The men and women of those long centuries had not the dazzling glow of two centuries of remarkable material development, bolstered by blind faith in automatic and inevitable human progress to hide from them the dangers of a relapse into disorder and anarchy.

It is a truth too easily forgotten that not only does artistic culture and political activity demand a certain minimum of social and economic stability, but also that the Church itself owes a grateful debt to the social context of an established order. Its organized worship, its institutional life, its buildings and its liturgy, its catechetical and theological conversation, all become precarious and endangered in revolution and civil war. No doubt the Christian Church draws its ultimate strength from other sources, and is able to persist, even to find renewal amid the disruption of an established order. Yet it is a romantic and pietistic error altogether to disregard such considerations and to talk glibly about the benefits to the Church of persecution and of worldly tribulation, themes on which the suffering are wont to be strangely silent.

It is perhaps natural that the Church has again and again sought stability in the maintenance and alliance with the existing social and political order, not without paying a high price. But here we are only concerned to note their excuse, which was real. If Tudor Englishmen set a high estimate on national unity and saw in the Christian Prince the symbol of its maintenance, they lived nearer than we to the Wars of the Roses. Luther did not 'let down the Peasants', for as they framed their cause, he had never taken them up, but he did read, as his critics never seem to read, the fanatic tracts of the peasant leaders who looked with some pleasurable anticipation to disorder and anarchy, in the midst of which, as Luther well knew, the real matter of the Reformation would have been engulfed.

The difference of title between Luther's *Liberty of a Christian Man* and Tyndale's *Obedience of a Christian Man* is due indeed to those events which intervened between 1520 and 1527. The Reformers had to face the charge of fomenting social and political revolution, and in his Preface Tyndale explicitly refers to this:

'Our holy prelates and our ghostly religious which ought to defend God's Word speak evil of it...that it causeth insurrection and teacheth the people to disobey their heads and governors and moveth them to rise against their princes, and to make all common and to make havock of other men's goods.'[1]

Tyndale's exposition of the obedience of subjects and of the office of the governor is imbedded in a treatment of the duties of children and parents, masters and servants, husbands and wives. His thought is not of the State as the preservative against chaos so much as of the 'powers that be' as executors of the law of God.

'The King is in the room of God: and his law is God's law, and nothing but the law of nature, and natural equity which God graved in the hearts of men.'[2]

'Heads and governors are ordained of God, and are even the gift of God, whether they be good or bad. And whatsoever is done to us by them, that doth God, be it good or bad.'[3]

'God therefore hath given laws unto all nations and in all lands, hath put kings, governors and rulers in his own stead, to rule the world through them.'[4]

---

[1] Tyndale, *Doctrinal Treatises*, P.S. p. 163.
[2] Ibid. p. 240.   [3] Ibid. p. 194.   [4] Ibid. p. 174.

They are still the instrument used by God, even when they abuse their office:

'If they be evil, why are they evil? Verily for our wickedness sake are they evil, because that when they were good, we would not receive that goodness at the hand of God...evil rulers then are a sign that God is angry and wroth with us.'[1]

For this reason Saul was not slain by David:

'For if he had done it, he must have sinned against God, for God hath made the king in every realm judge over all, and over him is there no judge. He that judgeth the king judgeth God: and he that layeth hands on the king layeth hand on God: and he that resisteth the king resisteth God and damneth God's law and ordinance.'[2]

This obedience is due even to a heathen ruler:

'Few of us would think, if we were under the Turk, that it were sin to rise against him, and to rid ourselves from under his dominion, so sore have our bishops robbed us of the true doctrine of Christ.'[2]

Tyndale insisted that the tyrant would be punished by God in God's way, and in God's time, and of course, that obedience must first be given to the law of God. He asserts in the very Prologue of this treatise:

'Let it not make thee despair...that it is forbidden thee to read the word of thy soul's health. But much rather be bold in the Lord, and comfort thy soul.'[3]

Historians of political theory have not done justice to the views of Luther and Tyndale, or to their agreement with later Reformers, when they have taken as their standpoint the later controversy about resistance and tyrannicide. They have not noted sufficiently this deeper agreement between all the Reformers, and of course, between them and their opponents, in the whole conception of Christian obedience in all walks of

---

[1] Tyndale, *Doctrinal Treatises*, P.S. pp. 194–5.
[2] Ibid. p. 177.   [3] Ibid. p. 131.

life. What emerged later were new problems of the application of this doctrine, as between one kind of rule and another, or in the light of such intolerable tensions as the beginning of Mary's reign, when Ponet, who was involved in Wyatt's rebellion, penned his tract *Of Politick Power* and inaugurated a new kind of literature. But Luther and Tyndale did not teach 'passive' but Christian obedience.

Has Tyndale anything to say about a modern problem, the difference between the ruler as ruler, and the ruler as Christian ruler? That is an issue which confronts us as between the Christian State and the Secular State. In the light of our democratic notions we are apt to decide the matter by counting heads. A State where Christians are a considerable majority may, we believe, attempt to put Christian principles into law, whereas the State where Christians are an insignificant minority lacks any such obligations.

Tyndale, like the other Reformers, thought within Christendom, amid conditions greatly differing from those of a secularized society. For him this problem existed on the outskirts of the world, where the unbeliever hammered at the gate. What, then, is the difference between the Grand Turk and the Christian Prince? According to Tyndale the Christian subject owes an obedience to both alike.

The Grand Turk, also, derives his authority from God:

'Such obedience unto father and mother, master, husband, emperor, king, lords and rulers, requireth God of all nations, yea of the very Turks and infidels. The blessing and reward of them that keep them is the life of this world...and as we see Turks far exceed us Christian men in worldly prosperity for their just keeping of their temporal laws.'[1]

'For God...will have all judged by his law indifferently and to have the right of his law, and will avenge the wrong done unto the Turk or Saracen: for though they be not under the everlasting testament of Christ, as few of us which are called Christians be...yet are they under the testament of the law natural, which is the law of every land made for the commonwealth there and for peace and unity that one may live by another: in which laws the infidels, if they keep them, have promise of worldly things.'[1]

That is, the duties of the Ruler come to him by reason of his office, and not of his faith. Grand Turk and Christian Prince, Christian State and Secular State owe their office to the providence of God. God has not a set of rules for the Christians, while leaving the pagans to their own will and devices. The Secular State has its duties towards God even when it acknowledges a false god or no god at all. That is a notion which would seem to bear upon our modern controversies. There is a further consequence, that the State must either accept its duties and perform them, or else usurp its commission and step into the place of Anti-Christ, and if this is something more clearly seen in the modern Church struggle in Germany than in the teaching of the Reformers, both would seem to agree that there is no such thing as the Neutral State.

Is there, then, no difference between the Ruler and the Christian Ruler? Tyndale implies there is a great difference, but it lies not in the office, but the person who holds the office.

'Father, mother, son, daughter, master, servant, king and subject be names in the worldly regiment. In Christ we are all one thing, none better than other, all brethren: and all must seek Christ and our brother's profit in Christ.'[2]

'Let kings, if they had lever be Christian indeed than so to be called, give themselves altogether to the wealth of their realms, after the ensample of Christ: remembering that the people are God's and not theirs: yea, are Christ's inheritance and possession, bought with his blood. The most despised person in his realm is the king's brother, and fellow-member with him, and equal with him in the kingdom of God and of Christ.'[3]

[1] Tyndale, *Doctrinal Treatises*, P.S. p. 204.
[2] Ibid. p. 200.   [3] Ibid. p. 202.

For Tyndale the office of government is an office of the law, and the king or judge must act in his official capacity according to that office. Tyndale puts the matter in words which will set the modern mind on edge:

'In time of judgment he is no minister in the Kingdom of Christ: he preacheth no Gospel, but the sharp law of vengeance. Let him take the holy judges of the Old Testament for an ensample and namely Moses which in executing the law was merciless: otherwise more than a mother to them.'[1]

Let those who cavil see whether, in their own mind, they do not eventually accept some division between public and private ethical action.

Outside his office and as an individual the Christian ruler, like all other Christians, is bound to frame his actions by the law of love. Thus the character of a Christian realm whose members own the 'everlasting testament of Christ' must greatly differ from that which knows only the 'testament of the law natural', even though neither can escape the operation of the laws of God.

That the law of God might itself demand a reconsideration of the ethic of public governance,[2] that to be 'merciless as Moses' might not be the final Biblical word, even for earthly judges, that within the orders of God the law of love would itself demand a profound transformation in the relationships of family and of industry and politics, some of the implications of these things lay beyond the horizon of Tyndale and his contemporaries. Yet even where his opinions most fidget us, he has much to tell us. And there is in his writing as in all Christian writing a tension between world acceptance and world

[1] Ibid. p. 203.
[2] Since Tyndale is here maintaining and expanding the same doctrine as that of Luther, whose distinction between 'person' and office he takes over, it should be emphasized that neither Tyndale nor Luther imagine an ultimate dualism since the whole of the Law is fulfilled in the command of love.

rejection, which as Troeltsch has shown, has been potent in the course of Christian history. In the long run it would be more deeply revolutionary than the doctrine of the Rights of Man that 'the most despised person in his realm is the King's brother, and fellow member with him, and equal with him in the kingdom of Christ'.

THE CHRISTIAN PRINCE

The literature evoked by the Royal Supremacy falls within another category than Tyndale's discussion of Christian Obedience, namely the ancient controversy between the spiritual and temporal power, and we shall not understand the elements of novelty without first recognizing the background. 'The earliest imitative impulse of those exponents of dawning national consciousness was to pour new wine into the old bottles of the papacy and empire, and to crowd a nation's growing in the parting garments and shrinking glories of a catholic and mediaeval world',[1] and so it was that Henry VIII could angle for the imperial title while his Chancellor Wolsey touted for the tiara.

There can have been few subjects in Christian history which have so continuously and over so long a period exercised men's minds as the controversy regarding the respective limits of spiritual and temporal authority. Whatever respect might be shown to Biblical doctrine or to Christian tradition, such doctrines were not conceived in a mental vacuum and from the earliest times account must be taken of notions derived from the Roman lawyers or the Stoic philosophers, while the ever-changing practical situation, that historic context without which theological controversy is but half explained, gave different patterns to diverse notions.

The medieval controversy between Pope and Emperor

[1] A. F. Pollard, *Wolsey*, p. 25.

stimulated a vast literature. Papal theory showed great variation, from the Gelasian doctrine of the separation of the two
powers, with the allegory of the two swords, to the Hildebrandine teaching with its significant preference for the figure
of sun and moon, up to the extreme limits of the claim of
Boniface VIII to hold within his breast the fountain of all
laws. On the secular side, from the time of Constantine
onwards, in practice and in theory there did not lack support
for the rights of the secular ruler. Ambrosiaster called the
King 'the Vicar of God' and claimed that he 'has the image
of God as the Bishop has that of Christ'. The medieval period[1]
saw the theme developed with great variation, from the cham-
pionship of the English crown by the 'Anonymous of York'
to Dante's imperialism, or the thoroughgoing Aristotelianism
of Marsilius of Padua. Alongside theory went fact, the life of
medieval Christendom with its innumerable compromises and
adjustments between Pope and Emperor, bishop and king,
monastery and township, priest and peasant, most of whom
cared very little, though they probably cared more than we do,
for fine-spun theory, and who often cut with the sword the
knot of disputation.

In making their appeal to the secular ruler to intervene, the
Reformers assumed three things. First, they took for granted
the common life of Christendom, that fabric of life without
which the Turk, within which the Jew, the heretic and the
unbeliever were the only insoluble elements. Even where,
with a new emphasis on the *koinonia* of the *Gemeinde*, the community of believers, the Reformers altered the emphasis of the
doctrine of the Church, they still thought in terms of a *Volks-
kirche*. They appealed to the secular rulers as fellow members
of a Christian church in a Christian world. Their assumptions
were greatly different, as we have already seen, from those of
a secularized society like our own.

[1] See Lagarde, *Naissance de l'Esprit Laïque au Moyen Âge*.

Next, the spiritual power of the Church was allied to a vast system of finance, law and administration which covered whole areas which would now be regarded as the province of secular authority, and had moreover intruded into that large 'no man's land' which was the subject of medieval litigation and debate. A good deal of the anti-clerical writing of the Reformers, as Tyndale's *Practice of Prelates* is concerned with this intrusion, and in asking the secular rulers to remove this, they were asking for the removal of something which often merited Luther's blunt words, 'thievery and robbery'.

Third, the Church had failed to reform itself, or had delayed so unconscionably that matters were critical. Luther's appeal to the 'Christian Nobility of the German nation' is grounded in the fact that the spiritual authorities had too long refused the initiative to reform which was their proper task, and since in this crisis the common priesthood of all believers must act, their fellow member, the magistrate, was specially fitted to act on their behalf, by reason of his office.[1]

In England, those considerations which moved the Continental Reformers were of less account than the political and personal events which brought about the English schism. The doctrine of the Royal Supremacy, which was enunciated by the 'Henricians' who included not only Foxe and Cranmer, but Gardiner and Tunstal, was as we might expect little concerned with the reform of the Church in head and members, and much more ready to take up the threads of an older controversy.

Edward Foxe, who at Cambridge had been called 'the wonder of the University' and as Royal Almoner, the 'darling of the Court', produced in 1534 a small tract, *Opus eximium de vera differentia Regiae potestatis et ecclesiasticae et quae sit ipsa veritas et virtus utriusque*.[2] He begins with the various views of

---

[1] See R. Sohm, *Kirchenrecht*, vol. 1. K. Holl, *Gesammelte Aufsätze. Luther. Luther u. das Landesherrliche Kirchenregiment* (1911).

[2] Thomas Berthelet. No author is named.

ecclesiastical authority, between those who regard the Papacy as *divino jure* and those who consider it to be *jure humano*. There are others who would confine ecclesiastical power to the ministry of the Word given by the apostles to the Pope and bishops, 'let them preach and teach what is given them in scripture and not add to or diminish that, as though divine providence which is absolute and ineffable needed supplementing by human industry so as to improve the salvation of man'. Yet others 'seek to stretch the confines of ecclesiastical power to the borders of heaven and hell' while others 'make all Christians equal, and what was said to the Apostles they ridiculously twist to fit everybody, confounding all degrees of Christians'. He then discusses Peter's Confession and the commission of the Church, that 'universa congregatio fidelium et vera Christianorum'. Not only has the Church no power to punish or constrain but Romans xiii excepts nobody from the civil jurisdiction 'neither Peter nor Paul, priest or bishop, nor cardinal nor patriarch or Pope'. The work concludes with a long historical section alleging many edicts of the Anglo-Saxon and Norman kings of England. The tract relies on the usual quotations from the Fathers and the *Glossa* and is in no way remarkable.

More original and much more famous was Stephen Gardiner's *De Vera Obedientia*. So stoutly did he champion the royal power that in his later life the book became a source of great embarrassment to its author, who could always be flummoxed by a timely quotation during the trials of the Marian Reformers. Gardiner sees the King as the natural head of a Christian realm.

'Seinge the Churche of Englande consisteth of the same sortes of people at this daye, that are comprised in this word realme of whom the king is called the headde, shall he not beinge called the headde of the realme of Englande be also the headde of the same men when they are named the churche of England...the kinge (say they) is the headde of the realme but not of the churche: whereas notwithstonding the Churche of Englande is nothing elles but men and women of the clergye and of the laytie united in Christe's profession, that is to say, it is justly to be called the churche because it is a communion of Christen people.'

Gardiner goes further than most in putting little limitation on royal power:

'But here some man will saye...who ever denyed that the prince ought to be obeyed?...but we must see (wil he saye) that the kinge doo not passe the lemites appoynted him... what manner of lemites are those that ye tel me of, seinge the scripture hathe non suche...but only hath preserved the obedience due to God safe and hole that we should not hearken unto any manne's word in all the world against God.'

He has little use for the Gelasian, Hildebrandine separation with its figures of sun and moon 'forsothe a blynde distinccion and full of darkenes'. 'What waye shall a Christian prince take in governement to leade christian people by? The waye of truth which leadeth unto life, or the way of lyes which hasteth to deathe, for there is no mydde waye found.' To confine the king to temporal matters 'is the most spedy waye to marre all, and ferre contrary from his office that occupieth Goddes rowme in earthe. Is this to fede the people?' It is the duty of the Christian prince 'to take charge, not only of humayne maters, but muche more of divine maters'.[1]

A third significant document is the lengthy exposition of the Sacrament of Orders in the Bishops' Book of 1537, which, on rather dubious grounds, has been attributed to Cuthbert Tunstal. It is a very good piece of work with a careful exposition of the distinction between the *potestas ordinis*, and the *potestas jurisdictionis* of the spiritual office. It contained a limitation on the royal power which aroused some discussion

[1] Janelle, *Obedience in Church and State* (1930), pp. 93–101.

and the statement with its controversial material was not carried over into the King's Book of 1543. Said the statement:

'We may not think that it doth appertain unto the office of kings and princes to preach and teach, to administer the sacraments, to absoyle, to excommunicate, and such other things belonging to the office and administration of bishops and priests'

but

'as chief heads and overlookers over the said priests and bishops, to cause them to administer their office and power committed unto them purely and sincerely, and in case they shall be negligent in any part thereof, to cause them to supply and repair the same again'.[1]

The fourth significant statement of Henrician doctrine, and the most thoroughgoing is Cranmer's famous reply to a question, in 1540:

'All Christian Princes have committed unto them immediately of God, the whole cure of all their subjects, as well concerning the administration of God's word, for the cure of their soul, as well concerning the administration of things political, and civil governance: and in both these ministrations they must have sundry ministers under them to supply that which is appointed to their several offices.'

Much of the wilful misunderstanding of Cranmer's career arises from not taking seriously these convictions. It is very easy for us to snort at such doctrines surrounded with examples of the perils of bondage of spiritual to temporal power: it is easy to forget that in the sixteenth century the prince seemed even more a deliverer than a captor. There is a worse bondage than subjection to the State, and that is when the Church becomes the tool of its own perverted power. Those who in our time conceive a 'Resurrection of Christendom' will have to spend more time than they have done so far, in considering

[1] Lloyd, *Formularies of Faith*, p. 121.

the office of a Christian prince, or magistrate. It is true, of course, that the Christian prince in the sixteenth century sorely tried any ideal description of his office. Josiah and Hezekiah emerged from the past trailing clouds of glory, but the roaring bully, who badgered poor Lambert or reduced Barnes to scared silence by his density, was not a pretty or an admirable sight. Yet the bond held, and while Henry VIII lived neither Cranmer, Tunstal, nor Gardiner weakened or wavered in their loyal obedience to the King.

So the 'Christian prince having the governance of a Christian people' steps into the foreground. For their theory, those who supported his cause turned not so much to the classical models of which Machiavelli and Marsilius are full, as to history and to holy scripture. They turned to the Old Testament because that, too, assumed a Christian commonwealth—unlike the New Testament world where the Church was a struggling minority. It was not that the Reformers were more Jewish than Christian in their outlook but that with Augustine and the Fathers they regarded themselves as comprehended with Israel within a covenant and promise. For them, as for all Christian thought, Church history began with Abraham, if not with Adam. They remembered also the first days of the Christian empire and it did not escape their memory that Constantine himself was of British origin. Yet after all, Constantine and Justinian were by no means perfect exemplars, and it is a pity that the Reformers did not know just a little more history, for they might have found more warning and less inspiration in these stories from the past.

CHAPTER VI

HENRY VIII AND THE GERMAN
PROTESTANTS

THE new role of the Christian Prince coincided with the swaggering patriotism of Renaissance heroism, and we have to consider the new as well as the old elements in the configuration of the time. When Henry grew to manhood and to power he came to hold a conception of his office not wholly derived from the tradition of his fathers, owing much perhaps to the Italianate notions of princely power which attracted some of his courtiers. Long ago More had warned Warham that 'if the lion knew his strength, hard were it for any man to rule him' and Henry soon learned to test his roars and his claws. It is not strange that it should be his divorce which complicated the English Reformation and made it the strangest compound of any ecclesiastical revolution.

Moreover, Henry was not only the Christian Prince, but that modern figure the eminent layman who fancies himself as a theologian. We shall find reason to suggest that his capacity in this direction has been exaggerated, but at least the interest was genuine enough. At any rate Henry decided himself to enter the lists against the heresiarch Luther. We know that he was anxious to gain prestige at the expense of the Emperor and the French King and that it chafed him that the one was the Most Catholic and the other the Most Christian King, while he lacked any such honorific title. He may have coveted for himself the title of 'Orthodoxus' and on the whole Englishmen, Catholic and Protestant, may be grateful for having been spared that embarrassment. But there is no reason to suppose that it was self-interest alone which inspired him to dash into this, the cheapest of all the Crusades. How much of his book was written by the King, we cannot say. His comments on the Bishops' Book of 1537 are far below the theological level of this book. There is not much proof that the King had either learning or leisure enough to produce the *Assertio Septem Sacramentorum Adversus Martin. Lutherum*. It is probable that the royal author had considerable assistance from More, Fisher and Lee and that the texts of Scripture, the linguistic evidence from Hebrew and Greek, the patristic citations and much of the argument were supplied by others.[1]

The work itself has not much more than an antiquarian interest. A modern Catholic[2] has taken one of its points as of note, the conception that the Testament of Christ embraced the Passion as well as the Last Supper. But this is noteworthy only as an aspect of the doctrine which fell into the background after the Council of Trent. Henry himself explicitly stated that the doctrine was no novelty: 'We have heard preachers over and over again who treat of these things...for they referred to that same testament not only what Christ did at the Last Supper, but also what he suffered on the Cross.' For the rest its arguments on behalf of the seven Sacraments will seem singularly weak or admirably cogent according to the presupposition of the reader.

The historical importance of the work is greater than its theological significance. Much or little as Henry wrote, it was coupled with his personal authority and bound up with his prestige. On this the seal was set by the title of *Defensor fidei* bestowed by a grateful pope, and received into this country with all solemnity. There were two results. First, it made all personal contact with Luther impossible. Secondly it tied the King to certain doctrinal statements which he could not retract without losing face. He must have regretted the running pen

---

[1] John Barlow was very sceptical about the King's share in it. See the narrative of Constantine, *Arch.* vol. XXIII.

[2] P. de la Taille, *The Mystery of Faith* (Eng. tr. London, 1941), pp. 77-8.

in such passages as: 'What serpent so venomously crept in as he who calls the Most Holy See of Rome, Babylon and the Pope's authority, Tyranny, and turns the name of the Most Holy Bishop of Rome into that of Anti-Christ?' What, indeed! That which followed aggravated the difficulties caused by the book. Luther who had already fought the Emperor and the Pope could hardly be expected to mince words with the King of England, and his reply though nothing to what he could do, gave the King a rough handling. So matters rested, until political interests forced Henry to turn his attention towards Germany. Then the King of Denmark with customary and well-intentioned tactlessness told Luther that Henry was now 'inclined to the Gospel' and that if Luther would make an apology he would be met more than half-way. Luther, well aware of his own vehement spirit, agreed, with that unfortunate result which invariably attended his attempts to roar as gently as any sucking dove. But he had some right to complain of the treatment he now received. It was not only that his private letter to the King was published, for the sixteenth century abounds with such breaches of confidence. But the letter was published with a treatise which claimed that Luther had retracted his doctrines. There is reason to suspect Sir Thomas More as its author for the same statements are repeated in his *Dialogue* of the same year, the scurrility about Luther's marriage and his alleged fatalism in the *De Servo Arbitrio* and the same libellous assertion that in it Luther makes God 'fountain, author and mover of all evil'. So that Luther had something to complain of when he grumbled: 'I hoped my letter would remain private with the King.' But there it was: King and heretic had made plain what they thought of each other and there could hardly be direct negotiation between them.

That the King changed his attitude towards the German Reformers was entirely due to political considerations, and not to any kindling sympathy with evangelical doctrine. The divorce brought new dangers to England and henceforth any rapprochement between Henry's enemies was fraught with anxious concern, while his supreme objective was to prevent any overwhelming coalition between them against himself. Henry had already shared in one war engineered by papal policy. He had no desire to view the next from the operating table.

He had also to reckon with the possibility of a reconciliation between the German Reformers and the Roman Church. Before the colloquy of Regensburg in 1541 the possibility was kept alive by theologians on both sides, and when the Papal Nuncio arrived at Wittenberg, to sound the German attitude to the Mantuan Council, there seemed some ground for alarm at the thought of a Council recognized by the German Reformers as 'free and Christian', at which a general condemnation of Henry might be part of the price of agreement. Nor may it be forgotten that Wittenberg and Rome were at one in their support of Katherine of Aragon, hence Henry's instructions to his envoys (Cranmer was to give Heath careful coaching in the matter) to conduct theological discussions about the Divorce such as would bring the Germans to a decisive verdict in his favour. That he continued to press for this after Katherine had been put away, and even after her death in January 1536 is proof that for Henry the whole matter was closely bound to his concern for the succession.

In what follows we shall be wise not to underestimate the personal influence of the King. Cromwell might scheme, Cranmer might advise, but in the end the Henricians were more, not less, subservient to the King's direction than ever Wolsey had been. And so, in 1534, Henry found it expedient to open negotiations with the German Protestants.[1] Francis I

[1] Mont and Heath (his first diplomatic mission) were sent to the German Princes in 1534 beginning with Bavaria, but they do not seem to have reached Saxony.

of France was in need of friends, and despite his persecution
of French Reformers now addressed a most apologetic letter
to the Germans which was published by Melanchthon. This was
followed by a warm invitation that Philip should visit France,
and the rumour that the invitation had been accepted, and
indeed that he was already on his way to France, thoroughly
alarmed Henry who determined to send a counter-invitation
that the prodigy of Wittenberg should visit England. Negotiation with Luther was out of the question and this scholar,
the friend of Erasmus, was the kind of man with whom Henry
felt he could deal, as one theologian to another, so to speak.
Even so, matters were delicate and Robert Barnes was sent on
an informal visit to Wittenberg, where he was *persona gratissima*,
formally to beg Melanchthon to initiate a correspondence.

The result was a tactful letter from Melanchthon which
walked delicately among the verities. He extolled Henry
whose patronage of letters could only be compared with
Ptolemy of Egypt, but pointed out how closely the reform of
letters was linked with change of doctrine, since in Germany
the same people despise letters who care nothing for religion,
and since letters are 'brought into odium on account of religious controversies' which might be mitigated 'if your Majesty
would lend his authority to incline other monarchs to modera-
tion: if indeed he would deliberate with learned men about a
form of doctrine'. The letter concluded: 'Dr Antonius disputed with us certain articles, showing the highest faith and
diligence and I have given him my judgment in writing. But
of this I wish to testify that I am not so enamoured of my own
opinion that if certain good and learned men having deliberated
together take exception to some part, I should prefer my
opinion before theirs.'[1]

The visit of Barnes was a success, and the next step was a
formal overture from Henry to the Elector John Frederick,

[1] C.R. vol. II, 1264; 4, 11 and 13 March 1535.

in which Barnes and Melanchthon acted as go-betweens.
Henry's immediate concern was to stop Melanchthon going to
France and provision was made for his journey to England,
with all expenses paid. But Melanchthon had replied so cordially to Francis that withdrawal was no easy matter. Luther
himself had written the Elector in favour of it 'who knows
what God will work, whose thoughts are always higher and
better than ours'.[1] But John Frederick clung to his theologians as lovingly as his predecessor had cherished the bones
of saints and he preferred that Melanchthon should be the
instrument of Providence on good German soil. The crisis
passed when Francis, having failed to gain anything useful
from the heretics, turned hopefully to the Turks. As his rival
cooled Henry became more eager, though Melanchthon could
be excused for a certain nervousness about Henry's burning
eagerness to see him.

The King decided to dispatch a formal mission. The envoys
were to have an assorted programme. They were to take with
them articles about the Divorce and conduct disputations with
a view to a favourable German verdict. As a side-line they
were to get into the territory of Duke George and publicly
refute his pet theologian, Cochlaeus,[2] once the ally of the
English in their attempt to destroy the English New Testament, but now a voluble opponent of the Royal Supremacy.
If they could not manage this, they were to publish works in
refutation of his arguments. They were also to negotiate with
the German princes with a view to the possibility of Henry
being admitted to the Protestant League, and if necessary they
were to discuss doctrinal articles with the Germans.

---

[1] Luther, *Letters*, W.E. vol. VII, p. 252.
[2]   'A littell pratye foolysshe poade.
        But although his stature be small
        Yet men say he lacketh no gall.'
                    (*Rede me* ... (ed. Arber), p. 43.)

In August 1535 Robert Barnes set out for Wittenberg. He bore two letters, one accrediting him to John Frederick as 'our beloved and faithful chaplain', and the other a safe conduct for Melanchthon's journey to England with twenty companions and servants 'or less', horses, apparel and all found. Meanwhile, Philip dedicated his new edition of his *Loci Communes* to Henry in the preface to which he reverted to his former theme: 'Certain chief articles of the Christian faith have long lain in deepest darkness...good and wise princes ought to seek a suitable remedy...for the Church will be torn in an infinity of ways unless some plan be devised by which a pure and pious form of doctrine may be handed down to posterity.' Melanchthon forwarded two copies of the work, one for the King and the other for Thomas Cranmer, by the hands of that restless spirit, Alexander Alesius, who had touted vainly for preferment in Germany and was about to descend on England.

On 6 September Luther reported the arrival of Barnes in Wittenberg and assumed him to be there in connection with Melanchthon's projected trip.[1] A week later it is clear that Barnes had opened other matters. Luther, Jonas, Cruciger and Bugenhagen wrote to the Elector on 12 September asking that Barnes might be granted a 'private or close audience, for there is good reason why what he has to say should not be made public before we know where we stand ('ehe man wuste wie oder was')'. The same letter favours the visit of Melanchthon to England and once again Luther asks: 'Who knows what God will work? His wisdom is better than ours and his will better than ours.'[2] But John Frederick was as sceptical of the virtue of English soil as he had been of French earth, and

---

[1] Luther, *Letters*, W.E. vol. VII, 2235: 'Nova nulla, nisi quod hic est Doctor Antonius ille niger Anglicus, legatus sui regis ad Principem nostrum et ipse petens M. Philippum in Angliam ad colloquium Regis.' Does 'niger' here mean 'unfortunate'?

[2] Ibid. 2240.

believed that God would speak, as his manner is, to his Germans in Germany, and this part of Henry's plan came to nothing. Meanwhile, Luther wrote to Chancellor Bruck in the most optimistic terms saying that 'the King is ready to receive the Gospel and to enter the alliance with the Princes and to set forth our Apology (i.e. the Augsburg Confession) in his Kingdom'. 'The matter of the King's marriage is in abeyance until the other legate comes who is going into it with our theologians as we cannot very well refuse to do. But that does not concern the Princes. I shall be very interested to see just why they want to make so sure in this matter.'[1]

On 13 September Frederick gave instructions for the reception of Barnes and the other legate who 'should be on his way' and asked that either Spalatin or Melanchthon should attend as the discussions would be in Latin. On the 17th Bruck replied that Barnes had gone to Wittenberg for a degree ceremony and was awaiting his summons to Jena. Somewhere about the 20th the interview took place either at Jena or at Hummelshain. A memo in the Weimar archives probably covers the points of the interview.[2]

First article

His Majesty is sending another envoy and asks that he may be given a good hearing.

His Majesty has confided certain articles to this envoy and requests that he may be given conference with learned men.

His Majesty will not refuse to join himself to the association of the Evangelical League.

To that end he asks that it may be indicated to him by his learned envoys what articles they will defend in the Council.

Fourth article

If the confederates receive His Majesty into the association of the League then he asks that they should not agree to a

---

[1] Luther, *Letters*, W.E. vol. VII, 2241.

[2] Ibid. p. 270. The editor of the Weimar edition wrongly identifies 'alius Legatus' with Cristopher Mont.

council without the common consent of the King and of the confederates.

That his Majesty would deliberate about amending ecclesiastical abuses.

To that end he asks that Dr Philip should be sent to him, whose counsel and doctrine he would hear.

The interview went well enough, and in reply the Elector gave favourable consideration to most of the points raised. The other ambassador would be well received, and arrangements would be made for his hospitality should the Elector be absent on his arrival. The theological discussions were not in any case to be held up, though political decisions would need to be deferred until his own return. The disorder into which Wittenberg had been thrown by the plague was a good excuse to avoid deciding about Melanchthon's visit to England. As to membership of the League, the Elector cautiously pointed out that it was not for him to make conditions without consulting his fellow members, and in a pointed hint reminded Henry that it was not primarily founded upon political interest but for the defence of the 'pious and pure doctrine of the Gospel', affirming his own complete adherence to the *Confessio Augustana*.[1]

The German theologians could now discuss dates and places and suggested a meeting at Torgau should Wittenberg still be dangerously infected. On 1 October Henry replied cordially to Melanchthon's dedication: he sent him two hundred crowns, and if this good work was not unexpected there was surely supererogatory virtue in the signature 'Vester Amicus, Henry VIII'. There followed weeks of delay,[2] and Barnes who

[1] C.R. vol. II, 1329, 1330.

[2] It is said that Foxe visited Strasbourg concerning the publication of books, which may have been the works in favour of Royal Supremacy which were to confute Cochlaeus. His own *De Vera Differentia* and Gardiner's *De Vera Obedientia* were the two most important defences of the Henrician view. See Janelle, *Obedience*, pp. xxv–xxviii.

had written earlier that Foxe need not hurry, on account of the plague, now began to be seriously exercised. During the interval, a picturesque event occurred. The Papal Nuncio had invited Barnes and Luther to breakfast with him,[1] but, Barnes declining, did not succeed in pumping Luther as to what this projected Covenant between Death and Hell might mean. Luther hugely enjoyed himself.

Not until the end of November did the English finally reach Erfurt. Barnes had now to give way to the senior members of the delegation. Edward Foxe as Bishop of Hereford and Almoner to the King had had long diplomatic experience since his training in the school of Wolsey's diplomacy, and had already been much employed about the Divorce and the Royal Supremacy. He was ably seconded by Nicholas Heath and if Foxe may be said to have arrived, Heath was regarded as a 'coming man'. Though at this time only an Archdeacon, he impressed the Germans more favourably than Foxe whom they judged to have a 'prelatical manner'.

In the early days of December, Luther wrote with relief of their arrival: 'I rejoice that Doctor Antonius has been freed from his anxieties...for I too had begun to fear the worst, since the other envoys have been so slow.'[2] On 15 December the delegates met Bruck and the newly appointed Vice-Chancellor, Francis Burchardt. In private and informal discussion they put forward four propositions, that Henry should be sent in return a 'stattliche Botschaft' which was to include a 'vortrefflich gelehrter Mann', that a statement should be made about the Council, that it must be according to God's Word and not the canons, and any other kind of council to be rejected. The King would not refuse to join the alliance if he were honourably received and the King would oppose the Pope.

On Christmas Eve, Foxe addressed the estates of the League,

---

[1] Luther, *Letters*, W.E. vol. VII, 2270, 2276.
[2] Ibid. 2276, 2278.

and Spalatin, told off for the purpose, took copious notes of the address.[1] In his opening words Foxe stressed the authority of his King: 'Defensore fidei et supremo sub Christo in terris anglicanae ecclesiae capite.' The Germans were a little puzzled by the emphatic insistence on this and were later moved to humorous comment upon it. The address laid stress upon the characteristics of the English schism but Foxe's insistence on the need and desirability of doctrinal agreement was playing to the gallery, for Henry certainly did not seriously intend to implement the suggestion that doctrinal unity was 'the one firm and solid basis of peace, unity and concord'.

By extricating England from the Papal tyranny, Henry had struck at the root of all abuses in the Church and so would not refuse a free and Christian council, 'but nothing could be more unhappy, unfortunate, or more calamitous than that a council should be held in which the ambition of the Roman pontiff were upheld', and for this reason the King of England 'seeks above all that the Princes, Estates and those belonging to them will take heed lest they consent to a council before they have agreed and established peace and concord of doctrine'. Since the princes were already agreed on doctrine, and since indeed the Augsburg Confession was the one indispensable basis of the League, and since the chief difference between them and Henry was the latter's refusal to accept unmodified this confession, this was pretty cool impudence. But no doubt it went down well and the effect of the speech survived even the flowery peroration. The result was that a series of political articles were presented on Christmas Day.[2]

The first article bound the King to promote pure doctrine 'according to that form which the Princes and Estates confederated confessed in the Diet of Augsburg' and defended

[1] C.R. vol. II, 1382.
[2] Strype, *Eccl. Mem.* vol. v, pp. 559 ff. Jacobs, *Lutheran Movement*, pp. 63-7.

'in their published Apology...unless certain things meanwhile may chance to merit correction and change according to the Word of God, by consent of the Most Serene King and the Princes themselves'. This is the doctrine to be defended in any council, but such a council must be assented to by all the members as a truly free and Christian council. Any council called without consent of the League is to be opposed by all means at the disposal of the alliance, who will cause public and formal protests to be made by their clergy by which they 'shall demonstrate the purity of their faith' and the decrees of such a council are to be null and void.

Henry, whose envoy had stressed his title 'Defender of the Faith', was now to be accorded the name 'Defender and Protector of the League', and the cynical might have noted that Henry's determination to be 'Defender of the Faith' was stronger than his certainty as to which Faith he wanted to defend. The other articles were political and financial in character and demanded from Henry a surety of 100,000 crowns with a further grant of the same amount in case of necessity, under an assurance from the Princes that the money would not be improperly diverted. The ambassadors remaining for the theological discussions were to convey Henry's reply. The articles were signed by the three Englishmen, followed by John Frederick and Philip of Hesse.

We can only guess Henry's reaction to them, but the comments of Gardiner upon his copy are characteristic and a shrewd attempt to sabotage the venture. He asserted that the first article would bind the King 'to the Church of Germany'. More cleverly he puts his finger upon a point which was in some confusion, the relative authority of the Princes and of the Emperor, since the Princes 'we know as no heads of their churches but as inferior members'. Gardiner also objected to Henry having any title less than that of 'Chief Head and Principal of the League' as derogatory to the dignity of the English crown. Of the monetary clauses he made the acid comment 'they be very good for the said Princes'. Finally, where they desire to have all things agreed before they send an ambassador to the King's highness 'they speak wisely therein...for their own commodity, for so shall they obtain the glory that they shall send to us, not to learn of us, but to instruct us and teach us, not to sue to us, but to direct our Church in such cere-monies as by their deliberation should be summoned and concluded'. Gardiner's series of 'doubts and scrupulosities'[1] handled with loving care a number of apples of discord, calculated to touch the pride of Henry and even to arouse the jealousy of John Frederick. Probably Gardiner only confirmed Henry's own sentiments and we may be sure the monetary clauses had not escaped the criticism of Henry and of Cromwell.

In the negotiations which followed, the English and the Germans had different interests and objectives. Henry was primarily concerned with the Divorce judgement, with the papal council and with the safety of his realm. What he least intended was a reform of English doctrine on the lines of the Augsburg confession such as should make it appear that the English church was in tutelage to Wittenberg. The Reformers were much less interested in the political theme. The Princes had an eye to the main chance in monetary matters and Philip of Hesse was far more of a politician than the Elector John Frederick. But what really dazzled the Germans was the prospect of an England won to the cause of the Reformation. Dazzle them it did, for no other explanation accounts for their patience in supporting the weary business of the spring of 1536, the delays, the rebuffs, the discourtesies they accepted of the embarrassed envoys, less and less sure as they were of a wel-come home, for every point of agreement with their hosts. The bright mirage led the Germans on, not without impatience for in this matter they were all zeal, all haste, whereas Henry

[1] Muller, *Letters of Stephen Gardiner*, no. 53, pp. 71-5.

could afford to wait, hoping for some change in the pattern of events which would enable him to attain his political ends without being too far committed to a distasteful entanglement.

It was the changing political situation which determined his steps to or away from the League until the moment when events themselves enabled him to be free of it altogether. His courtship of Anne of Cleves is a parable of his dalliance with Germany.

The first discussions were about the Divorce, despite the fact that both Luther and Melanchthon had already given earlier judgements against Henry.[1] It was the King Charles' head of all the conversations and the Germans found it difficult to get the English going on any other topic. It was a very nice theological question and the Reformers were at sufficient distance from London and Rome to regard it coolly on its theological merits. It was such a problem as makes the theologian lick his lips, for it involved just those questions of the relation between the Law and the Gospel which were favourite articles of sixteenth-century controversy. It was not at all a matter of New Testament exegesis, or of Our Lord's teaching of the bond of marriage. Rather it was concerned with the interpretation of two passages in the Pentateuch, the one forbidding marriage of a brother's wife and the other dispensing with it.[2] In what sense did the one abrogate the other? In what sense was the law of Moses binding upon Christians? Were these rules of natural and moral law and so universally binding, or were they human legislation? Did the Scripture afford practical precedent as well as theoretic guidance? Here were subjects about which an astonishing variety of opinion could exist, and where a very slight dif-

---

[1] Yet on 28 December Barnes could write (*L. & P. Henry VIII* (1535), vol. ii, 1030): 'Marten est multo aequior causae quam antea, Jonas non repugnat, Phylippus videtur nobiscum esse, solus Pomeranus mordicus resistit, sed non despero de felici successu.'

[2] Leviticus xx. 21. Deut. xxv. 5.

ference in theory might lead to a startlingly different practical conclusion. And Henry, we may be very sure, had not paid for an embassy to discuss nice points of abstract theology: he was interested in that practical conclusion.

Into the intricacies of that debate we need not enter. Melanchthon soon grew tired and withdrew, returning only when his presence was demanded by the Elector since the English made his presence a matter of good faith. On 19 January 1536 Luther wrote of the rumours of the death of Katherine: 'The Queen is dead and they say the daughter is mortally ill. But hers is a lost cause with all the world save with us poor beggars, the theologians of Wittenberg.'[1] The death of Katherine did remove one practical obstacle to any agreement with the Emperor, however, and in the light of growing hostility between the Emperor and the King of France, Henry felt himself in a stronger position than for some time.

Melanchthon, who like most self-conscious correspondents was not above using a good phrase twice, wrote to Veit Dietrich and to Camerarius in almost identical terms about these discussions: 'The English contend that the law about not taking one's brother's wife is indispensable. We, on the other hand say that it may be dispensed with. But you see how much easier it is for them to defend "to akribodikaion" than for us to relax the law...we have not yet disputed with them about evangelical doctrine except by the way. But we are coming to that now.'[2] He added: 'Nicholas the Archdeacon is a learned man, and apt for purer doctrine, but the bishop has the prelatical manner.' Meanwhile, he had written to Osiander at Nuremberg as an Old Testament expert, asking for Rabbinic authorities on the Levitical marriage law, and Heath himself visited that city, charming all by his mannered graces.

[1] Luther, *Letters*, W.E. vol. VII, 2287.   [2] C.R. vol. III, 1396, 1397.

The protracted discussions, the postponement of all talk about major doctrines, the sophistry of the English began to annoy the Germans who were not a little concerned at the expense with which their patron was now encumbered.[1] 'The English are disputing with us here, if hair-splitting is to dispute', complained Luther, 'and it is an annoyance to me that our prince should be burdened with so many feasts', and he added that this kind of sophistry could come to no good end as he had himself experienced with Zwingli and with Karlstadt. At the end of January the English attended a German debate on the subject of Private Masses, in the course of which Foxe made an intervention. After it Luther again addressed his Prince this time in even stronger terms. He reported that the English were prepared to defray their own expenses, but remitted the affair to the judgement of the Elector. Frederick in a calm reply sympathized with his theologians but expressed his willingness to continue as host. Once again Melanchthon had gone off on his own, this time to dispute against Anabaptists at Jena, and he had to be fetched back by Heath on 10 February. The final conclusions of the German theologians about the Divorce present a minor historical problem. It is certain that their difference from Henry was maintained, for on 30 March Melanchthon wrote: 'peri tes gunaikos apostasiou', 'we have not agreed with them'. But the memorial embodying their conclusions is extant in two forms, a shorter version in Latin and a longer in German, and the reply brought back by the English delegates would seem to have lacked the German opinion that there was dispensation from the Levitical law among the Jews, and so this command was even less binding upon Christians.

Nearly all conjectures about the different versions are unsatis-

[1] The expenses allowed the English envoys from home were: Edw. Foxe, 5 months, £373. 6s. 8d.; Heath, 4 months, £74. 13s. 4d.; Mont and Barnes, 40 days, £40.

factory. It has been suggested that the Germans, for the sake of an alliance, were agreeable to the omission of the last sentence. The latest German historian to discuss the matter makes the even less probable suggestion that this part was tactfully omitted by the English diplomats in their anxiety to report a successful mission.[1] Let alone the bad faith this would imply in three honourable Christian men, it would have been far too risky, and there were far too many chances of the truth coming out, to be followed by swift and dire disgrace. And of course Henry was not interested in minor points, and no concessions would please him while the German theologians would only consent with Luther that the Divorce was due to 'maximis et gravissimis causis' and refused to agree to Foxe's 'propter justissimas causas'.

Decisions now came swiftly. The legates presented Henry's reply to the Christmas articles. Nine of them he found satisfactory—he had nothing to lose where they were concerned, for they opposed the papal council. He suggested amendments to the financial clauses, but haggling had been expected and he did not refuse the idea of giving a subsidy. In any case it would be a long time before he had to pay up. In return he asked for 500 horsemen or 10 ships of war (Hamburg and Bremen belonged to the League) and that they should provide soldiers for whom he would pay. He would not refuse to be Protector of the League but he would not accept unmodified the Augsburg Confession, 'unless some things in your confession be modified in private colloquy and friendly disputation between his and your learned men'. He repeated the request for 'one of your most learned men to be sent to his majesty to confer diligently about changing statutes and ordinances'. The request for theological accommodation was difficult for the Germans to meet, since they had made their confession the platform for an uncompromising stand against

[1] Pruser, *England und die Schmalkaldener*, pp. 51 ff.

the Emperor and the Pope. But they agreed to see how far minor concessions could win general agreement.

So the discussions began on doctrine and proceeded apace. The Augsburg Confession may have been the starting-point, but there was gradually evolved another document which since its publication by Mentz in 1905 has been known as the 'Wittenberg Articles of 1536'. On 9 March Melanchthon wrote: 'We are now disputing with the English about doctrine', and on the following day he informed Prince George of Anhalt that 'we have been talking about all the articles of Christian doctrine and the legates seem not altogether averse from the study of purer doctrine'. On 20 March John Frederick reported that all the articles had been discussed except 'the four, marriage of clergy, communion in both kinds, the papistical mass, and monastic vows'.[1] On 28 March Luther informed the Elector that Burchardt had translated the articles that the Prince might see for himself how the discussions had gone, but warned him that the English delegates were uncertain whether their King would receive the articles.[2] Two days later an irritable letter from Melanchthon complained that 'Everybody thinks the Legates are staying too long...of the remaining articles of doctrine we had no light disputation, but none the less we agreed over many.'[3] The debates were concluded on 8 April and on the 9th Luther wrote to Thomas Cromwell praising the reports that the King's Minister had 'tam seriam et propensam in causa Christi voluntatem' but complaining of the abrupt departure of Barnes 'nor did he think fit to salute me or bid me farewell'.[4]

Later in the month the Princes gathered at Frankfurt and thither the other English delegates (Barnes had gone to England with the Divorce document) went up to take their

[1] Pruser, *England und die Schmalkaldener*, p. 296.
[2] Luther, *Letters*, W.E. vol. VII, 3003.   [3] C.R. vol. III, 1409.
[4] Luther, *Letters*, W.E. vol. VII, 3013.

leave of the assembly. Philip of Hesse was more inclined to the view that political agreement with the English might be made without theological agreement and was also of the opinion that his own pet theologians of the Strasbourg school should take more prominent share in the discussions, for it was apparent that the Germans were disappointed with the results of the long negotiations. On 8 April John Frederick had caused a letter to be drafted 'with extraordinary care' in which he addressed Henry in polite but cool terms, directing his attention to the four ecclesiastical abuses [1] and commending Heath and Foxe for their exertions. But his treatment of Foxe is the best indication of his real feelings and is in marked contrast to his warm, almost effusive, farewell to Barnes in the preceding year. He refused to grant Foxe the customary farewell interview, and Foxe wrote a letter revealing his chagrin and also, to his credit, his concern for the safety of his cause. It is customary, he wrote, at the end of important negotiations for an ambassador to take personal leave of the prince or monarch to whose court he is accredited, and to take leave with clasped hands, lest ill-wishers have excuse to say: 'Look, it is clear how badly things have gone between the illustrious Elector and the English envoys. For the most illustrious prince did not deign to give him his right hand or salute him ·or bid him farewell.' [2] Which, all in all, was exactly what the illustrious prince intended, for though he sent a perfectly correct and even cordial reply the interview was not given and for once Henry was repaid in kind. At Frankfurt, however, Philip of Hesse would not so easily give up and secured that the English met on 11 May the Hessian, Saxon and Strasbourg representatives, though no promise was made about the desired mission to England as a letter from Heath to Melanchthon on 27 August makes plain. 'We had to go home without

[1] See above, p. 106.
[2] Luther, *Letters*, W.E. vol. VII, pp. 401–2.

receiving any definite word as to whether the delegation would or would not be sent.'[1] This is important, for it shows that the fall of Anne Boleyn in the month following the Diet did not lead to the interruption of negotiations between England and Germany, but that the breach had already occurred and from the German side.

But it does also show that at the time when the 'Ten Articles' were passed, Henry could not afford to close the door to further negotiations with the German Princes and their theologians. The fact remains that when the Elector sought the advice of Luther in April 1536 Luther was firm: 'We can make no further concessions in doctrine other than those we have already admitted.' He would not refuse to make minor verbal changes but there could be no further compromise in respect of doctrine, for it would, he said, be great folly to grant concessions to the King of England which had been denied to the Bishop of Rome. He agreed that patience ought to be exercised with regard to the English and that latitude might be allowed as regards outward ceremonies. As for the political alliance, Luther true to his principles remitted that judgement to his prince 'since it is a temporal matter', but adventures none the less his private opinion that it is dangerous to seek an outward alliance when hearts are divided.[2]

In May came news of the fall and execution of Anne and the news came as a shock to the German theologians, while it caused alarm and despondency among the English Reformers. Barnes warned Melanchthon against visiting England. He need hardly have worried, for Melanchthon's enthusiasm needed little cooling and he was writing to his friends in evident relief at not having to fulfil the prospect of being an English Daniel come to judgement, if not also to a burning, fiery furnace. 'I am now altogether free from worrying about that journey

[1] Luther, *Letters*, W.E. vol. VIII, 3228, p. 221.
[2] Ibid. vol. VII, 3016.

to England.' On the day he wrote those words the Convocation met in London and Foxe and Heath, who had arrived in England in the last days of June, presented the results of their mission.

The Wittenberg Articles of 1536 and the Ten Articles

We noted the abrupt departure of Barnes from Germany and the reason may be sifted from a gossip-ridden despatch of Chapuys to the Emperor on 1 April. 'The prelates here are daily meeting in the Archbishop of Canterbury's rooms to discuss certain articles as well as the reformation of church ceremonies. I am given to understand that they do not admit of Purgatory nor of the observance of Lent and other fasts, nor of the festivals of saints, and worship of images which is the shortest way to arrive at the plundering of the Church of St Thomas of Canterbury and other places of resort for pilgrims in this country. And I am told that the above-mentioned prelates are now busily engaged in framing an answer to certain writings of Luther and his followers which this king's ambassador in Saxony, a bishop, had sent them, in which writings Luther and his disciples mention that the king's first marriage was permissible, but that whether or no, the legitimacy of the Princess can in no wise be questioned. ("Què le dict mariage estoit tollerable et que fut tel ou non sans nulle doubte la Princesse estoit legittime.") And moreover, it is an ascertained fact that the said ambassador, in order no doubt to please his master, has written to say that he fancies that Luther and his followers are of a different opinion, but dare not say so openly for fear of your majesty.'[1] It is probable that much work was done upon this side of the channel upon this document and

[1] *Cal. State Papers, Spanish*, vol. v (1536), p. 84. A. F. Pollard, *Cranmer*, pp. 102–3.

upon the Wittenberg Articles, and that it was not allowed to wait on the return of Foxe and Heath who only arrived shortly before Convocation.

The temper of that assembly can hardly be judged by the vigorous Latin sermon with which it seems that Latimer harangued its opening, still less by the presence in the chair of Thomas Cromwell acting for the King, with the ruling that in his absence the layman Petre might preside as proctor and deputy. Rather should it be gauged by a series of articles condemning irreverent and Sacramentarian expressions and a condemnation of Lutheran opinions. To this assembly Foxe presented a 'book of faith and articles' which may have been the Ten Articles.

When it was all over Heath sent an informative letter to Melanchthon in which it was suggested that things might have gone better, from the German point of view, had their embassy come to England immediately on the return of the English envoys, and while the Parliament and Convocation were in session. He speaks of the 'assembly which among us is called a parliament, one with the bishops, abbots and general clergy …for this is our custom that as often as parliament is held, so often and at the same time a synod of bishops and clergy is held'. He describes the attention paid by the parliament to the succession problem and to the legitimacy of the offspring of Katherine and Anne, concluding discreetly 'but to write many things about this matter is not expedient for your sake, nor safe for me'. 'In the synod', he continued, 'they discussed the quietening of tumult and murmuring which had arisen among the people and was filling the minds of the vulgar, owing to the dissension of the preachers. The synod took action by making and publishing certain articles in which a prescribed form is given to the preachers as to how far they may speak of those religious matters which are the subject of controversy.' He promises to send Melanchthon a copy of them in Latin, 'where, however, little care has been taken about their Latinity. For I wished that it should be translated word for word, as far as possible, that you might not only grasp the meaning, but have the words. Yet when they were put forward there were many who assented to the meaning of these articles only with great difficulty. And in the end it was necessary to obtain consent by the intervention of royal authority, and for the sake of concord and the appeasement of causes of tumult. So that if your legation had come in time, some things might have gone better.'[1]

What was the relation between the Wittenberg Articles which had evolved in the course of the earlier negotiations and the 'Ten Articles'? The basis of the Wittenberg Articles had been the Augsburg Confession and its Apology, since these were the doctrinal basis of the Protestant League. But although the Germans had taken their stand on the Confession, they could hardly refuse to discuss the possibility of any alteration, without placing their own tradition above the Word of God. Probably the first draft of the Wittenberg Articles was the work of Melanchthon and they bear evident traces of his theology as adumbrated in his *Loci Communes*.

There was a difference of intention between the Augsburg Confession and the Wittenberg Articles. The first was a confession of faith, the second an attempted *eirenicon*. The Wittenberg Articles are an illumination of the extent to which the Germans would make minor concessions, if only they might add England to the Evangelical Party.

The resultant document was in no way a theological masterpiece and it soon dropped into the background of reformation confessional literature. Pruser points out that in places it contradicted known sentiments of the German theologians. The statement 'est fides ipsa praecipuum opus' in the article concerning Good Works had been explicitly rejected by Luther

[1] Luther, *Letters*, W.E. vol. VIII, pp. 220–3.

in his disputation on 'Justification'. Luther had expressed disapproval of Anselm's definition of Original Sin as 'carentia justitiae originalis debitae' as being 'tenuis et obscura', and yet the·Wittenberg Articles could 'highly approve' this defini-tion. Mentz says that the number of concessions is surprising.

The influence of these articles upon German theology was negligible. If certain passages in the *Variata* of 1540 and the *Confessio Saxonica* of 1551 seem reminiscent of them, the resemblances are due to common authorship. In the story of the English Reformation they have rather more importance. For it was one result of the negotiations that, through this cloudy medium, the Augsburg Confession entered the back-ground of English confessional controversy. Next, there is the evident influence of them in the 'Ten Articles of 1536' and in the Bishops' Book of 1537. Last, they reappeared in the negotiations of 1538 and part of them got into the Thirteen Articles which emerged from those discussions and which were themselves made use of in the great Edwardian and Elizabethan confessions.

To admit this does not deliver judgement as to the Protestant or Catholic nature of the documents they influenced, nor answer the further question how much they owed to foreign or to indigenous inspiration. The negotiations between Henry and the Germans in 1535–6 show that the part played by the Augsburg Confession and the Wittenberg Articles in English confessional history is due to historical rather than theological fact in the first place, and to the need for a united front against the threatened council. But if political interest could elevate them into the forefront of debate they could, once more, become a means of theological influence.

We saw how full of misgivings the English envoys had been about the reception of this document by their King: they could have had little illusion about the attitude of the English clergy. The process by which the Wittenberg Articles were allowed to influence the Ten Articles can only be surmised. In any case the two documents were different in character. In the Wittenberg Articles there are long passages whose evident origin lies in theological disputation. But the Ten Articles were intended to appease controversy by settling plainly 'what all bishops and preachers should instruct and teach our people'. The agreement between the English and German theologians was too small for the Ten Articles to be any use as a bridge between England and Wittenberg. But that there could be any relation at all was, after all, something, and at least the door was carefully left ajar to further negotiation.

Nor were the agreements insignificant. In both the Wittenberg and the Ten Articles, the Bible and the three symbols are acknowledged as standards of faith. Baptism is defended against Anabaptist error: in both Penance is defended and expounded as a Sacrament, though with a decisive difference in the definition of it, the Ten Articles reverting to the traditional Catholic division. The article on Justification in the Ten Articles shows indisputable trace of the influence of the Wittenberg Articles. The use of images and the invocation of saints are more heartily commended in the Ten Articles, but the theological difference is not fundamental. Alone, the article on Purgatory has no parallel in the Wittenberg Articles, but this was in the forefront of English controversy. In both the Eucharist is given the same cautious definition, and the fuller statement in the Ten Articles has reference to the current teaching of the Sacramentaries which was a preoccupation of the Convocation in 1536.

In one further important respect the door was left open towards the Germans. In the Ten Articles, as in the theology of Martin Luther, as in the Augustana and the Wittenberg Articles, the number of Sacraments expounded is three. This is no negative concession, as some historians have suggested. These three were, according to the Protestant view (which was followed in the Bishops' Book), to be distinguished from the rest as being Sacraments of the Gospel, instituted by the Lord and proclaiming the Forgiveness of Sins. On the other hand it is remarkable that no mention is made of the four ecclesiastical abuses which so exercised the Germans. Henry would not meddle with them: whenever they were discussed the debate was broken off: they were the rock on which all future theological discussions were to founder. It is the more striking that Henry himself was to proceed drastically with practical measures which struck at some of them. He would dissolve the monasteries: he would not debate monastic vows. Perhaps it was because anything conceded here might have looked as though the 'Defender of the Faith' was in tutelage to Wittenberg. The result was that the Ten Articles were more garbled even than the Wittenberg Articles. Bishop Foxe's *Book of Articles* bore as little resemblance to the debates in Germany as a novel to its film scenario. 'Confusissime compositi', sighed Melanchthon, as he pondered his copy of them. The verdict may stand, and perhaps it would not be the last English confessional document to deserve it. It sometimes appears that in exalting the Middle Way the English Church has elevated confusion of thought to the level of a theological virtue.

NEGOTIATIONS, 1537–8

There was an interruption of relations between English and German theologians after Heath's letter of 1536. In England the autumn brought the serious open rebellion in the North which moved Henry to walk delicately. Yet he could not ignore the danger of the Papal council and issued a statement which the German reformers approved. There is an anxious note in this inquiry: 'What the States will do, if the Emperor, French King and the Bishop of Rome conclude upon a General council and do anything contrary to the Law of God?'

Once again Cristopher Mont set out for Germany and in February 1538 he attended a meeting of the League at Brunswick, where he asked for the long-awaited delegation. This time it was dispatched. The leader, Francis Burchardt, Vice-Chancellor of Saxony, was a man of parts, and one who could hold his own in theology and in politics. The theologian of the party was Frederick Myconius the Superintendent of Gotha. With them came a Hessian nobleman, George a Boyneburg. The delegates bore a letter from Luther to Edward Foxe, in which Luther tried to put the best interpretation on the silent interval, and hoped that the delegates might now bring back word that the English Church had embraced the Gospel. Luther had established cordial relationship with Foxe on the basis of their common disease, the stone, and had indeed exchanged remedies with him. But a higher authority had sealed the lips of the Bishop, for death had taken him four days before Luther wrote.[1] In the passing of Edward Foxe the Reformers lost a good friend. Though the Germans might find a 'prelatical manner' and a propensity for 'sophistry' in one who, after all had trained in the old diplomatic school of Wolsey, the months following his return to England showed him to have intervened with some learning and growing warmth in the evangelical cause. The difference between the Bishops' and the King's Book might have been mitigated had he been alive, for his was a healing and moderating influence, who was a friend of both Thomas Cranmer and of Stephen Gardiner.

The Germans found that the conduct of debate had been entrusted to three bishops, Stokesley, Sampson and Cranmer the 'archbishop of Kandelberg', and to four doctors, including Barnes and Heath. As a team they could not compare with the giants of Wittenberg, but Burchardt and Myconius far from home were soon hard pressed and so

[1] He died 8 May 1538.

exasperated by the 'papists' and the 'sophists'. The discussions proceeded on the basis of the Augsburg Confession and the Wittenberg Articles of 1536. These were gone through in order and various amendments suggested. Over 'Original Sin' there was swift agreement but over Justification such heat that, Myconius smugly reported, had the evangelical doctrine not been pure gold, it must have melted.[1] By August all the doctrinal articles had been traversed and a list of thirteen Articles compiled from the discussions. Melanchthon was moved to cautious optimism, and wrote to Brentz: 'there is hope that the English churches will be reformed.' Once again the discussion reached the four abuses, and stuck fast.

The ambassadors began to think of departing, and sighed for that home from which they had had no letters for long enough. Cranmer complained on their behalf: 'they are very evil lodged where they be, for besides the multitude of rats daily and nightly running in their chambers, which is no small disquietness, the kitchen standeth directly against their parlour where they daily dine and sup, and by reason thereof the house savoureth so ill that it offendeth all men that come into it.'[2] Doubtless their native haunts had not been all sweetness and light, but to the homesick exile strange sounds and unfamiliar smells can be an almost insupportable annoyance. Myconius fell sick. But this time Henry was not going to let them go until he was ready. Cranmer was set to persuade them to stay 'as gentilly as I could...after long reasoning...they condescended and were very well content to tarry for a month'. The debate continued. The Evangelicals raised the four abuses, the Catholics, the four remaining sacraments. To keep up their spirits the delegates were told tales of Henry's evangelical zeal, how he had even had the Augsburg Confession turned into English (they were not told that this was Cromwell's action

[1] Pruser, *England und die Schmalkaldener*, p. 315.
[2] Cranmer, *Works*, P.S. vol. II, p. 379.

and some twelve months old). Myconius was allowed to preach in the Austin Friars. But on the European stage the situation had clarified. Henry saw with relief that the imperial armament was directed against the Turk. So on 1 October with many compliments and a few presents the Germans were allowed to depart. Once again the bright mirage had led the Germans on: once again political interest furthered and ended the mission on the English side. Myconius aptly and bitterly summed it: 'Harry only wants to sit as Antichrist in the temple as God, and that Harry should be Pope. The rich treasures, the rich incomes of the Church, these are the Gospel According to Harry.'

NOTE. THE THIRTEEN ARTICLES OF 1538

The Thirteen Articles compiled during the negotiations of 1538 attained no measure of public authority whatever, but they have intrinsic interest, apart from the use made of them in the articles of 1552. The origin of them is threefold: the Augsburg Confession, the Wittenberg Articles of 1536, and the deliberations of 1538. The following note gives some indication of the extent to which those sources were blended, concerning which the publication of the Wittenberg Articles has given new information.

Art. 1. *De Unitate et Trinitate Personarum.* Verbally identical with Art. 1 of the Augsburg Confession (save for the change of person, 'damnamus' for 'damnant').

Art. 2. *De Peccato Originali.* Contains the greater part of Art. 2 of the Augsburg Confession adding the definition (from Anselm) of the Wittenberg Articles.

Art. 3. *De duabus Christi naturis.* Verbally identical with Art. 3 of the Augsburg Confession.

Art. 4. *De Justificatione.* The sense of much of Art. 4 of the Augsburg Confession is quoted and the last half verbally repeated, but the statement is amplified by the addition of part of the Wittenberg Articles: while at the end Art. 5 of the Confession is repeated verbally. It should be noted that the 'oportet' of Good Works becomes 'necessaria' in the Wittenberg and Thirteen Articles.

Art. 5. *De Ecclesia.* A definition of the Church was a notable omission from the Wittenberg Articles. This long article amplifies but does not contradict the Augsburg Confession and enunciates the distinction between the visible and the invisible church, besides including part of Art. 8 of the Augsburg Confession.

Art. 6. *De Baptismo.* Here the short statement of the Augsburg Confession is abandoned for the fuller statement of the Wittenberg Articles which is reproduced in full.

Art. 7. *De Eucharistia.* The article is that of the Wittenberg Articles but the important addition is made that the sacrament is received 'sive bonis et malis'.

Art. 8. *De Poenitentia.* Here extensive alterations have been made. Yet this is not an entirely new article and there are quotations from the Wittenberg Articles. But it differs from evangelical doctrine by its statement that auricular confession is 'valde utilem ac summe necessariam'.

Art. 9. *De Sacramentorum Usu.* Quoted verbally and in full from the Wittenberg Articles.

Art. 10. *De Ministris Ecclesiae.* Quotes Art. 14 of the Augsburg Confession verbally and in full.

Art. 11. *De Ritibus Ecclesiasticis.* Shows substantial differences from any German document but has traces of the words and more of the ideas of the Wittenberg Articles.

Art. 12. *De Rebus Civilibus.* Does not traverse the Augsburg Confession or the Wittenberg Articles but enlarges them, though most of the article is new. Is by far the longest of these articles.

Art. 13. *De Corporum Resurrectione.* 'De Judicio Extremo' is verbally identical with Art. 17 of the Augsburg Confession.

BREAKDOWN OF NEGOTIATIONS, 1539–40

The last years of the negotiations have less importance from our point of view, for, two long disquisitions on the 'four abuses' apart, they produced no important theological documents. In 1538 the danger to Henry VIII from foreign powers had receded, but the spoliation of the shrines sensationally stirred Catholic opinion. Cardinal Pole went to the imperial court to solicit aid against his schismatic kinsman. In Scotland, Cardinal Beaton received from the Pope a sword and the title 'Defensor Fidei', pointed compliments with their edge towards England. The King of France rudely interrupted the printing of English Bibles at Paris. Rumours reached England of an invasion fleet assembled at German ports, and of a plan to oust Henry and put the Duke of Orleans on the English throne. Once again Henry sought allies, but this time he looked elsewhere than the League, to the King of Denmark and to the nobles of the Palatinate and of the House of Cleves who stood without the League but favoured moderate reform. Once again Cristopher Mont went to Germany where the Reformers too were a little alarmed at the bristling armament of the Catholic powers.

There followed a warning from John Frederick to Henry about the Anabaptist peril, but Henry had his own grim methods and needed little advice on this subject. The question of a wider alliance then arose. Cromwell sought an alliance of anti-Catholic powers which would have a wider basis than that of the Schmalkaldic League and which would offer the advantage of political alliance without the disadvantage of theological entanglements. In 1538 Burchardt had discussed the possibility of a match between the Duke of Cleves and the Princess Mary, a match which John Frederick promised to further as far as in him lay. Cromwell now had a more elevated thought and suggested the match be between Henry and Anne, the sister of the Duke. Mont reported the idea to be so favourably received that Drs Wootton and Bird were sent to Cleves to gain information and to make personal acquaintance with the favoured lady. John Frederick was not so pleased and made the excuse that his painter, Lukas Cranach, was ill, to avoid sending Henry a portrait of the intended bride. The incident had unforeseen results, for it followed that the charms of Anne had to be presented in a written report. It was doubly unfortunate that Cromwell should touch up his envoy's pen picture from which, no doubt, all warts had already been removed. He went so far as to declare that the Princess Anne surpassed the Duchess of Milan (the other foreign candidate for Henry's favour) as the golden sun surpasses the silver moon. In any case, no Judgement of Paris was involved, since Holbein found the latter lady so uninteresting that her hands and her gown are the only interesting features of his famous portrait.

Barnes and Saint Leger were sent on embassy to Denmark to further Cromwell's design 'to see all professors of the same joined in an indissoluble knot' of political alliance. It seems that Cromwell was far more eagerly in the van of this programme than he had been in 1536–8, a fact which was to hold fateful consequence for himself. The German theologians had lost most of their interest by now. But Mont made the acquaintance of Erasmus Sarcerius and sent a copy of his *Loci Communes* to the King. The book pleased Henry perhaps because it was simple and printed scriptural references in full.[1] Melanchthon, perhaps feeling a little guilty about his persistent refusal to visit England, made atonement by bombarding Henry and his court with a series of letters of uniform burden. The Roman tyranny has been abolished in England, yet the superstitions remain. There are signs that the new Romish apologetic of Pole, Contarini, Sadaleto and Gropper is becoming popular among the English clergy. Such men derive their arguments from Pseudo-Dionysius and Durandus. The letter to Cranmer is the frankest of the series and that to Heath shows most restraint, perhaps because Heath was now leaning to the conservative side.

Mont returned with news that a German embassy was on

[1] Jacobs, *Lutheran Movement*, pp. 140 ff.

the way and Francis Burchardt and Ludwig von Baumbach arrived in London 23 April 1539. Cromwell was very well pleased. 'These orators shall be very formidable to the Bishop of Rome and to others of his adherents also. For doubtless if your Majesty shall happen to join with them, the papists shall be half desperate.' He did not dare put into words any reflection of what would happen should his Majesty happen to break altogether with the Germans. The discussions followed at Cromwell's house and a debate was arranged at St James' Palace in which Norfolk and Suffolk, Audley and Tunstal took part. Then came news that an agreement had been reached between the German Protestants and the Emperor, one article of which forbade the widening of the League by the admission of new members. This was a fatal, perhaps a deliberate, blow at the negotiations in England, and the embarrassed delegates tried vainly to impress Henry with the possible uses which the League might have, even in the new circumstances. But they left on 31 May and never had agreement seemed further away.

If this was a snub to the English, what followed was a resounding buffet for the Germans. So far from the 'four abuses' being eradicated, the new act of Six Articles named, commended and enforced them under savage penalties. The 'foreign policy' aspect of the Six Articles is not to be exaggerated, but it deserves to be noted. They ended all hope in the hearts of the Elector and the theologians of Wittenberg. It was now quite clear that Henry had been moved throughout by political motives. Indeed, John Frederick and Philip of Hesse could hardly believe the news and the latter roundly swore that if it were true 'he must certainly be according to my judgement, the most wretched being of whom I have ever heard'.[1] But the news was hastily confirmed by the swift

---

[1] Lenz, *Briefwechsel Landgraf Philipp's von Hessen mit Bucer* (Leipzig, 1880), p. 99.

appearance of Alexander Alesius at Wittenberg. That self-appointed Chorus to the English Reformation, though he felt the new measures dangerous enough to merit his own rapid withdrawal, did his best to exculpate Henry and put the blame on the English Bishops. The news that Barnes had failed in his mission to Denmark, and the arrest of leading English Reformers were other signs that the evangelical cause in England must be gravely imperilled.

Now the Cleves match was the only link between England and Germany. Duke William was still agreeable. Holbein went to take the portraits of sister Anne, and, just in case, of her sister Amelia. Two councillors from Cleves set out for London and John Frederick agreed to send two envoys. Now unexpected support came from the Landgrave Philip and his Strassburger theologians who were always glad of a chance to expend righteous indignation at the expense of Wittenberg. Mont visited Bucer and went on to John Frederick in Saxony. The Elector was adamant that there could be no alliance without theological agreement, and while the sinister Six Articles held law. Bucer plunged into his favourite fuss of peace-making, and in a letter of 16 September 1539 reported to his patron on the English situation, seeing Gardiner's hand at work in it all, and criticizing the Wittenberg theologians for their half-heartedness. Why had Melanchthon refused to visit England, again and again? Written treatises were no substitute for that personal argument which alone could defeat the 'sophistischen Griffe und Scheinargument'. Was it not the special mission of the Christian to seek out the erring?

'Our Lord Jesus left heaven to help us in his pity, and suffered bitter death: he left the ninety and nine sheep and sought the hundredth, he has richly dowered us and bidden us help others as freely as he has given to us: and said that he will repay us an hundred fold with eternal blessedness. That is: "Go into all the world and preach the Gospel to every creature." Yet we think that when somebody comes to us, that we have done and suffered everything for them that is needful. But that in this way we might win some for our Lord, that we do not understand as we should. The Lord help us to a better knowledge of it, and then we shall be better able to act for the salvation of others and of our own selves according to his will.'[1]

With these words he urged Philip of Hesse to secure that an embassy be sent to England, headed by Melanchthon and in a confidential postscript blamed Burchardt for the failure. He and Myconius were no match for the sophisters and had been in too great a hurry to get home. It was all very well for Bucer to talk like this at the eleventh hour, when the theologians of Wittenberg had borne the heat and burden of a long and wearisome day, but there was perhaps something in it.

At the same time Bucer wrote to Luther whose reply fore-shadowed the response of the other Wittenberg theologians. 'About the King of England', Martin wrote, 'I fear your hope is vain. We heard the English themselves complaining about their king when they were here, envying us our liberty.'[2] The fuller and more official reply bears the weight of their growing exasperation. The Germans have been forced to believe that Henry is acting deliberately against his conscience. There they did him an injustice: Henry never acted against his conscience which he had long educated to walk humbly with him. They added the comment upon the Six Articles: 'The King does not seek the honour of God, but wishes to do just as he pleases, as he told our Vice-Chancellor "He would rule his Kingdom himself".' 'We will write an expostulation to the King', they concluded, 'but further we are not bound to go. As for Master Bucer's quotation "Go ye into all the world..." we do that with our writings, and to leave our present calling is not

---

[1] Lenz, *Briefwechsel*, pp. 103–4.
[2] Luther, *Letters*, W.E. vol. VIII, 3394.

bidden us.' The letter was signed by Luther, Jonas, Pomeranus and Melanchthon.[1]

We must sympathize with their irritation. Luther's personal reply to his patron was even stronger. 'The King is a trifler and means nothing in earnest.' When the English first came the Germans had taken them seriously but finally 'like your Grace's purse, it was all gone for nought and everything turned on the King's pleasure'. They themselves had admitted 'Rex noster est inconstans' and again and again they had heard from Dr Antonius that 'our king really cares nothing at all for religion and the gospel'. It is as well that the hypocrisy of this king has been shown up, for now at least the Germans are not to be laden with his sins. As for the title 'Caput et defensor evangelii', 'away with such a Head and such a Defender!' 'Gold and money have made him think men must pray to him. Now he can carry his own sins unassoiled. We have enough of our own. He ought to be the Pope, as he already is as far as England is concerned.'[2] On 1 November Melanchthon's expostulation was ready.[3]

It bears all the marks of hurried composition and opens with some tactless historical parallels. Politely, Melanchthon refused to believe Henry responsible for the Six Articles. He must have been over-persuaded as was Darius by the satraps. But rulers need not be ashamed to retract unjust laws as witness such princes as Nebuchadnezzar, Darius, Asahuerus, Hadrian and the Antonine Emperors. The Bishops have been led astray by the sophistries of Contarini and Sadaleto. 'Confession must be retained', indeed! why not say right out that the enumeration of sins is necessary 'de jure divino'. The affirmation that the 'marriage of clergy is contrary to divine law' can only have one author, Stephen Gardiner: 'O wicked Bishop, O impudent Winchester!' He does not see how Henry can attack papal authority and yet retain the doctrines on which the papal

[1] Luther, *Letters*, W.E. vol. VIII, 3396.
[2] Ibid. 3397.   [3] C.R. vol. III, 1868.

tyranny has been built. He exhorts Henry to join the roll of princes who have been instruments of God, David, Josiah, Hezekiah, 'and Britain also gave a pious prince to the world in Constantine'. Finally, he appeals to the King to relax his severities, 'for Christ is going about hungry, thirsty, naked, bound, complaining of the madness of the bishops and the most unrighteous cruelty of many kings, begging that the members of his body be not wounded, but that true churches be defended and the gospel magnified. To recognize him, to receive him, to cherish him...this is the duty of a Godly king and the worship most pleasing to God.'

This letter, a mixture of argument, epigram and rather windy rhetoric, achieved nothing at all, but no doubt its writer felt better for having written it. If Henry did relax the enforcement of the legal penalties attached to the Six Articles it was not because he had been moved by German pressure. Meanwhile, the marriage negotiations must continue and Henry had no wish to break altogether with Wittenberg. Burchardt sent a hopeful report, causing concern only by his report that a clever forgery was going the rounds in England as it had done in France, in the form of a collection of garbled sentences from Luther and Melanchthon which made it appear that both had renounced their doctrines.[1]

The news that the first panic rumours of the effect of the Six Articles had been exaggerated secured a favourable hearing at the next Bundestag for Philip of Hesse's plea for a strong delegation to be sent to England. But the other cities refused to support the plea of Strasbourg and Burchardt returned to England with restricted powers. In January 1540 Cromwell's giant blunder with the Cleves' match was plain. Cromwell was now hemmed in by his enemies and had at last made the fatal

[1] Extracts are given in Jacobs, *Lutheran Movement*, pp. 158–67, and were wrongly taken as authentic by Strype, *Eccl. Mem.* p. 526. Both Dixon and Messenger wrongly suppose serious theological discussions to have gone on in spring 1539. Messenger, *Reformation, Mass and Priesthood*, pp. 271 ff. Dixon, *History*, vol. II, pp. 109 ff.

mistake of becoming identified with an unsuccessful line of policy. Hopes raised by the special mission of Baumbach at this juncture were soon dashed. They had to confess they lacked power to make any definite alliance and were sent packing.

Yet even now neither party could afford a final break while the imperial threat remained. At the Schmalkaldic Bundestag in March 1540 it was decided that the German theologians should draft a full reply to Henry on the subject of the four 'abuses' and that, if all went well, a place of disputation should be fixed in Germany or in England. On 16 March Melanchthon was preparing the necessary writings, though a month elapsed before they were sent to England with a polite covering note from the Electors.[1] Then bad news began to come back from England. Aepinus wrote to Pomeranus: 'In England Satan begins to rage and storm...the King has put Dr Antonius into prison because he would not sign the godless edict...and it is forbidden to bring the books of Luther or of Philip into England...there is little hope of Antonius's life.' From Hanover, Urbanus Rhegius reported 'the King of England has thrown 330 preachers in chains, and condemned all your doctrines and books'.[2]

Then on 10 June came the fall of Cromwell, among other things condemned as a 'detested heretic'. His fall was complete, but it was not the only cause of the events of these months. His fall marked the ascendancy of Gardiner and his party. The Germans lacked all power to interfere. Melanchthon could cry out in disgust at Henry as 'this viper' and tear out

---

[1] Pruser's suggestion that this is identical with the document C.R. vol. XXIII, pp. 667 ff. may be accepted. Those printed by C.R. vol. III, 1951 and by Gairdner in *L. & P. Henry VIII*, vol. XV, 509 (and so by Jacobs, *Lutheran Movement*, pp. 169–77) are really the last part of the Wittenberg Articles of 1536.

[2] These were rumours and very inaccurate but they are evidence of the kind of rumour which was current at the time. They are printed in Pruser, *England und die Schmalkaldener*, App. 22, pp. 341–2.

the dedication from his *Loci Communes*. Luther's own services to Robert Barnes were perforce confined to a handsome obituary notice paying tribute to the merits of 'saint Robert', but the canonization though well intentioned was perforce posthumous. And when the Reichstag was held and the Emperor confronted the Reformers, the English were represented by Stephen Gardiner.

This was the end: only once more, when in 1544 the Peace of Crespy left him in some danger, did Henry make any attempt to reopen negotiations. When he did, he attempted to use the concessions given in the *Variata* of 1540 as the excuse to get into the League on reduced theological fee. But the Schmalkaldic war stopped negotiations and the death of Henry soon followed. The story of the negotiations between 1535 and 1540 is fairly consistent. There was some truth perhaps in Bucer's complaint that the Wittenberg theologians might have done more, but one can hardly blame Melanchthon for not getting too close to so capricious and savage a prince as Henry could be. From start to finish, however, the Germans were consistent in maintaining that theological concord must precede political alliance. The only exception was Philip of Hesse, who had perhaps some fellow feeling for Henry as one also driven to strange devices in matters matrimonial. Above all the Germans were led on by the hope of an England won over to the evangelical cause. On the English side, it is apparent that the evangelical opinions of a small minority of Englishmen had little or no effect upon high policy. It may be difficult to assess the relative responsibility of Henry and Cromwell in directing that policy, but in any case the political motive was allowed to dominate. Despite all this, we have seen that there was some theological contact which was not without effect upon the English confessional development. And as a study in national temperament, the story of the relation between the English and German theologians has a sufficiently modern interest.

CHAPTER VII

CONFESSIONAL LITERATURE, 1537–47

ENGLISH CHRISTIANS of all communions may find encouragement, profit and warning in the study of this half century when the Church of England was in truth the mother of us all, and when, more than any time before or since, she approximated the ideal of a 'Comprehensive' Church. The decade under immediate consideration is a good illustration of this, for bishops and divines of the most diverse temperament, opinion, and allegiance worked together on the innumerable committees which produced various confessional documents in this period, and worked together if not altogether amicably, at least in a manageable way. And if the cynical find the underlying unity less in a sense of catholicity than in concern for the unity of the realm, and so the safety of their own skins, or their obedience to the King, and so the safety of their own necks, this is at least testimony to the fact that the Royal Supremacy had secured a real measure of stability for the national Church.

We cannot avoid using labels like 'conservative', 'reformer', 'evangelical', 'catholic', but too often those words have been given a nineteenth or seventeenth-century connotation, after our modern habit of dressing up the past. For they have been pressed into a dichotomy as though they were exhaustive categories. Yet we have only to consider to find that along different matters there were quite different alignments. The matter of the Royal Divorce places Robert Barnes with Gardiner and Cranmer against Tyndale, More and the German Reformers. The Royal Supremacy joins Cranmer and Foxe and Barnes with Tunstal and with Gardiner. Regarding the Sacra-

ment of the Altar, Bilney, Barnes and the Cambridge Reformers, Cranmer (in this period), were with Tunstal, Gardiner
and the King in their opposition to the radical doctrines of
Lambert, Frith and the other English Reformers.

In this period Thomas Cranmer, Archbishop of Canterbury,
played a part of supreme importance. In the years when
Reform had been stirring in Cambridge, there is no sign that
Cranmer played a leading part in the formation of what we
have called the Cambridge Movement. We hear that he had
an exceptional devotion to Biblical study, but we also know
that he refused to join that Adullamite assembly which Wolsey
transplanted from Cambridge to Oxford. And when we first
hear of his connection with Reform it is 'the King's matter'
of the Divorce, and of the Royal Supremacy which most concern
him. It is on his diplomatic travels in Germany that we first
glimpse his keen interest in the Reformers and above all in
their liturgical experiments. There he not only found a German
wife, but through her became a connection of Andreas
Osiander, the chief maker of the new Church Order at Nurem-
burg. Yet this seems to have been his chief connection with
the Reformer and as late as 1540 he could write to Osiander
'with the rest of your doctors my intimacy is of a lighter
character, and less close'. At the time of the negotiations with
Germany we catch glimpses of his work behind the scenes,
but when he sent for Nicholas Heath, to coach him in his
business, it was about the issue of the Divorce and not about
Reformed Theology.

Recent historians have paid tardy tribute to his great qualities,
and it may be hoped that the legend of the pusillanimous
courtier, tossed about by every wind of doctrine, has been
disposed of to all but those who read their history with their
emotions rather than their heads.

No time-server would have ventured, as Cranmer did, to
intercede for Anne Boleyn and Thomas Cromwell, in the

moment of their fall. No coward would have undertaken to discover to the King the infidelity of Catherine Howard, or to act as a go-between when pride made the one, and fear the other, and grief both of them, into tormented animals.

In theology, his writings show him to have been slow-moving but tenacious. The charge of instability is a frivolous one, unless to move from one belief to another be instability, in which case every theologian of worth would be guilty, from the Apostle to the Gentiles to St Thomas or Karl Barth. The limpid clarity of the *Homily of Salvation* is deceptive, for it is theological writing of first-class importance. And who, studying his notes in his commonplace books, reading the letters and the Eucharistic treatise, and above all watching the liturgical projects grow into living frame, could dismiss the man as a mere snapper-up of other men's ideas? One shudders to think what a botched business the English Liturgy might have been, or what would have happened had it been shoddy and second-rate. Liturgies affect history no less than Acts of Parliament and his was no mean workmanship which, quarried from many sources and fitly framed together, could sustain the long burden of a people's prayers.

He was, perhaps, a lonely figure, not a great party leader, not perhaps in the end, a leader of men at all, for they did not gather round him as they did round other Reformers. His personality made little impression upon the common people. That he was Archbishop of Canterbury gave him a responsibility which he could not disregard. On the other hand, it gave his position a strength which defied all the assaults upon it by Gardiner and his henchmen. He was doubly fortified in practice by the ungrudging and unfailing friendship of the King. It was a relationship, strange as it may appear, based upon mutual affection and respect. Cranmer knew his Henry better than any other man: nobody had better claim to be considered the keeper of the King's conscience, and if that conscience seems to us an unlovely and sometimes a dreadful thing, it was not unseemly that the Archbishop should find pity for its dark recesses.

The triumph of the Catholic Party in 1539 and after has been exaggerated. The Six Articles was something more than a scare, but its bark was worse than its bite. The fall of Cromwell was a complexity, and the balanced execution of Friars and Reformers in 1540 can scarcely be called a party triumph for any side. Meanwhile, Cranmer, far from being in disgrace, went on with the work of reforming his own clergy, and, as we shall see, presided, in making the 'King's Book', over the all-important committee on the Sacraments. The failure of the considerable 'Prebendaries Plot' against him in 1543 is something more than a personal success of Cranmer against Gardiner. If there is no striking change in this period comparable with the catastrophic acts of the preceding decade, there are some very significant pointers. There is evidence to show that the country stood on the edge of far-reaching changes at the death of Henry,[1] that Henry himself proposed to be their executor, and that the death of the King and the accession of Edward meant a weakening rather than strengthening of the cause of Reform, by the new instability it engendered. In any case, the reforms of Edward's reign were not after the order of Melchizedek: they did not spring suddenly into being but were the fruit of long and careful preparation in the preceding years. Some of those preparations we shall proceed to note.

THE ENGLISH PRIMERS, 1530–45

Simple devotional literature had circulated among the Lollards, and their expositions of the Lord's Prayer, the Commandments, the Seven Deadly Sins and the Works of Mercy may

---

[1] Cranmer, *Remains*, P.S. vol. ii, pp. 415–16.

have differed little from the orthodox productions of which there were many, and among which that of Sarum was most popular. Not long after 1520 a Primer made its appearance which had some significant omissions. Thomas Hytton, the mysterious Kentish martyr, confessed to having brought an English Primer into the country. More suspected Joye of being the author. 'The Psalter was translated by George Joye, and I hear say, the Primer too.' Excerpts from an heretical Primer were condemned by the bishops in 1530 because 'he puttith in the book of the vii Psalmes, but he leveth owt the whole Litany, by which apperith his erronyous opynyon agenst praying to saints latanie'.[1] This agrees with More's statement about Joye's Primer 'wherein the Seven Psalms be set in without the Litany and the Dirige is left'.

It is worth remembrance that the first publication to bear Luther's name and authority had been his edition of these Seven Penitential Psalms, and all that we know of this Primer suggests contact with the doctrines of the Reformers. No copy of the original edition has survived though More alleged that it bore the name of Thomas Hytton in place of St Thomas. The Abbot of Northampton exhibited a Primer in the Convocation of 1534 which contained certain suspicious rubrics and it is just possible that it contained other Lutheran material, e.g. his instructions for behaviour at Mass. The earliest extant copy dates from 1533–4 and was printed by John Bydell for the civil servant turned bookseller,[2] William Marshall. It became known, in its revised version, as *Marshall's Primer* though its title was *A goodly Primer in English*. Two characteristics mark it from orthodox compilations, the presence of a 'very large didactic element' and the omission of the Litany and the Dirige (Vespers, Mattins and Lauds for the

Dead). The revised edition of 1535 included those omitted prayers with a spirited retort to the 'divers persons of small judgement and knowledge in Holy Scripture who have been offended', a not over-respectful reference to the Archbishop and his colleagues? The new preface to the Dirige has some forthright words about Purgatory, 'there is nothing in the Dirige taken out of Scripture that maketh any more mention of souls departed than doth the tale of Robin Hood'.

Marshall's Primer has much Lutheran material. In 1523 Luther had published a *Bethuchlein* of expositions and devotional matter, which in its Latin form (*Encheiridion Pium Precationum*) had been introduced to England and a large section of this finds its way into Marshall's book. The opening admonition to the Reader has references to 'Eccius, Cochlaeus and Hocstratus books' which betray its origin and in fact it is the 'Admonition' of Luther's book. There follow Luther's expositions of the Commandments, part of which through *Marshall's Primer* were included in the Bishops' Book of 1537. The Primer follows Luther in dividing the Apostles' Creed into three rather than twelve articles and the exposition of the Lord's Prayer by means of several long prayers is a rendering of Luther which follows closely the original without being always a verbal translation. The Offices and, in 1535, the Litany follow, and also in that edition a long 'contemplation on the 51st Psalm' by Jerome Savonarola which had also been specially published by Luther with a preface commending its doctrine. There followed the story of the Passion according to the Gospel narratives, and a number of prayers. The interest of *Marshall's Primer* lies less in its intrinsic worth than in the fact that some of it passed over into the Bishops' Book, and indeed traces of it survived even until the King's Book of 1543.

It was inevitable that this unwieldy omnibus volume should be superseded, but Hilsey's *Manual of Prayers* (1539), which

followed, was not much more successful despite the commendation of Cranmer and Cromwell. It included some
material from Marshall, but was on more traditional lines.
'I have', he claimed, 'pointed and set forth the true life of a
Christian that as oft as he shall handle his Primer he may so
oft learn and remember the true life towards God which consisteth principally and wholly in faith, in prayer, and in good
works.' These are the three divisions of the Primer which
begins with the Creeds, continues with prayers and concludes
with a scriptural catena describing good works, mostly taken
from Marshall. Finally, in 1545, the *King's Primer* appeared,
and from it the didactic material had disappeared, perhaps
because this was now provided by the King's Book. The
result is a Primer along traditional lines, though it does contain
a vigorous defence of vernacular prayer.

THE INSTITUTION OF A CHRISTIAN MAN
('THE BISHOPS' BOOK'), 1537

We have already noticed the appearance of the Ten Articles
and the Bishops' Book during the negotiations with the
Germans, and come now to consider their domestic background.

The Ten Articles of July 1536 aimed 'to stablish Christian
quietness and unity among us' but were followed, not by an
agreeable stillness, but by the irruption of a series of rebellions
which reverberated until the following spring, and presented
the gravest threat to the security of the realm which Henry
had to face. The motives underlying them were by no means
wholly religious, and the rebels were not all adherents of 'the
old religion'. Sir Francis Bigod, one of the rebel leaders in
the last phase of the Northern Revolt, was a fourteenth-
century Lollard born out of due time, author of a violently
anti-clerical tract upon 'Impropriations'. But, of course, the

weight of the disturbances came from the conservative side, and the fact that all contact with the Germans was cut off during this time is perhaps a sign that the King had been moved to caution, while he gave the next theological document the cautious approval which might be given to a *ballon d'essai*.

The Ten Articles probably pleased few, and may thereby have increased rather than diminished tension. Alexander Alesius, the peripatetic Scot, sent a copy post-haste to Melanchthon. He himself, having got little from London save a small pension, had tried to find lodgement as a Divinity lecturer at Cambridge. A technical regulation of the University was made the pretext for dislodging him from his precarious footing there and he reluctantly shook its dust from his feet.

'I departed from thence, specially forasmuch as I perceived there were statutes sent forth from the bishops and from the whole council of the realm, which were such that it had been wickedness not to have spoken openly against them, and yet to have reproved them, it should have been made a point of sedition.' And Alesius, who was canny enough to think discretion the better part of valour, and had not perhaps great store of either virtue, withdrew to London to study medicine. That science, though not quite such a 'dangerous trade' as theology in the sixteenth century, was certainly safer for the practitioner.

But he was not so soon to be loosed from Divinity, and one day he met Cromwell in the street, on his way to inaugurate a theological debate between the Bishops in the 'Parlement house'. Cromwell, his head full of the precedents of the early Christian empire, took Alesius along and introduced him into the debate as 'the King's scholar'. The subject was important, nothing less than the raising again of the subject of the four sacraments which had been excluded from the Ten Articles, and Cranmer made it clear that the matter must be discussed in the light of the fundamental questions of the nature of a

Sacrament, and the relation of written and unwritten verities. It would in any case have been a heated debate, but Alesius seems to have provoked a rare unanimity among the Bishops by uniting them in dislike of himself. As he harangued them, no doubt with a raucous Scottish accent, even the Evangelicals began to wriggle, and Edward Foxe had to intervene by reminding the guest speaker that by the King's command the debate was to keep to the 'rule and judgement of scripture'. Foxe himself made an able contribution to the debate by claiming that scriptural knowledge had already shown itself the victor over sophistries. 'The lay people do now know the holy scripture better than many of us: and the Germans have made the text of the Bible so plain and easy by the Hebrew and Greek tongue that now many things may be better understood without any glosses at all, than by all the commentaries of the doctors.' He concluded with noble words: 'Truth is the daughter of time, and time is the mother of truth: and whatsoever is besieged of truth cannot long continue: and upon whose side truth doth stand, that ought not to be thought transitory, or that it will ever fall.' Then followed another wrangle between Stokesley and Alesius, until the unwritten English rubric that theological disputation must never interfere with meals caused Cromwell to interrupt his protégé and adjourn the debate. No doubt informal lobbying during the luncheon interval convinced him of his blunder. Alesius was too much for the bishops, and Wittenberg out of St Andrew's too dubious a pedigree: the voice of a stranger would they not hear. In the morning even Cranmer sent a note asking Alesius not to come, while Cromwell tried tactfully to cheer him by suggesting he write out the speech which he was now unable to inflict upon the fathers of the English Church.[1]

[1] Foxe, *A. & M.* vol. v, p. 380 and Alesius's own account in his tract *Of the curiosity of the Word of God...* and summary, *L. & P. Henry VIII* (1537), vol. i, 790.

The debate took place at some time between July 1536 and February 1537, probably nearer the latter. Confirmatory evidence that the four other sacraments were now discussed comes in a statement made by one Dakyn in that month, concerning his communication with the Archbishop of York:

'Hearing while in the City from Dr Waldeby and others, of dissension among the Bishops concerning the Sacraments omitted in the King's Book of Articles, I asked the Archbishop whether I should proceed according to his previous command, in declaring that book. He said "Yea", and added, "these four sacraments that were omitted be found again now, and we be concluded upon them yesternight, and the book shall be printed anew again: but in the mean season, let the curates declare the old book.'

The statement 'the book shall be printed anew again' is generally taken as referring to the Bishops' Book, but it is possible that at this time it was intended only to reissue the Ten Articles with the four additional sacraments. In the addenda to the *Letters and Papers of Henry VIII* for this year there is a draft preface for such a document. It begins: 'The Archbishops and Bishops of England to all and singular the Kings highness loving and faithful subjects, greeting', and refers to a book 'wherein we spake long sithence of baptism, penance and the eucharist,' and of their purpose now to speak of the other four.[1]

The undated drafts of four statements on these other sacraments are extant and historians generally have been content to place them between the Ten Articles and the Bishops' Book, i.e. between June 1536 and August 1537.[2] But we can date one of them, the important statement on 'Orders', with precision. For among the signatories is Dr Marmaduke Waldeby who had informed Dakyn of the dissension among

[1] *L. & P. Henry VIII* (1537), vol. 1, 789.
[2] Ibid. ii, add. 33.

the Bishops, and who was himself imprisoned in the Tower in April 1537 for his implication in Aske's rebellion. He must have been in trouble some time before this and we can with some confidence date the document as February 1537. It is likely that the statements on the other three sacraments are of the same date.

The suggestion that after the Ten Articles and before the making of the Bishops' Book, there was debate and definition of the four other sacraments finally finds confirmation in a letter of Cranmer to Cromwell in July 1537, when the Bishops' Book was almost finished: 'I with the other bishops and learned men here assembled by the King's commandment, have almost made an end of our determinations, for we have already subscribed unto the declarations of the Paternoster and the Ave Maria, the creed and the ten Commandments: and there remaineth no more but certain notes of the creed: unto the which we be agreed to subscribe on Monday next.'[1] It is striking that Cranmer, resuming the contents of the book, omits all reference to the Sacraments, but intelligible enough if the work had been done upon them and concluded months before. The Ten Articles had indeed gone rather far in omitting the four sacraments, and in the context of the rebellions the evangelical bishops concentrated on getting their distinction accepted between the three primary sacraments and the others, as indeed was included in the Bishops' Book.

But it was obvious that more material of a catechetical nature was needed. In July 1537 Foxe wrote to Bucer that 'the best of princes, . . . when he saw all appeased, immediately turned his mind to promulgating the gospel. He therefore charged the bishops and the doctors convoked for that purpose to compile certain rudiments of Christianity and a Catechism'.[2] This document was compiled by the labours of an 'assembly

---

[1] Cranmer, *Works*, P.S. p. 338.
[2] *L. & P. Henry VIII* (1537), vol. II, 410.

of bishops and learned men' such as performed so much of the
confessional labour of the English Reformation.

Edward Foxe took a leading part, and may be considered
editor-in-chief. Cranmer, though much pressed by other affairs,
did what he could. Latimer shared in the work, though he
chafed to be off to Kingston, and was soon wearied by ecclesiastical disputations which engendered heat and sound so
easily and light but smally. But Foxe was now a chronic
invalid, dying of the stone, and the work was interrupted. Then,
just at the critical stage when the work was shaped and when
the King would have been consulted, came the Plague. The
Bishops were forbidden to bring into the royal presence the
contagion of the 'smoky air' of London. Although Foxe
could write in July that the book was finished and 'wanteth
nothing but the Creeds' they were still unprinted at the end
of August, still unseen by the King.

Perhaps these delays rather than Royal guile account for the
manner of his half approval. 'We have caused your book to
be printed', he informed its authors, 'and will the same to be
conveyed into all parts of the realm...notwithstanding that
we are otherwise occupied, we have taken as it were a taste of
the book, and have found nothing therein, but that it is meet
to come from you, and also worthy our praise and commendation.' Book-tasting, 'as it were', aptly describes the royal
theological method, and the best measure of the theological
learning of the King lies, not in the sparkling erudition of the
treatise against Luther, but in the comments on the details of
the Bishops' Book which the King sent to Cranmer. Cranmer's
counter criticism should dispose of yet another legend, that of
the Archbishop's timidity, for he takes his royal master to task
as severely as if he had been back at Jesus, conning with tired
severity the efforts of the youngest in the Schools: now it is
clumsy English, then bad Latin, here redundancy of thought
exposed, there flat disagreement registered.

It was natural for the book to make use of existing didactic material and large portions of Marshall's Primer were incorporated in it. Through that means the Bishops' Book derived some teaching direct from Luther, while there are other passages which show a striking affinity with Luther's Catechism. It should be said that the teaching here borrowed was not of an immediately controversial nature. The borrowing of any material did not make it tractable to debate, and the clumsy expedient was adopted of appending a series of debated and agreed 'Observations' after each section of the work. The division of the Book into Creed, Sacraments, Commandments, Lord's Prayer was an obvious one.

The Book begins with an exposition of the Apostles' Creed, divided into the traditional twelve articles, as against the threefold division of Luther and Marshall. The 'Observations' deal with the doctrine of the Harrowing of Hell, perhaps with an intent to offset the emphasis in the text on the Divine Mercy, with the thought of the Divine Justice, but more probably to deal with a subject of current controversy, for Bale and others had recently attacked the doctrine on theological and critical grounds.

The discussion on the Church declares the Church of Rome to be a 'particular member' of the universal Church and affirms:

'I believe that these particular churches, in what place of the world soever they be congregated, be the very parts, portions or members of this catholic and universal church. And that between them there is indeed no difference in superiority, pre-eminence, or authority, neither that any one of them is head or sovereign over the other, but that they be all equal in power and dignity.'[1]

The declaration of the Sacraments begins with an exhaustive discourse on the nature of Matrimony which was paid the

[1] Lloyd, *Formularies*, p. 55.

compliment of reception, almost unaltered into the next catechetical work of the reign, the King's Book (1543). Its Sacramental character is affirmed:

'Although this Sacrament of matrimony be no new Sacrament instituted in the New Testament... but instituted by God and consecrated by his word, and dignified by his laws, even from the beginning of the world and before any other of the Sacraments were instituted in the New Testament yet the truth is that Christ himself did also accept, approve and allow the said institution.'[1]

Baptism is expounded in terms of the Ten Articles, Confirmation traced to the Apostles in the beginning of the Church, and to the primitive church: Penance and the Sacrament of the Altar are taken from the Ten Articles.

Though from the standard of pious instruction one of the least edifying, the section on Orders is one of the most interesting in the book. It is composed of two documents; the first that statement on Orders which had been debated and subscribed by February 1537; the second, a new section dealing with the controverted *potestas jurisdictionis* as distinct from the *potestas ordinis*, and there is some evidence that it was written by Cuthbert Tunstal.[2] It probably caused more discussion than any other part of the book in court circles and was much criticized by the King in his comments on the book. Of all the sections of the *Institution of a Christian Man* it was most severely handled in revision, and the treatment of this sacrament in the King's Book is almost a new treatise.

In fact, the treatment of this section warns us against judging the pronouncements of this period from any modern notion of 'evangelical' and 'catholic', 'conservative' or 'reformed'. It is possible that this section of the work was one reason why Henry withheld from it his full approval.

[1] Lloyd, *Formularies*, p. 86.
[2] *L. & P. Henry VIII* (1537), vol. XII, ii, 401.

'Christ and his apostles did institute and ordain in the New Testament, that beside the civil powers and governance of kings and princes which is called *potestas gladii*, the power of the sword, there should be also continually in the church militant certain other ministers or officers which should have special power, authority and commission, under Christ, to preach and teach the Word of God unto his people: to dispense and administer the sacraments of God unto them: and by the same to confer and give the graces of the Holy Ghost: to consecrate the blessed body of Christ in the sacrament of the altar; to loose and absoyle from sin all persons which be duly penitent and sorry for the same: to bind and excommunicate such as be guilty in manifest crimes and sins, and will not amend their defaults: to order and consecrate others in the same room, order and office whereunto they be called and admitted themselves, and finally, to feed Christ's people like good pastors and rectors (as the apostle calleth them) with their wholesome doctrine: and by their continual exhortations and admonitions to reduce them from sin and iniquity as much as in them lieth and to bring them unto the perfect knowledge, the perfect love or dread of God, and unto the perfect charity of their neighbours.'[1]

There are three reasons for this power: God has willed it: it is the ordinary means 'whereby he will make us partakers of the reconciliation which is by Christ...by his word and sacraments'. It has annexed to it 'excellent and inestimable things, for thereby is conferred the Holy Ghost'.[2] This Sacrament of Orders 'was given by Christ and His apostles unto certain persons only, that is to priests and bishops whom they did elect call and admit thereunto by their prayers and the imposition of their hands'.[3] Other rites and the divisions of the minor orders had been laudably instituted by the holy fathers.

'Yet the truth is that in the New Testament there is no mention made of any degrees or distinctions in orders, but only of deacons or ministers, and priests or bishops. Nor is

---

[1] Lloyd, *Formularies*, pp. 101–2.
[2] Ibid. pp. 102–3.   [3] Ibid. p. 104.

there any word spoken of any other ceremony used in the conferring of this sacrament, but only of prayers and the imposition of the Bishop's hands.'[1]

There follows the section on jurisdiction. To it belong three capacities: power to rebuke sin and to excommunicate open sinners; power to admit duly presented persons to preach and administer the Sacraments; power to make rules and canons. But this last power is cautiously defined. Rules and canons were made by the Apostles 'during the time when the Church was subject to infidel princes and before any princes were christened'.[2] As soon as Christian princes were available they 'did not only approve the said canons then made by the Church, but did also enact and make new laws of their own, concerning the good order of the Church and furthermore did also constrain their subjects by corporal pain and punishment to observe the same'.[3]

'The Christian Princes... did also give to priests and bishops further power and jurisdiction in certain temporal and civil matters like as by laws, statutes, immunities, privileges and grants made of princes in that behalf and by the uses also and customs of sundry realms and regions it doth manifestly appear. And therefore it always was and always shall be lawful unto the said Kings and princes and their successors with the consent of their parliaments, to revoke and call again into their own hands or otherwise to restrain all the power and jurisdiction which was given and assigned unto priests and bishops by the licence, consent, sufferance and authority of God and his gospel, whensoever they shall have grounds and causes so to do for the weal of their realms, the repressing of vice, and the increase of Christ's faith and religion.'[4]

On the basis of this argument Papal jurisdiction could be cut off: the Lord King had given, the Lord King had taken away the power of jurisdiction. 'The Bishop of Rome he

[1] Ibid. p. 105.
[2] Ibid. p. 113.
[3] Ibid. p. 113.
[4] Ibid. p. 114.

cannot pretend himself no more to be favoured or injured more therewith than the kings chancellor or any other his officers might worthily think the kings highness should do him wrong, in case he should upon good cause remove him from his said room and commit it unto another.'[1] What is striking is that the King criticized this statement on 'Orders' because of its limitation, not its extension of royal authority. It is significant that the paragraph excluding the King himself from priestly functions was not only omitted in the King's Book of 1543 but was the subject, in 1540, of a special questionnaire circulated among the Bishops and Divines.

It is interesting to note that in 1535 William Marshall had translated into English the *Defensor Pacis* of Marsilius of Padua,[2] which contains some ideas in agreement with this statement upon Orders. Marshall's version had some discreet omissions, such as that 'On the corruption of Princes': 'et propter quam causam qualiter et a quibus legem transgrediens arceri' which Marshall cheerfully explained as 'nothing pertaining to this realm of England'. Even more striking is the omission of two chapters on the 'limits of ecclesiastical power' as being 'not of much value and to avoid the offence of some spiritual persons, that bear pepper in their noses, and that judges every truth to be spoken of malice'. A year later he had to admit that the book was not selling, though 'the best book against the Bishop of Rome'.

Nevertheless, the book must have been read by some of the compilers of the Bishops' Book and the ideas of Marsilius were potent stuff. Its arid Aristotelianism may have had little attraction, but it was a mine of patristic and scriptural quotation. Thus Marsilius also says that 'the apostles instituted their successors by the laying on of hands and by prayer, giving power to consecrate the Body and Blood of Christ, to ad-

[1] Lloyd, *Formularies*, pp. 107–26.
[2] See Marsilius, *Defensor Pacis* (ed. Previté-Orton). C.U.P. 1928.

minister the sacraments by which they can bind and loose men
from their sins'. Marsilius states that 'in essentiali dignitate
presbyter episcopo non sit inferior sed in accidentali tantum-
modo'. The denial to the priesthood of coercive jurisdiction
and the extension to the laity of the power of excommunication
are hinted at in the full statement in the Bishops' Book, and
both points are made by Marsilius. Marsilius also proceeds
from the assertion of the equality of all Bishops to the denunciation of the Roman tyranny. The parallels are suggestive,
but nothing is easier, or less demonstrable, than this kind of
borrowing and we had better leave the point by showing that
these ideas were abroad at the time of the making of the Bishops'
Book, than by asserting that Marsilius also was among the
Henricians.

Returning to the Bishops' Book, the Sacrament of Extreme
Unction is suggested in the apostolic mission in the Gospels.
'Because of the rule of St James it shall be very necessary and
expedient that all true christian people do use and observe this
manner of anointing with oil in the name of God.'[1] Such
prayer must be made in faith, accepting whatever may be the
issue as the will of God, and the Christian must forgive his
enemies and confess his sins. But he is not to think his life
will be shorter, but that it may be prolonged by the sacrament.

The exposition of the Sacraments concluded with a distinction between the three chief sacraments and the rest.
Baptism, the Eucharist, Penance were instituted by Christ as
necessary for salvation, as commanded in their visible signs,
and as conveying grace whereby sins are remitted.

The Commandments and the Lord's Prayer are expounded
with the aid of Marshall's Primer. Luther's exposition of the
Commandments had included long lists of the divers offences
against each law and most of these find their way into the
Bishops' Book. The *Institution of a Christian Man* concluded

[1] Lloyd, *Formularies*, pp. 126–8.

with the two articles, on 'Purgatory' and on 'Justification' from the Ten Articles of 1536.

When the book was finished, Foxe wrote to Cromwell asking in what form and under what authority it should be published and suggested that Wriothesley might be asked to devise a suitable preface. Cromwell preferred that Foxe should perform that office, and he seems to have done so. The preface resumes the reasons for making the book, and emphasizes that it is 'in our mother tongue'. There is in this introduction a description of faith which may have influenced the very different formulation of the King's Book. But here faith is described as

'that singular gift of God whereby our hearts, that is to say our natural reason and judgement (obscured and almost extincted by original and actual sins) is lightened, purified and made able to know and discern what things be indeed acceptable and displeasant in the sight of God: and for because also that faith is the very fountain and chief ground of our religion, and of all goodness and virtues exercised in the same...we have begun with the Creed'.

The dedication ends with a complete submission to the judgement of His Majesty, in the best Henrician manner:

'without the which power and licence of your majesty we knowledge and confess that we have none authority, either to assemble ourselves together for any pretence or purpose, or to publish any thing that might by us be agreed on and compiled...we do most humbly submit it to the most excellent wisdom and exact judgement of your majesty, to be recognised, overseen and corrected, if your grace shall find any word or sentence in it meet to be changed, qualified or further expounded'.[1]

So the book was issued, lacking explicit royal authority, bearing only its maker's preface dressed as a clerical petition, and in the absence of any rival book, it was for three years the

[1] Lloyd, *Formularies*, p. 26.

authorized basis of instruction. The ambiguities of the book led both parties to claim it as the fulfilment of their programme as Cranmer's heated correspondence with a Kentish magistrate very clearly reveals. And yet he surely had a right to speak of its intentions. 'If men will indifferently read these late declarations', he wrote, 'they should well perceive that purgatory, pilgrimages, praying to saints, images, holy bread, holy water, holy days, merits, works, ceremonies, and such other be not restored to their late accustomed uses, but shall evidently perceive that the Word of God hath gotten the upper hand of them all, and hath set them in their right use and estimation.'[1]

INTERVAL, 1537-43

But before those three years were up, changes had taken place. The most sensational was the passing of the Six Articles which made explicit much which in the Bishops' Book had either been ignored or veiled in reticent ambiguity. Yet there was nothing in the Six Articles which explicitly and directly contradicted the *Institution of a Christian Man*. The extent of Catholic triumph has been exaggerated. Shaxton and Latimer resigned their sees, but both had been stormy petrels and never did bishop more eagerly lose his charge than Latimer, nor could happier days induce him to take again the burden. But Cranmer, Barlow, Hilsey and Goodrich all retained theirs, and there is much evidence that the King even went out of his way to show his favour to Cranmer. In 1549 Cranmer protested that the Act would never have been passed: 'If the King had not come into the parliament house' and that it was 'enforced by the counsel of certain papists against the truth and common judgement both of divines and lawyers'.[2] Yet in one point of

---

[1] Cranmer, *Remains*, P.S. vol. II, p. 351.
[2] Ibid. p. 168: 'Answer to the Rebels.'

the debate Henry sided with Cranmer against Lee, Tunstal and Gardiner—the divine institution of auricular confession. Perhaps Melanchthon's letters had had some effect after all, or was it that Henry wanted to show his undistinguishing regard for truth as against party? The events which followed, the breakdown of the Cleves match, the fall of Cromwell and the Howard marriage reinforced the Catholic Party. In 1541 it was Stephen Gardiner who represented the King at the important Diet of Ratisbon. Yet even at this time the Reformers had influential friends at court and among the nobility. At Canterbury, where Cranmer's reorganization of the cathedral staff had sharpened the antagonism of his enemies, there fermented the formidable intrigue engineered by Germain Gardiner, the kinsman of the Bishop of Winchester. Yet the fiasco in which this 'Prebendaries plot' ended recoiled on the heads of the perpetrators. Nor was Cranmer idle during the period, or the cause of further reform stayed. In July 1541 some superfluous saints' days and obvious superstitions were abolished: in the following year he was authorized to remove shrines and relics which were superstitiously revered and to prohibit the offering of lights and candles except to the Blessed Sacrament. In 1542 Cranmer defeated Gardiner's attack on the English Bible, after the latter had presented a long list of words which he wished to be retained in their catholic and invariably incorrect usage.

Active steps towards a revision of the Bishops' Book were taken as early as June 1540 when two commissions were appointed, one to deal with doctrine and the other with ceremonies. As before, questions were circulated among the Bishops and Divines concerning controverted matters and they centred on those parts of the Bishops' Book which had aroused the greatest dissatisfaction, not indeed among the common people but in the mind of the King and of the higher clergy. There was still difference of opinion about the number of the Sacraments and of the seventeen questions circulated which have survived, eight deal with this subject. The next five concern the question of Orders and centre on that part of the Bishops' Book which denied priestly functions to the King. Cranmer's answer has been summarized above, but scarcely less interesting is the degree to which the other bishops and doctors went further than the Bishops' Book in defining the royal power in ecclesiastical matters. Question 13 reads:

'Whether, if it fortuned a Christian prince learned, to conquer certain dominions of infidels having nothing but temporal learned men with him it be defended by Gods law that he and they should preach and teach the Word of God there or no? and also constitute and make priests or no?'

The reply to the first half of the question is the only unanimous answer among the Bishops and Divines: 'They do all agree that in such case he not only may, but ought to teach.' Moreover, the Bishops of Durham, St David's, Westminster, and Drs Tresham, Cox, Leighton, Crayford, Symmons, Redmayn and Robertson admitted that in such case laymen might have authority to administer the sacraments and make priests. London, Carlisle, Hereford, with Dr Coren thought that direct guidance would be granted from Heaven in such dilemma. Only the Archbishop of York and Dr Edgeworth ventured a direct negation.[1]

The 'Necessary Doctrine and Erudition for any Christian Man' (The King's Book), 1543[2]

In April 1543 various committees were appointed to consider the various parts of the new book. Although the Catholic Party were of great influence at this time, it may be noted that the chairman of the all-important section on the Sacraments was the Archbishop Thomas Cranmer.[3] We find Gardiner

[1] Burnet (Pocock, vol. 1, (ii), pp. 314–69).
[2] Lloyd, *Formularies*. Lacey, *The King's Book*.
[3] *L. & P. Henry VIII* (1543), vol. xviii, (i), 365, 507.

with the Bishops of Rochester and Westminster reporting on the 'Lord's Prayer' and the 'Ave Maria' and the same bishops examining the exposition of 'Faith'. This time the King kept in close touch with the makers of the book and it is clear that full and respectful use had been made of his comments on the Bishops' Book. The *Necessary Doctrine and Erudition for any Christian Man* does not reflect a 'triumph for the Catholic party', even though Canon Mason went too far in asserting its evangelical character. Many changes were simply due to exigencies of style, spacing and general arrangement. As Foxe had complained, the Bishops' Book had greatly swollen in its last stages and would have gained by condensation. Many of the King's suggestions were of this character, and were adopted, notably the printing in full of the quotations from Scripture, and the full list of those prohibited degrees of marriage on which the King was by now an authority.

The book begins with a definition of Faith on Augustinian lines. It admits a distinction between a 'living faith' which includes both hope and charity and that faith which is 'persuasion and belief'. The clumsy 'Observations' on the Creed and Commandments which had been an untidy feature of the Bishops' Book were wisely omitted and the whole declaration on the Creed is enormously improved in matter, style and rhythm. The article on the Holy Ghost, with a few changes, benefits enormously and is a little masterpiece of clear thought and graceful arrangement.

Once again the definition of the Church is of interest:

'Beside the inward and secret calling which God hath used and yet still doth use, he hath also ordained an outward calling of the people unto him, by preaching of his most holy word: upon which outward calling the people yielding, assenting and obeying the same Word of God, and receiving it also with true faith and the sacrament of Baptism (as Christ's law requireth) be named in scripture "ecclesia", that is to say, an assembly of people, called out from others, as from infidels or heathen, to one faith and confession of the name of Christ, which word in English is called "church".[1]

The equality of the churches is affirmed, and the apostolicity of the church is said to belong to such churches as 'follow such teaching as the apostles preached with ministration of such Sacraments as be approved by the same'. It concludes with a statement of curious theological implications:

'And so every Christian man ought to honour, give credence, and to follow the particular church of that region so ordered...wherein he is born or inhabiteth.'[2]

It is claimed that it belongs to Christian Kings and Princes:

'not only to provide for the tranquillity and wealth of their subjects in temporal and worldly things, to the conservation of their bodies, but also to foresee that within their dominions such ministers be ordained and appointed in their churches as can and will truly and purely set out the true doctrine of Christ and teach the same and to see the commandment of God well observed and kept, to the wealth and salvation of their souls'.[3]

Into the section on Baptism there is interpolated part of the 'Lord's Prayer' section of the Bishops' Book, in language ultimately deriving from Luther. The Catholic definition of Penance is retained, but the familiar threefold division is slightly disguised by the opening definition: 'Penance is properly the absolution pronounced by the priest upon such as be penitent for their sins and so do knowledge and show themselves to be'—a statement which Henry had strongly criticized when made by one of the Bishops.

The exposition of Matrimony is taken from the Bishops' Book without much change, so that one omission is the more striking:

'the other thing to be noted is, that Christ saith here unto his disciples "Non omnes capiunt verbum hoc sed quibus datum

[1] Lloyd, *Formularies*, p. 244.
[2] Ibid. p. 248.   [3] Ibid. p. 249.

est, qui potest capere capiat" by the which words Christ
seemeth to exhort such as he shall endue with his grace and
virtue of continence whereby they shall be able to abstain from
the works of matrimony to continue sole and unmarried'.[1]

By deliberately omitting these lines the makers of the King's
Book deliberately refused to underline one of the few points
where their subject-matter touched that of the Six Articles.

The statement on Orders has been shattered to bits and
remoulded nearer to the royal desire. It deals only with the
potestas ordinis and avoids all those thorny questions which
were raised by the section on the *potestas jurisdictionis* of the
Bishops' Book. Much of the new statement seems derived
from a statement drawn up in 1538 which affirms the equality
of Churches and repudiates the councils of Constance, Basel
and Florence. It is affirmed that it belongs to the Christian
Princes:

'to endeavour themselves to reform and reduce the same again
unto the old limits and pristine estate of that power which was
given to them by Christ and was used in the primitive Church'[2].

The Sacraments of Confirmation and of Extreme Unction
are more succinctly expounded than in the Bishops' Book,
while most of the treatment of the Commandments is taken
from that source.

One change seems to contradict the Bishops' Book. Where
that reads: 'we be utterly forbidden to make or have simili-
tudes or images'; the King's Book has 'we be not forbidden'[3]
and yet the context proves that both books have the same
material point that we be 'forbidden to do godly honour to
them'. The long prayers which in Luther and Marshall's
Primer had expounded the Lord's Prayer were now abandoned, and the Ave Maria is little changed.

---

[1] Lloyd, *Formularies*, p. 88.   [2] Ibid. p. 287.
[3] Ibid. p. 299.

The King's Book concluded with four doctrinal articles: on Free Will, Justification, Good Works, and Prayer for souls departed. The first bears some marks of compromise and of the three is the nearest the reformers in theology. True, the commandments and threatenings of God in Scripture are said to declare that man 'hath free will now after the fall of our first father Adam'. On the other hand two definitions of this free will are allowed, first that it is

'a certain power of the will joined with reason whereby a reasonable creature, without constraint in things of reason, discerneth and willeth good and evil', 'but it willeth not that good which is acceptable unto God, except it be holpen with grace but that which is ill it willeth of itself'.[1]

The second is 'A power of reason and will by which good is chosen by the assistance of grace, or evil is chosen without the assistance of the same'. The effects of the Fall are then described:

'great is in our nature the corruption of the first sin and the heavy burden bearing us down to evil. For truly albeit the light of reason doth abide, yet is it much darkened and with difficulty doth discern things that pertain unto this present life: but to understand and perceive things that be spiritual and pertain to everlasting life it is of itself unable.' 'And so likewise although there remain a certain freedom of will in those things which do pertain to unto the desires and works of this present life, yet to perform spiritual and heavenly things free will is of itself insufficient.'[2]

This is not immeasurably distant from Article XVIII of the Augsburg Confession: 'Man's will hath some liberty to work a civil righteousness and to choose such things as reason can reach to: but it hath no power to work the Righteousness of God, or a spiritual righteousness without the spirit of God.'[3] But the similarity does not mean that this article was the work

[1] Ibid. p. 359.   [2] Ibid. p. 360.
[3] Schaff, *Creeds*, p. 3.

of the evangelical Party, for there are evident marks of compromise upon it.

The article on Justification moves within the Catholic framework and affirms that final justification is attained by 'baptism, penance and the daily spiritual renovation'. The need for grace is asserted and the fact that it is given gratis is stressed, and also in line with St Augustine and St Thomas, the need for good works which shall be 'inward and spiritual works, motions and desires as the love and fear of God, joy in God, godly meditations and thoughts, patience, humility and the like'.[1]

Again there are marks of compromise, but on the whole the theology of the articles on Justification and Free Will is probably as Protestant and as Catholic as St Augustine.

The article on 'Prayers for souls departed' is of another spirit. It repeats much of the similar article in the Bishops' Book. Prayers and masses for the dead are still commended. But it is urged that in the state of man's ignorance these should be general rather than directed for specific persons, and that they be offered on behalf of the universal church. Finally, it is declared that it is now necessary 'that we should therefore abstain from the name of Purgatory and no more dispute or reason thereof'.[2] It may seem that here is no more than the avoidance of contention. What's in a name? Yet this was the tenth year since the death by burning of John Frith, who on the eve of his death had penned the articles for which he died: 'I count it for no necessary article of our faith necessarily to be believed under pain of damnation whether there be such a purgatory or not.'

Thus there is enough compromise in the shaping of the King's Book to have enabled the Reformers to hope that the Word of God had not lost the upper hand.

[1] Lloyd, *Formularies*, pp. 373-75.   [2] Ibid. p. 376.

Part Three

INTRODUCTION

THE years 1520–88 saw the making of the English Protestant tradition, so that the colour and direction of the life of the English people were changed and pointed in a new way, and the character of religion and of people in this island received another and deep impress. In its making, as in the making of all the great currents in the human story, many things combined, saints like Tyndale and Bradford, sinners like Thomas Cromwell and his royal master, politicians like Cecil and his royal mistress, Sir Thomas Wyatt and Francis Drake, the fires of Smithfield and the dispersal of the Armada, self interest and defiant charity, cynicism and fanaticism, stupidity and prophetic vision. But these things alone do not add up to the full sum. There are two other facts, and with these the remaining chapters of these studies will be concerned.

First, there was the propagation of creative and liberating truths imbedded in the primary Christian gospel, but readjusted to a new age. We shall examine that doctrine of 'Justification by Faith' which was the foundation of their proclamation.

Second, the new values were incarnate in the life and witness of living men, who suffered to proclaim them. Dead men, they say, tell no tales. But here, between 1520 and 1558, is a tale which is told by dead men, which perhaps only dead men could tell with sufficient force to impress succeeding generations. Our last chapter will call attention to the martyrs, because the root of this great matter then and now lies in the real world of living men, and because these things happened for our example. We shall mend neither Christendom nor the Church without their like.

CHAPTER VIII

'JUSTIFICATION BY FAITH' AND THE ENGLISH REFORMERS

'The doctrine of "Only Faith Justifieth",' wrote Stephen Gardiner in 1547, 'if it were true as the Homily declareth, it is no more necessary for the present state of the Church than to know whether the burden of Our Lady and Christ only were as perfect as the burden of Our Lady and Christ with a flea sitting upon Our Lady's Head, which the solemn doctors of Paris so earnestly entreated of.'[1] He did not deny that 'in knowledge it be a grave matter, and such as for the entreating of it, many have wept even here at home, besides those that have wept in Germany'. But he thought it remote and academic in face of the searing problems of English social, political and religious life, and for all practical purposes irrelevant, since all Christian men 'are justified in Baptism'.

Yet precisely there is revealed the difference between the Reformers and their opponents. For them Justification by 'only faith' was the very ground bass of all their gospelling, while their adversaries either could not make out what all the fuss was about, or took their definitions to be polemical hair splitting as when Sir Thomas More misunderstood Tyndale's doctrine of saving faith to be 'an evasion, by means of a distinction of Melanchthon, in which distinction as in a mist he walketh away'.[2]

We can easily go astray if we stretch the utterances of the Reformers to fit any ready-made pattern, whether of Protestant or Tridentine orthodoxy. Ritschl correctly pointed out that they did not begin with the formal categories of systematic theology. If they penetrated with force into the Biblical world,

[1] Foxe, *A. & M.* vol. VI, p. 49. [2] More, *Works* (ed. 1557), p. 693.

and even with uncanny accuracy into the Biblical vocabulary, it is because Luther, like Paul, found his theology in the historical context of an acute crisis.

The Apostle to the Gentiles faced ultimate theological questions, but those inquiries, 'how may guilty sinners stand in the presence of the Living God?', 'What is the Church of God?' were faced in the more immediate form of 'What is a Jew?', 'What then is the real Israel?', questions implicit in the most urgent, grimly practical of all problems of the Apostolic age, the question of the terms on which the Gentiles might become members of the Church of God. It is as Paul faces these questions in the new dimension of the Christian revelation that he strains and tears an inherited vocabulary and opens up new worlds of theological exploration. For Paul, too, there was a Scriptural background. He did not invent his themes. In the Old Testament the consideration of individual integrity and national destiny both had come to involve questions of theodicy. God is Lord, and God is Righteous, and what He is has been made known in his Mighty Acts, of which the Exodus is the archetype. Yet it seems that despite his laws and promises to His Covenanted people, the wicked prosper, the ungodly triumph, the innocent, the 'poor man' is oppressed, and the fate of Israel among the Nations becomes ever more dubious and desperate. The Righteousness of God, His own saving might and the integrity of his promises need publicly to be vindicated in the sphere of human history. In the great crime story of history suspicion has fallen on the Great Detective.[1] But just because faith proclaims that God is Righteous and God is Lord there is involved the hope that his Righteousness will be displayed by acts of salvation, a hope

[1] It is doubtful whether the Book of Job deals with 'the problem of...' anything in our modern sense, but if it does it is less with our obsession, the problem of innocent suffering, than with this problem of Righteousness. How profoundly Ezekiel deals with the theme on the national scale was finely shown long ago by A. B. Davidson.

that is the heart of the developing eschatology. On the one hand the thought of the Righteousness of God retains the rich ethical content of the prophetic witness. It does not cease to concern the individual who guards the testimonies and keeps the law. Yet, compared with the New, the Old Testament could not sufficiently weigh the gravity of sin, and in any case the Old Testament thought of the Righteousness of God covers much more than the forgiveness of individual transgressions. The Righteousness of God is God's own saving activity, and while the technical vocabulary may evoke legal associations, the Biblical theme involves the whole Divine economy and seeks to justify the ways of God to man.

St Paul, we have seen, faced a practical problem, which called in question his own ministry, and indeed the whole foundation of the Church. He faced the question 'What is a Jew?' and he knew one answer to that question, knew it thoroughly as it had been the warp and woof of the existence of Saul of Tarsus, a Pharisee of the Pharisees. He knew that answer was wrong, but he also knew that this repudiation was enormous. If Israel after the flesh had failed, then all other human answers must fail too, and all approach from the human side to the Divine Righteousness must be excluded. In the end the religious man in the religious community, who could look with horror at the impious idolatries of the pagan world, he too was locked in the universe, Jew and Gentile in the one pattern of a world shut up in disobedience, responsible, guilty, justly condemned under the Judgement and the Wrath of God.

But now Paul had been shown another Righteousness, the Righteousness of God bestowed upon sinful men by God's own kindness declared publicly to men in Jesus Christ, and precisely, 'in his blood'. And this was given to man, not on the ground of human merit or desert but on the ground of faith. It goes without saying that for Paul this Righteousness of God is no abstract quality but God's own saving action,

His Love and Grace going out to men in the declaration of their forgiveness, in their reconciliation to Himself. The balance of the doctrine is preserved in a phrase which might have saved later theology from many pitfalls 'that He might be Just and the Justifier of him that believes'.

It is not our purpose to expound the teaching of St Paul, but it should be pointed out that his doctrine has a width and balance which may be missed by those who come to it out of the preoccupation of modern evangelical religion with the moral problems of the individual. For St Paul sets that subject within a Divine Action extending to all men in their corporate as well as in their private existence, and he turns naturally to the great antithetical phrases, 'In Adam', 'In Christ'. When he attempts to explain the inexplicable fact that guilty sinners become the children of God, and describes the indescribable dealings of God with men, he turns to metaphors (which he invariably strains and often breaks) which are corporate in their suggestion. Those who complain of his figures as abstract, and as unsuited to express personal relationships, might walk through the City of London, past the Royal Exchange, the Old Bailey and the Cathedral of St Paul. They will find there, as in the heart of any city from the most ancient times, those same figures, the market, the law court, the temple and be reminded that the language of transaction, of judgement and of sacrifice sums up a good deal of the life of man in its corporate existence.[1] Moreover, St Paul knew this salvation to be no innovation, no Divine improvisation: this must be the

---

[1] Dr Vincent Taylor in his discriminating discussion of New Testament teaching ('Forgiveness and Reconciliation', p. 46) says that 'the associations of λογίζομαι are unfortunate...the association is commercial'. But he puts up a very good defence for the use of the forensic δικαιόω. The same arguments would seem to justify, or not to justify all the Pauline metaphors, and I do not think that the doctrine of 'imputation' is to be discredited on these grounds alone, though one must admit the force of much of Dr Taylor's other criticism of it.

meaning of God's handling of his creation from the beginning, 'In Christ' must be the key to the life of Jew and Gentile, to all laws and promises, in the light of which all past and future history must be re-edited. Its horizons are as wide as the universe itself, for because of it the whole creation is in travail, eagerly straining to glimpse the appearing of God's sons.

Martin Luther did not rediscover St Paul's teaching in the sense that one may discover a pavement of Roman mosaic beneath a later floor, and he did not by any means discover the whole of St Paul. But he did apprehend the theme of Justification with a depth of intuition and a richness which has not been surpassed. But for him the whole Reformation movement, which apart from his intervention could not have been long delayed, must have taken another and more disastrous direction, and centred in those secondary issues which occupied the Lollards and were to obsess the 'Schwärmerei', if indeed the whole matter of Reform had not been swallowed in a dark tide of human greed and pride, the full force of which can hardly have been pondered by those who glibly speak of a preferable Reformation 'on Erasmian lines'.

Yet we must beware. The older historians loved to portray Luther as the lonely pioneer, wrestling with his sins, or poring over God's Book until the moment of illumination. There may have been such a moment. There may have been, but the evidence for it is confused and unconvincing. There may instead have been a long process of inquiry beginning when the fact of Death (rather than the fact of Sin) drove him to the religious vocation, and culminating when as a Professor he was occupied by the tedious business of making lecture notes. We need not be so modern as to deny the importance of his spiritual problems or his Biblical study. But his 'discovery', we repeat, was not like some scientific invention, a theological spinning jenny to be passed round, adapted, improved and finally patented by others! It was rather as when a note plucked on an instrument will set a hundred objects jangling that he struck his theme, and the vibrations reverberated through Christendom.

But others might, probably did hit the same note, for it was already present in the Scriptures. It is likely that Thomas Bilney found his new evangel apart from Luther's teaching. Zwingli himself probably was honest and correct when he claimed to have made his own adventure upon it. Luther did not make a theological discovery in an historical vacuum and then proceed to 'apply' it to a particular situation. What took place in his cell or study was as private, but also as public a church event, as what took place on the steps of the Schloss kirche of Wittenberg, and that is why it became the pivot of the Reformation.

'Sunt loci maxime cognati, doctrina poenitentiae et doctrina justificationis' profoundly remarked Melanchthon. Christian penitence involves an antinomy which persists from the original Christian gospel. In one sense the salvation offered in Christ is already achieved and bestowed. Christ has conquered Sin and Death and Principalities and Powers. The Christian is dead, he has been buried with Christ in baptism, baptized in truth into the death of Christ: now he is risen with Christ, raised where Christ sits at the right hand of God. Hence the new ethical imperative: 'Be what you are!' Yet, as is painfully clear, the Christians still fall into sin, Christians die, and in the world the sway of Principalities and Powers seems but little diminished. There is therefore a deep contradiction between what the Christian has by Faith and what he has by sight. It brought a series of problems to the Church, but none more acute than what John Wesley called 'Sin in Believers', of the relation of the grace received in Baptism to the sins of the baptized believer. The Epistle to the Hebrews and the 'Shepherd of Hermas' show how, in the early church, it was easier to mark the problem than to resolve it, but in the end the medieval penitential system was an impressive attempt to grapple with it, theologically by its doctrine of Grace, practically in the discipline of the Sacrament of Penance.

Its theology of Grace was carefully poised, and more of St Augustine is carried over into St Thomas than Protestants have always realized. Yet it is beyond controversy that towards the end of the Middle Ages there existed a good deal of confusion and much real perversion. For one thing there were parts of Christendom where the careful distinctions of the Angelic Doctor were less widely known than the aberrations of schoolmen like Gabriel Biel whose teaching was paramount in the schools where Luther got his training. Nothing could be farther from the truth than the attempt to show that it was from such that Luther drew his new teaching. Those who read the lectures or the Cathedral sermons of Gabriel Biel will find that he is not largely preoccupied, to say the least, with the problems of the 'bruised conscience'.

The notion that Christ had made satisfaction for Original Sin, but that for actual sins committed after Baptism the Christian must offer his own satisfaction, may have been the monstrous aberration of a single theologian (there is evidence that it was more than this). But at least the separation between the remission of sins before and after baptism was sharpened by the extension of the penitential system, and even as expounded by orthodox Catholics, it can be seen how the way lay open to popular perversion. Thus Sir Thomas More:

'Although one drop of Christ's precious blood had been sufficient to satisfy for all the sins of the whole world, and for all the pain also, that were in any wise due to the same, yet hath it not so pleased Him to order it... He leaveth ordinarily some temporal pain to be sustained for the evil act passed, and that to be suffered either here by good works of penance so doing or other satisfactory pains or good works, either in this world here, or after this world in purgatory.'[1]

[1] More, *Works* (ed. 1557), p. 438.

'We shall see that fasting and other bodily afflictions either taken by the commandment of God and his Church, or willingly taken of our own good mind done for our sins, done in true faith and devotion with purpose of amendment, is one of the very special things that obtain remission of the sin, release of the more pain with getting greater grace and the increase of God's favour.'[1]

When this doctrine is set against the doctrines of condign and congruous merit and of the doctrine of purgatory, it can easily be seen how the grossest medieval abuses centred on the matter of Christian penitence. But in effect the problem, which on the vulgar level was framed in the hawking of the indulgences by the Dominican Tetzel, was at another level, the problem of the religious vocation. The reader of Luther's early works will perhaps note with surprise that there is more cruel satire of open scandal in the pages of Erasmus or of the *Epistolae Obscurorum Virorum*. Luther seems to reserve his vehemence, as Grisar observed, for the practices of the 'little saints', the Observants of his own order who were less relaxed than most of their contemporaries. There was a reason. Luther too had sought the Righteousness which comes by human endeavour. He knew the lot of the Christian Pharisee to be the most desperate of all legalisms, since it made prison walls out of the very economy of Grace and turned the gracious promises of God into ireful dooms, whose knell had sounded in his ears, in his cell, in choir and at the altar.

Luther, too, could say:

'Nel mezzo del cammin di nostra vita
Mi ritrovai per una selva oscura
Che la diritta via era smarrita.'

That the Church of God could become a dark wood in the midst of which fear overwhelmed hope, and the very path of evangelical perfection a road in which a man might lose his

[1] Ibid. p. 369.

way, has been difficult for many to understand. Catholics have pointed out with what comfortable words the Canon of the Mass and the Divine Office are replenished, and how skilled were such men as Staupitz, Luther's own director, to relieve too scrupulous souls. Did not Luther misunderstand these things? In one sense he did. In another he saw through them. For he stands, like St Paul, as a question mark against the humanity of the Church. Just as the Apostle set on the summit of human disobedience the religious man, the man within the orbit of redemption, the man who has heard and thinks he possesses the promises of God, and so turned an occasional writing into a tract for all times of Christian history, so Luther marked the same taint as it corrupts the highest aspiration of all, the desire for that holiness without which no man can see the Lord.

Denifle did grievously err when he mistook Luther to mean bodily lust by 'concupiscentia' and interpreted the teaching of the Reformer as the rationalization of a moral impotence, of pride which ended in a bestial depravity. Luther was no beast, nor yet an angel, and his sins were the common sins of Christian men, if not of theological professors. But he knew what others failed to understand, that the Divine Righteousness demanded perfect integrity, and this in the inner man and the secret motive, and he used the word 'concupiscentia' to mark the inward taint. And as he looked about him, he was appalled to see men lulled into an easy self-deception, knowing neither the gravity of sin nor the cost of Grace. He watched them being fobbed off with the cheap grace which touted the divine mercies, or he saw them seeking to escape, by ascetic severities, a judgement in the light of which the most devoted human sacrifice must appear trivial and irresponsible.

Then he, too, found a liberating Righteousness in the word of the Cross. Guilty men stand before the living God, not on the ground of their own merits, not by reason of their character, however supernaturally endowed 'fide formata caritate' but on the sole continuing ground of the Righteousness of God declared in Jesus Christ and precisely 'in his blood'. He saw that relation between God and Man in Christ Jesus, of which the divine side is Grace and the human, Faith, to be the ground of Christian existence from the beginning to the end. This Righteousness spoke to him of freedom from guilt and condemnation and bondage and fear, as it brought him acceptance with God and renewal in the inward man through the gift of the Holy Ghost, with the assurance that forgiving mercy would be about him until his perfecting. And he put the problem of Christian penitence at the only place where it may safely linger, as part of the theology of the Cross, the theology of the Grace, the theology of the glory of God.

The doctrine of Justification by Faith therefore is closely associated with the problem of Christian penitence, for 'tota haec doctrina ad illud certamen perterrefactae conscientiae referenda est. nec sine illo certamine intelligi potest'.[1]

Catholic doctrine also associated Christian penitence with Justification. 'We are all justified in Baptism, when we are younglings, and falling after baptism we must arise by the Sacrament of Penance', wrote Stephen Gardiner. But, as a good Catholic, he understood Justification to mean that 'making righteous', and to include within itself that process of inward regeneration which the new categories of Protestant doctrine were to bring under the office of the Holy Ghost and to describe as 'sanctification'. Sir Thomas More spoke of a first and second justifying, but it was with sound instinct that Tyndale questioned the possibility of such distinction. The Divines at the Council of Trent very properly refused to accept a distinction made during the debate of a threefold justification, though it does underlie the divisions of the decree in chapters 7-9, 10-13 and 14-15.[2]

For that distinction, if pressed, severs the doctrine from its

---

[1] Augsburg Confession, Art. XX.
[2] Denzinger, *Enchiridion*, pp. 269-75.

eschatological root in the New Testament. Justification is a Divine action, and when God justifies men, then He justifies them and we cannot properly speak of His justifying us once, or twice or in a threefold mode. Justification, as God's verdict upon us, must be as Cranmer's *Homily* says 'full and perfect'. In an important sense it must be final. That is why every serious discussion of a theology of Grace must consider also the doctrine of Predestination. The problems still remain of sin in believers, of the possibility of a fall from Grace, of the ultimate tribunal, but at least we ought to beware of trying to mark off the Divine action in terms of temporal divisions.

What has been said should have answered the common misrepresentation of Protestant teaching as being concerned only with a legal verdict of Divine acquittal, and with the imputation of Righteousness which leaves the believer wallowing in his sins. So far is this from being the truth that, in the first period of the Reformation the opposite charge might more plausibly be brought, of a too great emphasis upon the subjective appeasement of the bruised conscience, and the consideration of Faith.

Neither charge can stand. In declaring that Biblical word 'Justify' to have an original forensic sense and to mean 'to declare righteous' and not to 'make righteous', the Reformers had recovered an authentic Biblical meaning and a use which modern critical exegesis has established.[1] But, in fact, it is only after the appearance of Melanchthon's *Commentary on Romans* in 1532 that the forensic definition is allowed to stand alone in the foreground of Protestant interpretation, and even then it is made clear that in Justification, 'remissio' is joined with 'acceptatio'.[2]

---

[1] Cf. Kittel, *Theologisches Wörterbuch*, vol. II, pp. 176–229. Sanday and Headlam, *Romans* (I.C.C.), pp. 28–31. C. H. Dodd, *The Bible and the Greeks*, pp. 42–59. V. Taylor, *Forgiveness and Reconciliation*, pp. 34–82.

[2] 'Justificatio, remissio peccatorum, reconciliatio, regeneratio, renovatio': Melanchthon uses these words almost promiscuously. Loofs, *Leitfaden*, p. 833.

In his *Apology* for the Augsburg Confession Melanchthon had written: 'Justificari significat ex injustis justos effici seu regenerari et justos pronuntiari seu reputari',[1] while Luther himself said at the Disputation of 1535: 'Justificatio est revera regeneratio quaedam in novitatem.'[2] And these are no isolated sentences. Justification is not to be separated from the regeneration of the believer, or from that gift of the Holy Ghost which makes him apt to the new obedience: 'ideo justificamur ut justi bene operari et oboedire legi Dei incipiamus.'[3]

In speaking of the non-imputation of sin and of the imputation of the merits of Christ, the Reformers turned again to a Pauline word used at an important point in the Apostolic argument. For the Reformers the doctrine had several uses.[4]

First, it ensured that the theology of Grace was also a theology of the Cross. Justification is a Divine act, but it may never be regarded as an arbitrary fiat of sovereign Will such as would reduce the work of Christ to irrelevance. In one of Luther's earliest extant letters he writes:

'Therefore, my sweet brother, learn Christ and him crucified, learn to sing to him, and despairing of thyself to say to him: Thou Lord Jesus art my Righteousness and I am thy sin: thou hast taken me and given me thyself: thou hast taken upon thyself what thou wast not, and given me what I am not.'[5]

Second, it balanced the subjective doctrine of Faith with an objective doctrine of the merits of Christ.

[1] Melanchthon, *Apol.* 100, 72.
[2] *Disput. de fide*, 1535. Drews, *Disput.* p. 13.
[3] *Apol.* pp. 146, 227.
[4] V. Taylor, *Forgiveness and Reconciliation*, pp. 52–6. The Reformers did not keep as close to Paul here as in their use of *justificare*. In one way their use of 'imputation' was healthier for it kept the doctrine of Justification close to the preaching of the Cross. In another it was less fortunate, for it brought to the centre a phrase which did not disturb the Pauline setting by its associations.
[5] Luther, *Letters*, W.E. vol. 1, no. 11, 8 April 1516.

'The Scripture doth say that Faith alone justifieth because that it is that alonely whereby I do hang of Christ, and by faith alonely am I partaker of the merits and mercy purchased by Christ's blood.'[1]

Third, it is the nearest the Reformers come to a theological explanation of the paradox of Christian penitence, the fact that guilty sinners, while still imperfect, enjoy the glorious liberty of the children of God, 'semper justus simul peccator'.

'Coeptus est enim justificari et sanari...interim autem dum justificatur et sanatur, non imputatur ei quod reliquum est in carne peccatum propter Christum.'[2]

But neither in the doctrine or Justification nor in the thought of the imputation of the merits of Christ does Luther intend us to forget the personal relationship established through faith:

'The popish divines do dream that faith is a quality cleaving in the heart without Christ. This is a devilish error. But Christ should be so set forth that thou shouldest see nothing beside him, and shouldest think that none can be more to thee or present within thee than he is: for he sitteth not idly in heaven, but is present with us working and living in us.'[3]

This thought of the Christ as man's indwelling Righteousness became distorted in the teaching of Andreas Osiander, who produced the first Protestant heresy about the doctrine of Justification. Yet Osiander sounded an authentic note from early Lutheranism,[4] at a time when it was in danger of being overlaid in the systematization of Lutheran theology carried out by Melanchthon, who emphasized the objectivities of the doctrine of imputation. This does not mean that in this matter

[1] R. Barnes, *Works* (ed. Foxe, 1573), p. 241.
[2] *apud* Loofs, *Leitfaden*, p. 730.
[3] Luther, *Commentary on Galatians*, p. 245 (Eng. tr. E. Middleton, 1807).
[4] 'ego soleo ut hanc rem melius capiam, sic imaginari, quasi nulla sit in corde meo qualitas, quae fides vel caritas vocetur, sed in loco ipsarum pono Jesum Christum et dico "Haec est justitia mea".' C.R. vol. II, 502.

at least Melanchthon is to be regarded as a perverter of the earlier teaching. It is simply that the first period was coming to an end, and that a certain looseness of vocabulary was being clarified. What was more important, a new church situation had emerged. The setting of the medieval church with its penitential system, its abuses of doctrine and practice had been superseded by a new context. Just as the one must never be forgotten in reading the earlier writings of Luther, so the other with its new disciplinary problems, has to be considered in the next period.

It was inevitable that Luther and his friends should read back their own world into that of the Bible. Because of this they naturally missed much, misunderstood more, and perhaps apprehended some truths which the men of the first century never knew. All the same, they did succeed in raising those very problems of Grace and responsibility which had been at the heart of the Pauline inquiry. They made sure that if warfare had to come within Christendom, it should be the right war at the right place. The word 'restatement' has been so grossly abused that it is probably never advisable to use it, but something very like it occurs when a new theological framework is erected, which results in new adjustments of truths in relation to one another, so that even the technical vocabulary has a new content.

Dr Whitney acutely remarked that the mediating theologians on the Catholic side 'should not therefore be held to have reached their view, through a compromise with Lutheranism, but to have based it upon some of the many elements in the mediaeval views'.[1] There is a sense in which the arguments of Eck and Cochlaeus and More have more weight against Contarini and Gropper and Pighius than against the Reformers, since all these Catholics accepted a common philosophic and theological background.

[1] J. P. Whitney, *History of the Reformation* (rev. ed. 1940), p. 172.

The Reformers had a changed background even when they used an already ancient vocabulary. Their fundamental distinction was that which divided Justification from Sanctification. That inward regeneration which Catholic theology includes under 'Justification' belongs now to that Sanctification which is the work of the Holy Ghost. The doctrine of 'Only Faith' depends from that distinction, guarding the gospel of free Grace, while involving no denial of that inward renewal which makes the Christian ready for the new obedience, which is to walk according to the law of love. And because the Christian is still imperfect, since sin includes not only outward transgression but inward motive, the doctrine of 'imputation' reminds him that this relationship with Christ is still maintained until the Christian made perfect in love is made righteous.

We have given no idea of the richness or the fullness of this doctrine of Justification as it is expounded in the writings of Martin Luther with an abundance of prophetic insight that has not been exhausted, or even fully explored. Nor may we stay to indicate the ramifications of the doctrine throughout the whole field of Christian truth, for indeed 'the article of Justification is master and chief, lord, ruler and judge of every kind of doctrine, and one which preserves and directs every doctrine of the Church';[1] and its presentation involves a modification of the doctrine of the Church, of the meaning of Word and Sacraments and Church order, of the vocation of Christian men upon the earth, while by its emphasis on the life of faith it gave back to the Church its true nature as 'ecclesia militans ac peregrinans', and something of the original tension of the New Testament eschatology.

We have set ourselves to explain certain points in the teaching of the Reformers because if they are misconceived we can have no just estimate of the English Reformers. We have

[1] Luther, *Disput. de fide* (1537), vol. I, p. 6. Drews, *Disput.* p. 119.

concentrated attention on Luther and Melanchthon during this period, not only because their teaching was in many ways more profound than that of later Protestant orthodoxy, but also because it was this teaching which made most fruitful contact with the teaching of the English Reformers. Zwingli and Calvin, like the other Continental Reformers, differed hugely from Luther and Melanchthon about many things, differed not inconsiderably about matters derivative from Justification, but about the fundamental teaching enshrined in the watchword 'Sola Fide' there was among them all a striking and substantial unity, a unanimity we may venture to assert to be shared by the English Reformers from William Tyndale to Richard Hooker. As one who had cause to know, and one of the latest and greatest of them, John Jewell defined it:

'As for those persons whom they upon spite call Zwinglians and Lutherans, in very deed they of both sides be Christians and good friends and brethren. They vary not betwixt themselves upon the principles and foundations of our religion, nor as touching God, nor Christ, nor the Holy Ghost, nor the nature of Justification.'[1]

NOTE TO CHAPTER VIII

'SOLA FIDE—PROTESTANT OR CATHOLIC?'

[Some Reflections upon *The Doctrine of Justification in the Anglican Reformers*, by the Rev. A. H. Rees, M.A. (*Theology*, Occasional Papers, No. 2).][2]

'A historian that favours his own side is to be forgiven though he puts a little too much life in his colours when he sets out the best sides of his party and the worst of those from whom he differs, and if he but slightly touches the failings of his friends and exaggerates those of the other side, though in this he departs from the laws of an exact historian, yet it does not blacken him: but if he gives his imagination full scope

[1] Jewell, *Works*, P.S. vol. i, pp. 69–70. [2] S.P.C.K. 1939.

...he ought not to think it strange that others take pains to expose him to the world.' (G. Burnet, *Answer to Mr Varillas*.)

Gilbert Burnet thus aptly defines the proprieties of historical controversy and of polemical divinity. Both have often scandalized the world, and the prospect of the followers of the Prince of Peace squabbling about the merits of His death has in all centuries seemed unsavoury and unedifying. Yet if we confess that all men are liars, ourselves included, that we are sinful men and never more so than in the search for truth, that in our every judgement upon the Reformation loyalty and faith are both engaged, there is room for honest controversy.

The pamphlet of Mr A. H. Rees, *The Doctrine of Justification in the Anglican Reformers*, bears the imprimatur of an 'Occasional Paper' in connection with the periodical *Theology* and as such claims serious attention. The trend of the work is to suggest that the Anglican formularies and the teaching of the Divines who framed them are to be understood in terms of Catholic, rather than of Protestant definition.

Mr Rees and the still higher Anglican school to which he belongs roam the sixteenth century in search for ancestors to add to an uneasy pedigree. Since their distinctive origin was with the Oxford Movement, they have no difficulty with the nineteenth century, and in the eighteenth they can find forerunners of their views, especially among the High Churchmen of the Convocation Controversy. By means of a one-sided catena of quotation they can claim for their Fathers the Caroline Divines.[1] But in the sixteenth century they face a quandary. Their spiritual ancestors are the men like Stephen Gardiner and Cuthbert Tunstal, but these were men who held the Henrician view of Church and State, and opposition to Erastianism of all kinds is the hall mark of the still higher Anglican. The alternative is to nail the colours of the Reformers to their mast and claim them as the fathers of modern Catholic doctrine. We will not ask whether the Henricians were not more logical than they, whether in the end any non-Roman system of Catholicism can evade a high doctrine of the authority of

[1] The Agreed Syllabus in Religious Education is abhorrent to this school. Yet the case for it rests not on Latitudinarian presuppositions but on the distinction made by the Caroline Divines between the fundamental and secondary portions of the Christian Revelation?

the State without becoming pietistic and sectarian. We have the right to dissent from the particular thesis of Mr Rees. The answer to him must lie in a just appreciation of the true doctrine taught by the Continental Reformers (Catholic doctrine is not in question) and then by the English Reformers themselves.

We have already asserted that between the Continental and the English Reformers there was striking and substantial agreement about the teaching of Justification by Faith. We now add as corollary that, whatever marks of compromise may lie upon the Anglican formularies, their teaching about Justification is unintelligible apart from the Protestant doctrine and confessions, while they can only be made to reach the definitions of the Council of Trent by being arbitrarily stretched and twisted from their proper setting.

The positive answer to Mr Rees must accordingly lie in the documents themselves, and we have tried to give sufficient citation and interpretation to enable the reader to see where the final demonstration must lie. The negative duty remains of dealing with certain points in the pamphlet itself. There are parts of it with which we have no need to quarrel, since in the very definitions of Trent there is a good deal that is common to both Protestant and Catholic. It is with the remainder of his argument that we shall try to reckon.

In the first place, it will be noted that although he gives abundant reference to the debates and definitions of the Council of Trent, he has no first-hand quotation from any Continental Reformer or from any Protestant confession. Or rather, he has no intentional quotation, for we shall find him engaged at several points in refuting the teaching of the Lutherans by quotation (albeit in ignorance) from their own writings. In the main, however, he is content to caricature Protestant teaching in a series of half truths the cumulative effect of which is wholly misleading.

Thus for Luther 'the actus justificationis is the external pronouncement by God of the sinner's justification' (p. 4); 'for him and for Calvin it does not free the sinner from sin, but only from its penalties' (p. 4); 'the word "impute" so characteristic of Protestant doctrine' (p. 6); 'the Lutheran conception of fiduciary faith' (p. 14); 'the Lutheran conception of faith as a sentiment of confidence without rational preamble or practical fruit' (p. 19); 'the Lutheran teaching that Justification is equal in every one' (pp. 24, 27).

By making the teaching of the Continental Reformers to be a legal doctrine of acquittal and imputation, by turning faith into a human sentiment, and by excluding every thought of inward regeneration from either, it is comparatively easy to show that the Anglican Reformers never held such an impoverished and starveling doctrine. They never did. Nor did Luther or Melanchthon or Calvin.

In the pamphlet itself the following points deserve comment:

Page 5. The definition of Justification in Cranmer's *Homily of Salvation* (referred to in Art XI of the XXXIX Articles) is quoted as: 'The forgiveness of man's sins and trespasses in such things as he hath offended...and this justification or righteousness which we so receive by God's mercy and Christ's merits embraced by faith, is taken, accepted and allowed of God for our perfect and full Justification.'

On this the author comments, 'the language here is ambiguous and the definition is insufficient compared with the previous pronouncements of the Church of England'.

(i) There are few tracts in English theology of like clarity with Cranmer's Homily, and it is surprising to have to supplement it by citation from the Bishops' and the King's Books, whose chequered and ambiguous background we have already sketched. The supplement indicated is the definition of the Ten Articles which was carried over into the Bishops' Book, viz.: 'the remission of our sins, and our acceptation or reconciliation into the grace and favour of God, that is to say, our perfect renovation in Christ'.[1]

(ii) But there is a demonstrable debt of this definition to the Wittenberg Articles of 1536 which were signed by Luther and Melanchthon, viz. 'Justificatio est renovatio et regeneratio'.[2]

(iii) Does not 'perfect renovation in Christ' imply a Catholic addition to this? That on the contrary it suggests the teaching of the Reformers is proved by Henry VIII's marginal correc-

---

[1] Lloyd, *Formularies*, p. xxvi.
[2] Mentz, *Die Wittenberger Artickel* (1905), Art. IV.

tion at this point, for he alters 'perfect renovation in Christ' to 'by Christ'.[1]

(iv) As it happens, we know what Cranmer thought about it too, for in his annotations on the King's comments he has a long excursus at this point, the Protestant character of which is obvious.[2]

(v) The statement in Cranmer's Homily is only ambiguous to those who wish to read into it something other than the teaching of the Reformers.

Pages 5–6. 'The Ten Articles of 1536 and the Institution of a Christian Man (the Bishops' Book) of 1537 both put out by royal authority...in 1543 after the visit of the Lutheran divines to England and as a direct corrective to the doctrinal confusion which had followed the royal injunction of 1538 setting up the Bible in England in parish churches, a further statement of doctrine was published, this time with the authority of both Convocations and entitled the *Necessary Doctrine and Erudition for any Christian Man*. This work commonly known as the King's Book....'

(i) The curious statement will at once be noted:

The Bishops' Book was put out by Royal authority— hence it was known as the Bishops' Book?

The King's Book was put out with clerical authority— hence it was known as the King's Book?

The facts are that the Ten Articles had the authority of Parliament and of Convocation, and that Henry VIII deliberately withheld from the Bishops' Book the authority he had given to the Ten Articles and was to give the King's Book. Mr Rees and his friends ought not to judge the sixteenth century with categories which echo the Convocation controversy without indicating at least why the Bishops' and King's Books got their popular titles.

(ii) 'In 1543 after the visit of the Lutheran divines.' I cannot account for this reference unless it be intended to add an air of artistic verisimilitude....No mention has been made of the important Anglo-German theological discussions of 1535–6, and 1538–9: in 1543 there had been no such debate for nearly

---

[1] Cranmer, *Remains*, P.S. vol. II, p. 112.   [2] Ibid. p. 113.

three years. Moreover, as the preamble to the Ten Articles makes plain, governmental concern at the confusion of doctrine was evident in 1536 and long before the injunctions of 1538.

Page 6. The statement on Justification in Cranmer's Homily is declared to be 'not inconsistent' with the King's Book.

(i) Mr Rees' quotation is ambiguous enough. But the doctrine of this section of the King's Book is quite at variance with that of the *Homily of Salvation*.

(ii) Let those who doubt it read the agitated letters with which Stephen Gardiner bombarded the government in 1547, and the account therein of his interview with Cranmer about the new Homily, and of Gardiner's almost desperate attempt to pin the government down to the teaching of the King's Book on Justification, and to refuse the doctrine of the Homily. 'As for my Lord of Canterbury's *Homily of Salvation*, it hath as many faults as I have been weeks in prison, which be seven, besides the general that the matter maketh trouble without necessity and is handled contrary to the teaching of Parliament.'[1]

Gardiner was kept in the Fleet, in part by reason of his antagonism to the teaching of the Homily. His comment on the suggestion that its teaching was 'not inconsistent' with that of the King's Book would have been devastating.

Page 7. A phrase in the Homily indicates 'that Justification may be effected through Baptism which is also the teaching of a "Sermon on Baptism" which Cranmer set forth in the first edition of his Catechism in 1548'.

(i) It was not a happy moment when Mr Rees strayed from the safe fold of the General Index to the works of the Parker Society for his references, for this Catechism (as any up-to-date work on the period would have told him) in which he finds 'Justification by Baptism' is none other than the Lutheran catechism of Nuremberg the work of Justus Jonas, the friend and disciple of Luther, and whose son was staying with Cranmer in 1548. Anybody who can find 'Justification by Baptism' in a Lutheran catechism can find it anywhere.

[1] Foxe, *A. & M.* vol. VI, p. 35. See also pp. 41, 42, 43, 47, 49, 51, 53.

(ii) But there is worse to come. On p. 8 he tells us that Tyndale has a passage in which he 'expressly denies Justification by Baptism'. And this passage proves, on examination, to be directly translated from a sermon by Martin Luther (as any up-to-date biography of Tyndale would have told him).

(iii) Thus on succeeding pages the doctrine of Justification by Baptism is found in an official catechism of the early Lutheran Church, and then its complete repudiation in a sermon of Martin Luther. Mr Rees can hardly wonder if our faith is shaken in his capacity to interpret the teaching of the Reformers, or even to recognize it when he meets it.

(iv) And, in fine, the three words in Cranmer's Homily are perfectly compatible with the teaching of the Reformers of the relation of Baptism to Justification.

Page 7. 'The Lutheran doctrine of Justification is expounded in the early Reformation period by Tyndale and Hooper. For both, Justification is simply the forgiveness of sins.'

Yet of the two immediate quotations, one adds to 'forgiveness of sins'—'and the favour of God', and the other—'sealeth thee with his Holy Spirit and maketh thee heir of everlasting life', theological conjunctions of some importance.

Page 8. The next statement is of importance for the author's main thesis. He asserts that John Bradford taught 'a different doctrine'. Two pieces of evidence are produced:

(*a*) The statement that Justification 'precedeth regeneration from whom we may discern it, but not divide it, no more than heat from the fire'.

(i) This is no departure from the teaching of the Reformers. We have already cited Luther's reiterated: 'Justificatio est revera regeneratio.'

(ii) And here, in Calvin is an even closer approximation: 'Righteousness and Sanctification are inseparable...the sun with his heat giveth life and fruitfulness to the earth, with his beams he giveth light and brightness. Here is a mutuall and unseparable conjoyning: yet reason forbiddeth to convey to the one that which is peculiar to the other.'[1]

---

[1] Calvin, *Inst.* Bk. 3, c. 11, p. 351 (Eng. tr. Thomas Norton, 1611).

(b) His second quotation is even less apposite. It is from that document which Bradford and his fellow prisoners drew up, which speaks of an 'inherent righteousness, which is to be discerned in the article of Justification from the righteousness which God endueth us withal in justifying us although inseparably they go together'.

(i) But who are these men putting their hands to a 'different doctrine' from Luther or Tyndale? Well, they included Miles Coverdale who spent years with the Continental Reformers, who translated many of their writings, including Luther's hymns: John Philpot who translated the Homilies of Calvin and who was to ask at his trial: 'Which of you are able to answer Calvin's Institutes?' John Rogers, the friend and literary heir of Tyndale who studied at Wittenberg, was pastor of a German church, and translated some of the writings of Melanchthon: and finally Bradford himself, the friend of Martin Bucer, the translator of Melanchthon's Prayers and of his *Loci Communes*, of which there are traces in this very document. It is not perhaps very likely that such men should choose this occasion to teach a different doctrine. In fact the full quotation of the paragraph reveals the opposite intention.

(ii) 'The Righteousness which God endueth us withal in justifying us, although inseparably they go together. And this we do not for curiosity, or for contention sake, but for conscience sake that it might be quiet; which it never can be, if we confound without distinction forgiveness of sins and Christ's Justice imputed to us, with regeneration and inherent righteousness.' [1]

(iii) It is wholly wrong to suppose that the Reformers left no room for the thought of an inherent righteousness, though the phrase was so liable to be misunderstood that they used it sparingly. But it underlies Tyndale's explanation of the differences between St James and St Paul. It recurs in the systematized exposition of Peter Martyr, in the safe framework of the rest of Protestant doctrine:

[1] Bradford, *Works*, P.S. vol. i, p. 372. See also the beginning of this paragraph: 'Fourthly, we believe and confess concerning Justification, that, as it cometh only of God's mercy through Christ so it is perceived and had of none which be of years of discretion otherwise than by faith only....'

'The dispute is not about some righteousness inherent in us, which indeed is spread throughout the whole man, but of that justification which is the condonation of sins and that in truth hath no place or seat in our souls, but alone in God.'[1]

'We say that our Justification cannot be in that righteousness and renewal in which we are refashioned by God' ('in ea justitia et instauratione qua reformamur a Deo').[2]

Page 9. On even less evidence, still more important consequences are drawn from Thomas Becon. There are two quotations from his *Demands of Scripture*. Of the first, as Mr Rees admits, and indeed could not well deny, there is a statement of the doctrine of 'non-imputation'. But of the second he comments: 'In the second part of the work, however, he writes: "What is Justification? Of Unrighteous to be made righteous by the righteousness of Christ which we conceive by faith."'[3] And from this Mr Rees draws the amazing conclusion:

'Though this last phrase [to be made righteous] is ambiguous, the phrase "to be made Righteous" indicates an approximation to the Catholic doctrine of Justification towards which a reaction had set in by this time. The Anglican church was seeing her way through the mists of controversy to a statement of her own doctrinal position.'

We reply:

(i) There is no evidence at all that Becon changed his doctrine of Justification, and a comparison of his works shows him to have held all the categories of the other Reformers in respect of it. Here is one passage in his *Dialogue between a Knight and Satan*:

'Austin writing upon John agreeth with us when he saith "All that are justified by Christ are righteous, not in themself but in him"...thou seest that our justification in this life can be no personal perfection and full accomplishment of the commandments of God, but a free merciful forgiving of our disobedience, and an imputation or reckoning of Righteousness for Christ's sake.'[4]

[1] Peter Martyr, *Loc. Comm.* p. 398.   [2] Ibid. p. 380.
[3] More correctly a second version of the first work.
[4] Becon, *Works*, P.S. p. 638.

(ii) 'Catholic doctrine towards which a reaction had set in by this time' is an unsupported assertion which begs the very question under discussion.

(iii) But let us for a moment grant that the quotation proves what the author asserts, and let us mark this point, at which the Anglican Church in 1563 had emerged from the mists of controversy. It emerged apparently at this point, which parallels exactly the operative words of his quotation,

'Justificari significat ex injustis justos effici seu regenerari.'

That is, to the *Apology* for the Augsburg Confession and to the theology of Philip Melanchthon? But no, the 'Anglican church was seeing her way through the mists of controversy' —or was it just Mr Rees taking a short cut?

(iv) We have had to deal at length with the Bradford and the Becon quotations because on the strength of these mis-interpretations the summing up at the end of the pamphlet, p. 26, can say: 'a fuller notion of the process of Justification is found in Bradford's teaching of an inherent righteousness', and that 'By the date of promulgation of the 39 articles this view had been supplemented with the doctrine of imparted Right-eousness'!!!

Page 14. Of the definition of Faith in the Second Homily of the Passion: 'this definition approaches the Lutheran concep-tion of fiduciary faith: but elsewhere in the Homilies Faith is spoken of as "the root and wellspring of life", a phrase reminiscent of the Tridentine decree which speaks of Faith as the "beginning of man's salvation, the foundation and root of all Justification"'. The acute mind will indeed observe without difficulty that the word "root" is common to both. But the resemblance has a simple explanation: both quotations derive from well-known descriptions of Faith in St Augustine and St Ambrose, quotations in common use by Reformers as well as Catholics.

Page 18. The distinction between the first and second Justification: 'the distinction found no place in the decrees of the Council, but seems to have been in the minds of the Fathers'.

(i)   A misleading statement because the twofold justifying which was a feature of the theology of Gropper and Pighius has nothing to do with this, which was part of a threefold elaboration made at Trent, but wisely omitted from the decrees.[1]   He adds that 'much confusion in the controversies of the time would have been avoided had the word justification been confined in meaning to the first justification and the word sanctification to the second' as though this were not the very distinction refused by Catholic theology.   He adds that 'Luther spoke of faith as justifying in the second sense of the word, i.e. as effecting man's final justification, for which according to his teaching, works were of no avail'.   But how could anybody use the word in the second sense without including also the first?   And how does Mr Rees account for Article XII of the Augsburg Confession?

'Damnant Anabaptistas qui negant semel justificatos posse amittere Spiritum Sanctum.'[2]

(ii)   Or explain such sentences of Luther as:

'Deus est adhuc in actu justificationis, non completo: tunc autem complebitur cum resurreximus a mortuis.'[3]

'Cotidie justificamur immerita remissione peccatorum.'[4]

'Justificatio nondum est completa, est in agendo et fieri.'[5]

'Justificatio est revera regeneratio quaedam in novitatem': 'nam fides incipit ad justitiam, sed deus reputat ad perfectionem; est igitur duplex regeneratio, imperfecta per reputationem, perfecta per suam naturam seu in ipso esse.'[5]

(iii)   To prove this against Luther yet another quotation is given from the Lutheran catechism of Nuremberg, set forth by Cranmer in 1548.

---

[1] For a valuable survey of Catholic doctrine, see *Dict. Théol. Cath.* vol. VIII, pp. 2042–227, art. 'Justification' (J. Rivière).   Also Jos. Hefner, *Die Enstehungsgeschichte des Trienter Rechtfertigungsdekretes.* Denzinger, *Enchiridion,* pp. 266–81.

[2] Schaff, *Creeds,* vol. III, p. 14.

[3] Luther, *Disput.* 1537. Drews, p. 154, *apud* Loofs.

[4] Ibid. p. 49.

[5] K. Holl, *Ges. Aufsätze.* Luther, pp. 128 ff., 156 ff.

Page 19. Mr Rees defines the Lutheran conception of Faith:
'A sentiment of confidence without rational preamble or practical fruit.'

(i) None of the Continental or the English Reformers ever
thought of Justifying Faith as a mere human sentiment, and
they would have thought the suggestion blasphemous. From
first to last they speak of the 'donatio fidei' through the Holy
Ghost.

(ii) As for rational preamble, saving faith for the Reformers
involved knowledge of the articles of faith:

'Nam hi non credunt omnes articulos fidei non enim credunt
remissionem peccatorum.'[1]

'Nec vero excludimus notitiam historiae de Christo ut
quidam calumniantur: cur enim dicimus fiduciam misericordiae
promissae propter Christum, certe omnes articulos fidei com-
plectimur.'[2]

(iii) As for 'practical fruit':

'Faith is a lively thing, valiant and strong, ever doing, ever
fruitful so that it is unpossible that he which is endued therewith should not always work good works without ceasing.'[3]

At least John Wesley did not misapprehend the practical
nature of it when this description of saving faith was the
occasion of his evangelical conversion in May 1738.

Page 20. The passage in the *Homily of Faith* describing faith
is said to describe 'substantially the same process which is
described by Trent in Chapter vi'. This is true in the sense that
all descriptions of the regeneration of the human soul through
the divine action are bound to coincide in some particulars.
Of the deep contradiction between these Homilies and Catholic
definition the letters of Stephen Gardiner are better proof than
Mr Rees's dubious points of contact.

Page 21. 'In contrast to the excessive reaction from Pela-
gianism which marked much of the Reformation, Anglican
formularies and Divines emphasise the importance of works.'

[1] Mentz, *Die Wittenberger Artickel* (1905), Art. IV.
[2] Melanchthon, *Loc. Comm.* C.R. vol. xxi, p. 422.
[3] Tyndale (Luther), *Prologue to the Romans* (N.T.). Cambridge, 1938,
R.S.L.

So they did, to be sure, and we have almost begun to expect how Mr Rees will prove it, as he does by quotations from Tyndale, all of which are direct translations from Martin Luther. All the Reformers from Luther onwards admitted the need of good works, and the statement to the contrary is the silliest superstition of the modern Catholic caricature of Protestantism. As the Augsburg Confession said: 'Docent nostri quod necesse sit bona opera facere' (Art. XX).[1]

Page 24. 'Anglican Reformers are agreed in opposing the Lutheran teaching that Justification is equal in everyone.'

(i) We have already commented[2] on this and given quotations from Luther to the contrary. Mr Rees will find many others in the pages of Karl Holl, including such phrases as 'justificatio magis et magis', 'justificat in verbo suo dum nos tales facit'.

(ii) But in any case Mr Rees once more proves his assertion by two apt quotations:

(*a*) From Luther's preface to the Romans which Tyndale included in his New Testament.

(*b*) By yet another quotation from the Lutheran Catechism (Cranmer, 1548).

Page 25. He finds in Art. XVI of the XXXIX Articles that Justifying Grace may be lost. And it is to be found there, as it was in Art. XII of the Augsburg Confession.

Page 26. Hooper is referred to as 'an extremist' and as not 'representative'.

(i) However radical his views might be with regard to the use of vestments or the Eucharist, there is not a shred of evidence to show that his doctrine of Justification was regarded by any of his contemporaries as 'extreme' or in conflict with those of Tyndale, Cranmer or Bradford.

(ii) The fact that Hooper deals at more length with the subject of 'imputation' is because it occurs in his work, the *Description of the Office of Christ*, where of necessity it comes into prominence.

---

[1] Schaff, *Creeds*, vol. III, p. 24.   [2] Above, p. 181.

Page 28. In some ways the climax of the argument:

'The specific doctrines of Luther...were excluded from the articles dealing with Justification, works before Justification, and Sin after Baptism.'

But this is too modest. For Mr Rees has shown that the 'doctrines of Luther' were not only excluded from the XXXIX Articles: they were excluded from the teaching of Martin Luther as he has completely demonstrated by an admirable catena of quotations from Luther's sermons and from the Catechism of one of Luther's most ardent disciples.

(i) But if we seriously consider the genuine teaching of Luther,

Why, if there was this change from an early Lutheran taint to Catholic doctrine on the part of the Church of England, was not all reference to the *Homily of Salvation* dropped from Article XI?

(ii) Even more cogent, why did it not abandon that phrase which was the bugbear of the Catholics (anathematized in Canon 9 of the Council of Trent), and was the famous watchword of all the Reformers, why did the Anglican Church not abandon the watchword 'Sola Fide'?

Page 29. 'Justification the Church of England did not define beyond what had been said in the King's Book.' Does this mean that the teaching of the King's Book is to be preferred where it clashes with that of Article XI and the *Homily of Salvation*? It is a very great pity that Article XI did not refer to the King's Book for fuller explanation instead of to the *Homily of Salvation*, if this were so. It is a greater pity that this pamphlet was not available four hundred years ago, to let Gardiner out of the Fleet, to reconcile him and Cranmer by making Cranmer a Catholic and Gardiner a Reformer and finally, by most apt quotation from Luther to show that the teaching of the great heresiarch was 'not incompatible with the Council of Trent'. It is to be feared that the truth is otherwise and that whatever else Mr Rees and his friends may understand, it is not the teaching of the Reformers, Continental or English.

Says the King's Book:

'And truly this way and form of doctrine is to be observed,

which is the very trade of scripture, wherein men be taught first to leave their sins and to return by works of penance unto God and then shall they receive remission of their sins and Justification.'[1]

A Roman Catholic historian hails this as a good specimen of Catholic orthodoxy. He is very welcome.

But on the other hand, says Article XI of the XXXIX Articles: 'Quare sola fide nos justificari doctrina est saluberrima ac consolationis plenissima, ut in Homilia de Justificatione fusius explicatur.' That is another world, of which the English Church has really no need to be ashamed.

THE ENGLISH REFORMERS

To demonstrate a doctrine by citing from an extensive literature is a hazardous enterprise, and conditions in the sixteenth century when the vocabulary of both Catholic and Protestant was shifting and confused, make the task more difficult. It would be possible by judicious selection to show that Cranmer and Gardiner, in their great Eucharistic debate, held one another's views!

All we can fairly do is to indicate where the demonstration must lie, and repeat that there was striking and substantial agreement among the Continental and English Reformers about the doctrine summarized in the watchword 'Sola Fide'. That doctrine is best studied, not in snippets from this or that work, but in such tracts as Tyndale (Luther)'s *Wicked Mammon* and *Prologue to the Epistle to the Romans* or in Robert Barnes' *Justification* in the period 1526–35, and in Cranmer's Homilies *Of the Salvation of all Mankind*, *Of True Lively and Christian Faith* and *Of Good Works*.

If the report of Cranmer's speech to the divines in 1537 be anything like accurate, it reveals him as keeping close to the Biblical setting of the doctrine.

[1] Lloyd, *Formularies*, p. 372.

'There be weighty controversies now moved and put forth, not of ceremonies and light things, but of the true understanding, and of the right difference of the Law and of the Gospel: of the manner and way how sins be forgiven: of comforting doubtful and wavering consciences, by what means they may be certified that they please God, seeing they feel the strength of the Law accusing them of sin: of the true use of the Sacraments, whether the outward work of them doth justify man, or whether we receive our Justification by faith.'[1]

It seems preferable for us to approach the doctrine of the English Reformers along these categories than in the formal divisions of the later systematized theology. Accordingly we begin with the offices of Law and Gospel and the problem of what Bunyan later called the 'bruised conscience'.[2]

Law and Gospel

'Note the difference of the Law and of the Gospel. The one asketh and requireth, the other pardoneth and forgiveth. The one threateneth, the other promiseth all good things to them that set their trust in Christ only...all is not gospel that is written in the gospel-book: for if the law were away, thou couldest not know what the gospel meant: even as thou couldest not see pardon and grace, except the law rebuked thee, and declared unto thee thy sin, misdeed and trespass.'[3]
'The law and the Gospel may never be separate: for the gospel and promises serve but for troubled consciences, which are brought to desperation, and feel the pains of hell and death under the law and are i.. captivity and bondage under the law. In all my deeds I must have the law before me, to condemn mine unperfectness. For all that I do (be I never so perfect) is yet damnable sin when it is compared to the law, which requireth the ground and bottom of mine heart.'[4]

---

[1] Foxe, *A. & M.* vol. v, p. 380.
[2] 'Tota haec doctrina ad illud certamen perterrefactae conscientiae referenda est, nec sine illo certamine intelligi potest.' Augs. Conf. Art. XX. Schaff, *Creeds*, vol. III, p. 23.
[3] Tyndale, *Preface to the New Testament* (1526), P.S. p. 389.
[4] Tyndale (Luther), *Pathway into Holy Scripture* (1526), P.S. p. 11.

'The Commandments of God lay our faults before our eyes, which putteth us in fear and dread, and maketh us to see the wrath of God against our sins...and maketh us sorry and repentant that ever we should come into the displeasure of God and the captivity of the devil. The gracious and benign promises of God by the mediation of Christ sheweth us (and that to our great relief and comfort) whensoever we be re-pentant and return fully to God in our hearts, that we have forgiveness of our sins, be reconciled to God, and accepted and reputed just and righteous in his sight, only by his grace and mercy which he doth grant and give unto us for his dearly beloved son's sake, Jesus Christ.'[1]

'The conscience, burdened and charged with sin, first seeketh remission thereof. For this thing the conscience laboureth and contendeth in all fears and terrors of sorrow and contrition... but forsaking her own justice, offereth Christ, dead upon the Cross, and sitting at Gods right hand. Nothing maketh it the cause wherefore this mercy should be given, saving only the death of Christ.'[2]

'For there is no man, but he knowethe that the lawe worketh anger, and causeth hatred. Butt lo, Christ maketh intercession for us,...and now wheare this tender mercy and incomparable goodnes of God is knowne, greace and hoape and stedfast trust in God dayly moare and moare floweth into mannes conscience.'[3]

Justification 'the office of God'

'Justification is not the office of man, but of God: for man cannot justify himself by his own works...but Justifica-tion is the office of God only.'[4]

This divine work is threefold:

'Upon Gods part, his great mercy and grace: upon Christs part, justice, that is the satisfaction of Gods justice or price of

---

[1] Cranmer, *Annotations on the 'Institution of a Christian Man'*, P.S. vol. II, p. 113.

[2] Hooper, *Early Works*, P.S. p. 50.

[3] W. Roye, *Dialogue between Father and Son* (ed. Wolf, 1874), pp. 41–2.

[4] Cranmer, *Homily of Salvation*, P.S. vol. II, p. 131.

our redemption, by the offering of his body and shedding of
his blood with fulfilling of the law perfectly and thoroughly:
and upon our part, true and lively faith in the merits of Jesu
Christ, which yet is not ours, but God's working in us.'[1]

The Merits of Christ

'The Scripture doth say that faith alone justifieth because
that it is that alonely whereby I do hang of Christ. And by
my faith alonely am I partaker of the merits and mercy purchased by Christ's Blood, and Faith it is alonely that receives
the promises made in Christ. Wherefore do we say with blessed
Paul that faith only justifieth imputative: that is, all the merits
and goodness, grace and favour and all that is in Christ to our
salvation is imputed and reckoned unto us because we hang
and believe on him.'[2]

'But our Justification doth come freely by the mercy of God
and of so great and free mercy that whereas all the world was
not able of themselves to pay any part towards their ransom,
it pleased our heavenly father, of his infinite mercy, without
any our desert or deserving, to prepare for us the most precious
jewels of Christ's body and blood whereby our ransom might
be fully paid, the law fulfilled, and his justice fully satisfied.
So that Christ is now the Righteousness of all them that truly
do believe in him. He for them paid their ransom by his death:
he for them fulfilled the law in his life: so that now in him,
and by him, every true Christian man may be called a fulfiller
of the law; forasmuch as that which their infirmity lacketh,
Christ's justice hath supplied.'[3]

'So that faith doth not only show us Christ that died, and
now sitteth at the right hand of God: but also applieth the
merits of this death, unto us and maketh Christ ours: faith
laying nothing to gage unto the justice of God but the death
of Christ and thereupon claimeth mercy and Gods promise,
the remission of sin and desireth God to justify and deliver
the soul from the accusation of the Law and right of the devil
which he is bound to do for his promise sake.'[4]

[1] Cranmer, *Homily of Salvation*, P.S. vol. II, p. 129.
[2] Robert Barnes, *Justification* (*Works*, 1573), p. 241.
[3] Cranmer, *Homily of Salvation*, P.S. vol. II p. 130.
[4] Hooper, *Declaration of Christ and his office* (*Early Works*, P.S.), p. 50.

'By justifying understand...'

The numerous definitions of Justification in the works of the English Reformers are often casually employed and not intended as exhaustive:

'We do give to faith and to Christ's blood that glory that belongeth to them only that is to say, "Justification, remission of sins, satisfying of God's wrath, taking away of everlasting vengeance, fulfilling of the law with all like things".'[1]

'God's truth justifieth thee: that is forgiveth thee thy sins, and sealeth thee with his holy spirit, and maketh thee heir of everlasting life through Christ's deservings.'[2]

'That wherewith a man fulfilleth the law declared him justified.... By justifying him understand the forgiveness of sins and the favour of God.'[3]

'Saint Paul when he saith that we be justified by faith...he meaneth that we have remission of sin, reconciliation, and acceptation into the favour of God.'[4]

'Justification, that is to say... remission, pardon and forgiveness of... sins and trespasses.'[5]

'To be justified is not to have our sins imputed to us, but to have them forgiven in Christ and for Christ.'[6]

Peter Martyr accepts this common conception but has an interesting addition:

'For justification and eternal life are so joined to one another that one is often taken for the other. And in truth justification is nothing else than eternal life dwelling in us.'[7]

'True Lively and Christian Faith'

'The faith in Christ's blood, of a repenting heart toward the law doth justify us only: and not all manner faiths.... There is a story faith, without feeling in the heart, wherewith I may

---

[1] Robert Barnes (*Works*, 1573), p. 239.
[2] Tyndale, *Works*, P.S. p. 262, also p. 192. [3] Ibid. p. 192.
[4] Hooper, *Early Works*, P.S. p. 49.
[5] Cranmer, *Remains*, vol. II, p. 128.
[6] Becon, *Works*, P.S. vol. III, p. 603.
[7] Peter Martyr, *Loc. Comm.* p. 383.

believe the whole story of the Bible and yet not set mine heart earnestly thereto.'[1]

The Homily of *True, Lively and Christian Faith* also discriminates: 'Believing of the word of God that it is true...as he that readeth Caesar's commentaries...believeth the history of Caesar', but

'Another faith there is in scripture...which as the other vain faith is called a dead faith, so may this be called a quick or lively faith...a sure trust and confidence of the mercy of God through our Lord Jesus Christ and a steadfast hope of all good things to be received at Gods hand.'[2]

'And mark this manner of speech: fide justificamur: hoc est fiducia misericordiae sumus justi: this word faith doth comprehend as well as persuasion and confidence that the promise of God appertaineth unto him for Christs sake, as the knowledge of God.'[3]

'The faith of the true believers is that God justifieth or forgiveth and Christ deserveth it: and the faith or trust in Christ's blood receiveth it and certifieth the conscience thereof, and saveth and delivereth her from fear of death and damnation.'[4]

This faith does not exclude belief in the articles of Faith:

'For those who do not believe all the articles of God cannot believe in remission of sins.'[5]

'For the right and true Christian faith is not only to believe that Holy Scripture, and all the foresaid articles of our faith are true.'[6]

'What thing is faith? It is a full and perfit confidence and trust in God through Christ engendered in our heart by hearing the word of God.'[7]

'What is faith? An assured confidence and trust in the truth of God, in the merits and promises of Christ, conceived through Christ by hearing of his word.'[8]

[1] Tyndale, *Answer to More*, p. 196. Greenslade, *Tyndale*, p. 179.
[2] Cranmer, *Remains*, vol. II, p. 135.
[3] Hooper, *Early Works*, P.S. pp. 50–1.
[4] Tyndale, *Expositions*, p. 11.
[5] Wittenberg Articles, 1536 (ed. Mentz).
[6] Cranmer, *Homily of Salvation*, P.S. vol. II, p. 133.
[7] Becon, *Works*, P.S. vol. III, p. 602.   [8] Ibid. p. 615.

Faith and Baptism

'The work of Baptism, that outward washing...justifieth us not. But God only justifieth us actively, as cause efficient or workman. God promiseth to justify whosoever is baptized to believe in Christ and to keep the law of God: that is to say, to forgive them their fore sins and to impute righteousness unto them, to take them for his sons and to love them as well as though they were full righteous...and faith doth receive it, and God doth give it and impute it to faith and not to the washing. And the washing doth testify and certify us of it.'[1]

'Justificatio est Renovatio'

'But the faith that shall justify us must be of another manner of strength for it must come from heaven and not from the strength of reason. It must also make me believe that God, the maker of heaven and earth is not alonely a Father, but also my Father, yea and that through the favour that Christ hath purchased me from the which favour neither heaven nor earth, tribulation nor persecution, death or hell can divide me. But to this stick I fast that he is not alonely my Father, but also a merciful father, yea and that unto me merciful and so merciful that he will not impute my sins unto me, though they be never so great so long as I hang on the blessed blood of Christ Jesus and sin not of malice but of frailty and of no pleasure. He is also a liberal father, yea and that unto me liberal which will not alone promise me all things, but also give them to me whether they be necessary to the body or to the soul. He is not alonely liberal but mighty to perform all things that he promiseth to me. Briefly this faith maketh me to hang clearly of God and of his blessed promises made in Christ and with his sweat and precious blood...finally of a fleshly beast it maketh me a spiritual man: of a damnable child it maketh me a heavenly son: of a servant of the devil it maketh me a free man of God.'[2]

[1] Tyndale, *Expositions*, p. 90.
[2] Robert Barnes (*Works*, 1573), p. 235.

Good Works the Fruit of the Spirit

'Right faith is a thing wrought by the Holy Ghost in us, which changeth us, turneth us into a new nature, and begetteth us anew in God...and maketh us altogether new in the heart, mind, will, lust and all our affections and powers of the soul, and bringeth the Holy Ghost with her. Faith is a lively thing, valiant and strong, ever doing, ever fruitful so that it is unpossible that he which is endued therewith should not always work good works without ceasing.'[1]

'The Spirit which looseth the heart, giveth lust to the law, and certifieth us of the goodwill of God to us-ward.'[2]

'Faith bringeth pardon and forgiveness freely purchased by Christ's blood and bringeth also the spirit: the spirit looseth the bonds of the Devil and setteth us at liberty.'[3]

'The Spirit of God accompanieth faith and bringeth with her light, wherewith a man beholdeth himself in the law of God and seeth his miserable bondage and captivity and humbleth himself and abhorreth himself: she bringeth Gods promises of all good things in Christ...and as faith entereth and the word of God is believed, the power of God looseth the heart from the captivity and bondage under sin and knitteth and coupleth him to God and to the will of God: altereth him, changeth him clean, fashioneth and forgeth him anew: giveth him power to love and to do that which before was impossible,...for him either to love or to do and turneth him unto a new nature so that he loveth that which he before hated and hateth that which before he loved; and is clean altered and changed and contrary disposed and is knit and coupled fast to God's will and naturally bringeth forth good works.'[4]

'Deeds are the fruits of love, and love is the fruit of faith. Love and also the deeds are great or small according to the proportion of faith. Where faith is mighty and strong, there is love fervent and deeds plenteous, and done with exceeding

[1] Tyndale (Luther), *Prologue to Romans* (N.T.). Cambridge, 1938.
[2] Tyndale (Luther), *Wicked Mammon*, P.S. p. 52.
[3] Ibid. p. 48.   [4] Ibid. p. 54.

meekness: where faith is weak, there is love cold and the deeds few and seldom as flowers and blossoms in the winter.'[1]

'Faith only maketh a man safe, good and righteous and the friend of God, yea and the son and heir of God and of all his goodness and possesseth us with the Spirit of God.'[2]

'Sola Fide': 'Sed numquam est sola'

'Yet nevertheless, because by faith we know Gods mercy and grace promised by his word, (and that freely for Christs death and passion sake,) and believe the same, and being truly penitent, we by faith receive the same, and so excluding all glory from ourselves, we do by faith transcribe the whole glory of our justification to the merits of Christ only...therefore...it is said of faith in ancient writers, "we be justified only by faith" or "by faith alone" and in St Paul, "we be justified by faith freely without works".'[3]

'Yet that faith doth not exclude repentance, hope, love dread and the fear of God, to be joined with faith in every man that is justified, but it excludeth them from the office of justifying.'[4]

'And although it be necessary and requisite that in the justification of a sinner contrition be present, and that necessarily charity and a virtuous life must follow: yet doth the scripture attribute the only remission of sin unto the mercy of God, which is given only for the merits of Christ and received solely by faith. Paul doth not exclude those virtues to be present, but he excludeth the merits of those virtues and deriveth the cause of our acceptation into the grace of God only for Christ.'[5]

'And thus ye see, that these three [faith, hope and love] inseparable in this life, have yet separable and sundry offices and effects: as heat, and dryth, being inseparable in the fire

[1] Tyndale (Luther), *Wicked Mammon*, P.S. p. 57.　　[2] Ibid. p. 59.
[3] Cranmer, *Notes on Justification*, P.S. p. 210.
[4] Cranmer, *Homily of Salvation*, P.S. vol. ii, p. 129.
[5] Hooper, *Early Works*, P.S. p. 50.

have yet their separable operations. For the dryth only expelleth the moistness of all that is consumed in the fire: and heat only destroyeth the coldness. For dryth and cold may stand together: and so may heat and moistness. It is not all one to say the dryth alone and the dryth that is alone. Nor all one to say, faith only and faith that is alone.'[1]

'For I must believe the mercy, ere I can love the work. Now faith cometh not of our free will: but is the gift of God, given us by grace, ere there be any will in our hearts to do the law of God. And why God giveth it not every man, I can give no reckoning of his judgments. But well I wot, I never deserved it, nor prepared myself unto it: but ran another way clean contrary in my blindness and sought not that way; but he sought me and found me out, and showed it me, and therewith drew me to him. And I bow the knees of my heart to God night and day that he will show it all other men, and I suffer all that I can, to be a servant to open their eyes.'[2]

[1] Tyndale, *Expositions*, pp. 14–15.
[2] Tyndale, *Answer to More*, p. 192.

CHAPTER IX

THE PROTESTANT MARTYRS OF THE UNIVERSITY OF CAMBRIDGE, 1531–58[1]

IT is an ancient and honourable supplication of the Christian Church to pray that its members 'being hurt by no persecutions may evermore give thanks in Thy Holy Church', and in this prayer is the wisdom of long, deep and painful experience. Those who in our time speak smoothly of the benefits of persecution, of its power to stimulate flagging energies, and to weed the faint-hearted, would find little encouragement in the real story of the Church suffering here on earth. It is the fact that persecution has often been terribly successful. It is the fact, that even where it has failed, it has left its own peculiar legacy of spiritual diseases. How many ills of the fourth-century church are due, not to that much-abused conversion of Constantine, but to the tangled legacy of the preceding persecutions? Who, looking at French Protestantism with sympathy, cannot but feel that it has been cheated of its contribution to the religious life of Europe by the effect of the persecutions it has undergone? It is the fact that to live through a time of persecution—the Church under the Cross in modern Europe attests it beyond dispute—means to undergo strains and stresses which take grievous toll of spiritual and moral energies.

It would be an unreal picture of our period, therefore, which ignored the Protestant martyrs out of undue tenderness to the modern reaction against an Evangelical tradition which sicklied o'er the sturdy vigour of John Foxe with a gloss of sentimentalism. The great German Reformers died safely in their

[1] Much of this chapter was read as a paper to the Cambridge Antiquarian Society, March 1943.

beds, but nearly all the first makers of English Protestantism
suffered violent death. And for most of them this was the
climax of a life of enmity, uncertainty, peril, in which the
common joys of human life had at all times to be loosely held.
The authorities made no nice discrimination of station or
learning. The 'known men' and their successors, the book
agents, the merchants and tradesmen paid their toll. But there
is reason to single out the Cambridge men from among them.
Members of that University played a coherent part in the
making of the English Protestant tradition. At least twenty-
five of them were executed in as many years, all of some
standing, some of pre-eminent distinction. One may wonder
whether any other University in Europe could make this
contemporary claim.

The Reformation in Cambridge began with love of letters,
among a company devoted to the New Learning and whose
excitement at the new text established by Erasmus was the
ferment of the new reform. Its leading members included
some fine classical scholars, as well as notable musicians, two
eminent physicians and the 'father of English Botany'. But
it had a religious centre, that band of young men whose
activities remarkably anticipate that 'Holy Club' which pre-
ceded the Evangelical Revival in eighteenth-century Oxford.
Some of their friends and allies turned back to the old ways,
offended like Stephen Gardiner by the imagined improprieties
of the Continental doctrine, or like Nicholas Heath impressed
by the mediating theology of Pole and Contarini and Sadaleto.
Of those who stayed the course the majority died before
their due time. Master George Stafford, the pioneer of Reformation Biblical study, died of the pestilence caught while
on an errand of mercy. Clerk and Sumner, who performed
similar offices in divinity at Oxford, died in gaol. But our
concern here is with those who suffered execution at the hands
of the authorities.

The names of the twenty-five martyrs are these:

THOMAS BILNEY, *Fellow of Trinity Hall*
RICHARD BAYFIELD, *Corpus Christi College*
THOMAS DUSGATE, *Scholar of Christ's and Corpus Christi College*
WILLIAM ROYE, *of the University*
JOHN FRITH, *Eton? and King's?*
WILLIAM TYNDALE, *of the University?*
JOHN LAMBERT (*alias* NICHOLSON), *Fellow of Queens'*
ROBERT BARNES, *of the University*
THOMAS GARRARD or GARRETT, *of the University*
WILLIAM JEROME, *of the University?*
GEORGE WISHART, *Corpus Christi College*
JOHN ROGERS, *Pembroke*
LAURENCE SAUNDERS, *Eton and King's*
ROWLAND TAYLOR, *Principal, Borden's Hostel*
ROBERT FERRAR, *of the University*
JOHN HULLIER, *Eton and King's*
GEORGE MARSH, *of the University*
JOHN CARDMAKER, *of the University*
JOHN BRADFORD, *St Catherine Hall and Pembroke*
ROBERT GLOVER, *Eton and King's*
JOHN BLAND, *Eton and King's (? St John's)*
HUGH LATIMER, *Clare*
NICHOLAS RIDLEY, *Master of Pembroke*
THOMAS CRANMER, *Jesus*
RICHARD YEOMAN, *of the University* [1]

THOMAS BILNEY,[2] perhaps the leader of the Cambridge Reformers, was involved in their earliest troubles with the authorities in 1526 and was arraigned in the following year. He was persuaded by his friends to make a curiously guarded submission, but ended a period of inconsolable grief at this betrayal, as he conceived it to be, of the good cause, and he

---

[1] It will be seen that this is an approximate list. Two of them quite possibly belonged to Oxford, despite tradition. If the Thomas Heytton (*Grace Book*, Gamma, p. 168) of 1518–19 were to be identified with the priest Thomas Hytton, burned at Maidstone in 1530, Cambridge could claim the protomartyr of the English Reformation.

[2] Foxe, *A. & M.* vol. IV, pp. 619 ff. Cooper, *Ath. Cant.* p. 42.

finally suffered as a lapsed heretic at Norwich on 19 August 1531. Of his two friends, Robert Barnes postponed his death by a decade by escaping overseas, while the third, Hugh Latimer, no less zealous than Bilney, no more discreet than Barnes, stumbled upon a sovereign talisman, that royal favour which alone in the sixteenth century could cover a multitude of indiscretions.

The authorities could deal easily enough with single heretics. When THOMAS DUSGATE[1] went off to Germany to consult Luther, he returned a violent convert, and nailed theses on English church doors, but it was simple for the authorities to demonstrate the difference between Exeter Cathedral and the Schlosskirche of Wittenberg by burning him outside Exeter in 1531. It was another thing to combat a widespread organization, the ringleaders of which were either merchants of repute or scholars in exile in the Low Countries. Their Society of Christian Brethren was a forerunner of the Religious Book Club, but its activities were wider. It subsidized scholars, ordered the translation and arranged the printing, transportation and sale of forbidden books and employed agents in an adventurous traffic which passed to and from the Rhine and the ports of the Low Countries to the ports of London, Lynn and Bristol, and from there to the Universities and to certain large religious houses like Reading and Bury St Edmunds. Some of the book agents proved malleable enough when caught and some of Sir Thomas More's most triumphant invective is based on their confessions. RICHARD BAYFIELD[2] was made of sterner stuff, and since his conversion to the evangelical cause (Robert Barnes had rescued him from the gaol of the abbey at St Edmunds and sent him to Cambridge) had been one of the most active agents of the society. He was caught red-handed, condemned and degraded and burned at Smithfield in 1531.

[1] Cooper, p. 43.   [2] Ibid.

The headquarters of this contraband traffic may well have been at Antwerp, where Lambert and Rogers were chaplains of the English House in which also Tyndale resided. WILLIAM ROYE[1] made contact with the society, probably after his brief and unsatisfactory association with Tyndale in the production of the English New Testament. The evidence connecting him with Cambridge is slight, and it is only a bit of gossip from Sir Thomas More and Tyndale which attests his martyrdom in Portugal in 1531.

Of WILLIAM TYNDALE,[2] the 'captain of our English heretics' and 'warden of their guild', tardy recognition has been made in recent years. We who speak the tongue which Shakespeare spoke because Tyndale made the English New Testament, have given him his best memorial in that English Bible which incorporated his best work. Had his work been botched, how different might that vernacular Bible (and a good deal of English religion) have been! There is no evidence that he was at Cambridge comparable with the proof that he was at Oxford, and perhaps we need not grudge that University the full glory of its slender contribution to the flowering of the Reformation. The martyrdom of JOHN FRITH,[3] three years before his friend Tyndale was strangled outside Brussels, was in some ways the supreme tragedy of the first decade. He was the prodigy of the Reformers, who in his early twenties had got rather the better of Sir Thomas More in theological controversy, and had at any rate driven him to the desperate device of the argument by seniority, and a spate of references to 'this young man'. And at the end, he battled mightily in a debate on patristic authorities, showing himself better versed in the

[1] Cooper, p. 44. See also introduction to *Rede me and be not wroth* (ed. Arber, 1871).

[2] J. F. Mozley, *William Tyndale*. S.P.C.K. 1938. Tyndale died at Vilvorde, 6 October 1536.

[3] Cooper, p. 47. Foxe, *A. & M.* vol. v, pp. 1–16; vol. VIII, p. 695. *Works* (ed. Foxe, 1573).

Fathers than were the opposing bishops, and sowing seeds which bore later fruit in the mind of Thomas Cranmer who reluctantly let him be done to death.

The other martyrs of the Reign resemble Sir Walter Raleigh in ' 1066 and all that', who was executed, be it remembered, for 'being left over from the previous reign'. These died because they had been left over from their previous troubles. JOHN NICHOLSON or LAMBERT,[1] despite a defence prodigious in its learning and eloquence, was saved in 1533 only by the death of Archbishop Warham, and he was burned in 1538 for Sacramentarianism, after a trial in which Henry forced Cranmer and Barnes to share, and in which the King personally intervened, showing off his very lay theology in one of his most rampaging moods.

ROBERT BARNES,[2] THOMAS GARRARD or GARRETT,[3] and WILLIAM JEROME[4] were the Lenten preachers at Paul's Cross in 1540, but there was more to their deaths than the matter of their sermons, or the fact that they made an ambiguous and face-saving recantation. Barnes had been partly rehabilitated during the negotiations with the German Protestants, but he had been ominously ill-rewarded. He became entangled in a verbal brawl with Stephen Gardiner, which was followed by an even more calamitous interview with the King. Thomas Garrard had only escaped death by the clemency of Wolsey, for he had been the most active of the book agents who infested the new Cardinal College at Oxford. He, too, was a man with a 'past'. The antecedents of William Jerome are more mysterious, but he had been a Black monk at Canterbury, chaplain to the executed rebel, Sir Francis Bigod, and had close connection with Thomas Cromwell who resided in his

[1] Cooper, p. 67. Foxe, *A. & M.* vol. v, pp. 181–236.
[2] See above, p. 31. Also Cooper, p. 74. Foxe, *A. & M.* vol. v, pp. 414–38.
[3] See above, p. 20. Also Cooper, p. 75.
[4] Cooper, p. 76. Ellis, *Letters*, 3rd ser. vol. III, p. 258.

parish of Stepney. They were all condemned by Act of Attainder without trial or cause of death being shown. They were burned on 30 July 1540 in company with three papists 'pour encourager les autres'.[1]

The changed climate of 1553 must be our measure of the intervening years. The attempt to put the Lady Jane Grey on the throne of England was the desperate remedy of desperate men, and the people welcomed Mary as Harry's daughter, even when they might fear the loyal daughter of the Church. In 1553 probably most of her Protestant subjects agreed with Underhill of the Gentlemen Pensioners who, though a Protestant who merited his nickname of 'the hot gospeller', declared that 'he went not forth against her majesty…nor liked those doings'.[2]

Two leading Reformers were irretrievably compromised. Ridley had openly championed the Lady Jane, and it was unlikely that Mary had forgotten his attempt to convert her, or his melodramatic departure from her presence which, if it made his admiring chaplain's hair stand on end, only roused in her that temper which was the one legacy which Henry VIII bestowed on both his daughters. Everybody expected the speedy death of Cranmer and of Ridley, but the government was nervous.

When a dagger was flung at the Bishop of Bath during a sermon at Paul's Cross in August, the presence of the Lord Mayor did not quell the resulting uproar, which only subsided when the Reformers John Bradford and John Rogers intervened, between whom the frightened preacher scampered to safety. Later that day the government meditated extreme measures against the City, and Bradford rebuked the citizens

[1] The story of George Wishart (Cooper, p. 88) belongs to Scotland. He was burned at St Andrews, 1 March 1546, and his execution led directly to the murder of Cardinal Beaton. His even more famous disciple was John Knox.

[2] Nichols, *Narrative of the Reformation* (Camden Soc.), p. 142.

for their unruly and seditious behaviour. The government, thinking twice, arrested Bradford instead. In the next weeks a band of Reformers was arrested, all but two of them Cambridge men, leaders of the second generation of the Reform, knowledgeable about their Melanchthon and their Calvin. In the various prisons they contrived to maintain communication by means of smuggled letters or by such clandestine meetings as were connived or winked at by their keepers. 'I would gladly meet my good brother Bradford', wrote Laurence Saunders, 'about eleven o'clock, before that time I cannot start out, but then they will be at dinner.'

'Depend upon it, sir,' said Dr Johnson once, 'when a man knows he is going to be hanged to-morrow, it clears his mind wonderfully.' Perhaps for this reason there is a rare integrity about the last writings of this little band. JOHN ROGERS,[1] the first to adventure upon the fire, was the literary heir of Tyndale, and the compiler of Matthew's Bible. But at the last it was not his literary remains that concerned him so much as the wife with her eleven children who formed the tragic little retinue at the place of execution. LAURENCE SAUNDERS[2] was a scholar in Greek and Hebrew much esteemed by the Reformers, but he too was gravely concerned for the fate of wife and child. 'Wife, you shall do well not to come often to the grate where the porter shall see you. Put not yourself in danger.' 'Wife, I would you would send me my shirt, whereunto you know where it is consecrated: let it be sewed down on both sides and not open: God bless thee, good wife, and thy poor boy also.' DR ROWLAND TAYLOR,[3] that portly and distinguished lawyer and divine, was condemned, after a memorable brush

[1] Cooper, p. 121. Foxe, A. & M. vol. VI, p. 611, 'carried between 10 and 11 of the clock into Smithfield with a great company of the guard'. Machyn, Diary (Camden Soc.), p. 81.

[2] Cooper, p. 122. Foxe, A. & M. vol. VI, p. 628.

[3] Cooper, p. 123. Foxe, A. & M. vol. VI, p. 700. Stokes, Med. hostels in Cambridge (C.A.S. 1924).

with his judges, and sent back to die at Hadleigh: 'and coming within a mile or two, he leaped and fet a frisk or twain, as men commonly do in dancing: "Why master Doctor" quoth the Sheriff, "how do you now?" "Well, master sheriff, never better for now I am almost home. I lack not past two stiles to go over, and am even now at my Father's house."' A passage where fact surpasses even the last pages of Bunyan's *Pilgrim's Progress*.

ROBERT FERRAR,[1] Bishop of St David's, had been imprisoned under Northumberland as the result of a plot among enemies in his diocese, enemies who included George Constantine and Roger Barlow, under an extraordinary series of charges 'that he surveyed Milford Haven, where he espied a seal-fish tumbling and he crept to the water side, and continued there whistling it by the space of an hour'; and that 'he spoke in the pulpit to the reviving of strife between the Welsh and English and to revive the singing of old Welsh rhymes'. He was not butchered to make a Welsh Eisteddfod, but he had been Somerset's chaplain and a technical *praemunire* kept him in prison until he answered contrary charges under Mary. He was handed over to his old enemies and burned at Caermarthen in May 1555.

The deaths about this time of JOHN HULLIER and GEORGE MARSH[2] are witnesses that not only the English Bible but the English liturgy had its red baptism. Marsh, formerly the curate of Laurence Saunders, tells how in prison 'I every day did read Morning and Evening Prayer with the English litany' while a congregation joined in outside his prison walls. When books were thrown into the fire which burned John Hullier on Jesus Green, Cambridge, 'by chance a Communion Book fell into his hands, who seeing it, joyfully opened and read it until the force of the smoke and flame caused that he should see it no more'.

---

[1] Foxe, *A. & M.* vol. VII, p. 26.
[2] Ibid. vol. VII, p. 53; vol. VIII, p. 131.

The brief submission of JOHN CARDMARKER [1] is a reminder of the strain that was put upon these men and also of the efforts made by the authorities to secure their conversion. What JOHN BRADFORD [2] meant to the Reformers and their cause is best shown by the lengths to which his judges went to win him, and in an ascending series of visitors sent to him, friends, theologians, bishops, archbishops and finally two Spanish Friars whom the devout Mary ranked but little lower than the angels. His end came suddenly. 'The keeper's wife came up, seeming much troubled, almost windless and said "O Master Bradford, I come to bring you heavy tidings...to-morrow you must be burned and your chain is now a-buying and soon you must go to Newgate".' To Newgate he was hurried by night, and next day to Smithfield. [3] In that place, twenty years before, the death of John Frith had made a deep impression upon the beholders. There, now, by the Grace of God went John Bradford, Latimer's convert, Bucer's pupil, theologian, divine, preacher and a saint beside whose shining integrity even Sir Thomas More, in some lights, contrives to look a trifle shabby.

THOMAS CRANMER, HUGH LATIMER and NICHOLAS RIDLEY [4] were kept till last. No dramatist could have invented a better contrast than the pairing of Ridley and Latimer, who were tried and executed together. Latimer was an old, old man, racked by his chronic illnesses, memory failing and grown something querulous: 'My Lords, I beseech you set a better order here at your entrance: for I am an old man and have a very evil back.' He was long past disputation, but now and again there was a flash of his old wit, and once when the laugh

---

[1] Foxe, *A. & M.* vol. VII, p. 82.

[2] Ibid. p. 194. *Works* (ed. P.S.), 3 vols.

[3] 'By eight of the clock in the morning, with a great company of people.' Machyn, *Diary* (Camden Soc.), p. 91.

[4] See their *Works* (ed. P.S.), and Foxe, *A. & M.* vol. VIII, Index. Cooper, pp. 130, 135, 145.

went against him he hushed the great crowd in that grand manner which had made his the most famous tongue in England. 'Why masters,' he piped, 'this is no laughing matter. I answer upon life and death. You look for learning at my hands which have gone so long to the school of Oblivion, making the bare walls my library: keeping me so long in prison without book or pen or ink: and now you let me loose to come and answer to articles.' Ridley in the maturity of his intellectual vigour gave a magnificent display of cut and thrust in patristic and scriptural quotation: it was magnificent, but it was not war, and this tribunal had not come to argue, but as a court martial of the Church militant, to condemn. So they went out, in contrast, to the end. 'Ridley had a fair gown furred and faced with foins and a tippet of velvet, a velvet night-cap on his head and a corner cap of the same, going in slippers... after him came Master Latimer in a poor Bristol frieze frock, with his buttoned cap and a kerchief on his head and a new long shroud hanging over his hose and down to his feet.'

At the last it was his quavering resolute voice which spoke the immortal words which outpaced all his sermons. He was the last survivor of the old guard, and the old guard died but did not surrender. And perhaps Ridley needed the comfortable words, as the flames choked the finest mind of all the Reformers, for they badly bungled his fire and the description of his shrieking agonies is too horrible to have been invented. We do not read that anybody laughed who beheld that scene. Cheap jokes about it began with the Oxford Movement.

Cranmer had done so much towards the Reformation that we read his character in the manner that we read that story. His heart had been the home of many lost causes, who had dared to plead with Henry VIII for Cromwell and for Anne and Katherine Howard; but now he faced an implacable foe, the bitter woman whose blood was gall towards him. Those who have been deeply moved by the Trial Scene in Bernard

Shaw's *St Joan* should understand how an old man might
behave as she did, for something of her reasons and with the
same tragic end. The hand that signed the recantations went
first into the fire: it was the hand that shaped the English
liturgy, with all that 'matchless beauty of the shapèd syllable'
and as though that too must be saved so as by fire. The last
of the Cambridge Martyrs, who may have been an undergraduate when Latimer and Cranmer were in their cradles,
RICHARD YEOMAN,[1] had seen the break of the first dawn of the
Reformation, and lived until its first sunset, to make a good
end.

The martyrs came from various Colleges, and Eton and
King's can claim the largest number of them, though it would
be going a little far to suggest that this battle, too, was won
upon the playing fields of Eton. There are many glimpses of
their connection with their University. It was their love for
Trinity Hall that made Stephen Gardiner and Bishop Nixe
slacken the wheels of justice for Thomas Bilney. Thomas
Dusgate seems to have taken a new name, Bennet, out of
affection for Corpus Christi, Bene't's college. When JOHN
BLAND[2] was tried at Canterbury he found an old pupil,
Dr Faucet, among his judges: his own condemnation was
certain, but there was one devastating weapon left him and he
used it, 'I was once his tutor', Bland told the court, 'but I was
never able to do him any good.' ROBERT GLOVER[3] was asked,
as a layman, whether he was learned: 'I said I was but basely
learned', which all in all was a modest remark for a Master of
Arts and a Fellow of King's.

The earliest extant letter of Latimer is occupied with University business and he remained its constant friend. Ridley's
services to the University were still more eminent, not only as

[1] Cooper, p. 176.
[2] Foxe, *A. & M.* vol. VII, p. 301. Pote, *Reg. Eton*, p. 9.
[3] Foxe, *A. & M.* vol. VII, p. 394.

Master of Pembroke, but also when as Royal Visitor in 1547 he prevented the government project to amalgamate Trinity Hall with Clare and form one lawyers' college. It took some courage to quote Naboth's vineyard to a Tudor government and whatever the rights or wrongs of that case, we may be grateful that he stood his ground at a time when many other liberties of the University were in danger. His farewell is a famous and gracious tribute:

'Farewell Cambridge, my loving mother and tender nurse ...thou didst bestow upon me all thy school degrees: of the common offices, the chaplainship of the University, the office of the proctorship and of a common reader. And of thy private commodities and emoluments in colleges what was it thou madest me not partners of? First to be a scholar and then to be a fellow and again to a mastership of a right worshipful college.'

His farewell to that right worshipful college of Pembroke is still more celebrated. Cranmer seems chiefly to have remembered, in private duty bound, the college of Jesus of which he was twice made Fellow:

'I send you here a buck to be bestowed among your company among the college. And forasmuch as you have more store of money than I and also less need than I at this season, therefore I bequeath you a noble of your purse towards the baking and seasoning of him.'[1]

There were worse deaths than burning in an age which suffered many things from many physicians, and knew the dread meaning of 'sundry plagues and diverse kinds of death'. But this was bad enough, and sometimes horrible. Fires were often an unconscionable time a-kindling: the wood might be too green, or the wind contrary, or the bags of gunpowder which well-meaning friends tied round the prisoner's neck failed to take, or worse, half finished their work. There is more

---

[1] Cranmer, *Remains*, P.S. vol. II, p. 247.

than one reason for the fact that Foxe's 'Last words' of his
martyrs are stereotyped and patterned: it was no moment for
note taking or memorial. It was a cheap expedition. A com-
posite Bill from the three deaths at Oxford would read:

100 of wood faggots	6*s.* 0*d.*
100 and a half of furze faggots	3*s.* 4*d.*
A post	1*s.* 7*d.*
A chain	1*s.* 4*d.*
A staple	3*d.*
Two labourers	1*s.* 4*d.*

We have begged two fundamental questions in this account
of them, in assuming that they were Protestants and that they
were martyrs. The first, I think, is demonstrable. The second?
There is another reading of the story and if you take it you
will find little to interest and less to edify in the tale of the exit
from this transitory life of this miscellaneous collection of an
invalid, two schoolmasters, and a number of unfrocked clergy-
men of the Church of England. I do not think it will do. The
judges of these men admitted them to have more than the
savour of learning, and did not deny but tried to explain away
their godliness. Between them, these men and their friends
produced a Bible and a liturgy and confessions of faith which
have worn pretty well. One way and another they laid
quickening fingers on some of our most treasured liberties.

Yet to call them 'martyrs' involves more than the judgement
of historical criticism. Says Mr Eliot: 'a martyrdom is no
accident...a martyr is always made by the design of God for
his love of men, to warn them, and to lead them back to his
ways.'[1] Our men are not unworthy glosses on that text. For
in truth Foxe's *Book of Martyrs* is not accidental to English
Protestantism; it holds a unique place in the making of the
English Protestant tradition, one by which the memorial of
events became itself an event. Foxe's *Book* counted in English

[1] T. S. Eliot, *Murder in the Cathedral*, p. 49.

history as much as Drake's Drum. For the martyr is to the Protestant what the saint is to the Catholic, an example held up to the believers. But he is not so exampled as a pattern of human goodness, however supernaturally endowed that goodness be. He is first and last the 'martus', the witness whose significance points always beyond himself to a Divine Passion and Action. In that sense these men are Christian martyrs. Robert Glover, desperately ill, yet fearful lest he die before his execution; Laurence Saunders preparing a shroud as though he feared to be found at the last without his wedding garment; Nicholas Ridley at his last supper: 'To-morrow I must be married'; John Bradford bidding farewell to his University: 'Dear mother, receive the admonition of one of thy poor children now to be burned for the testimony of Jesus.' They are part of a pattern wider than Cambridge or the English Church, the pattern of the Roman catacomb and the African arena, the Norwegian prison and the German concentration camp, they witness that the true church is the Church under the Cross, by whose witness the Word goes free, conquering and to conquer:

'Of their seed springs that which forever renews the earth, Though it is forever denied.'

SELECT BIBLIOGRAPHY

ALCUIN CLUB. *The Rationale of Ceremonial* (ed. Cobb). 1910.

ALLEN, J. W. *Political Thought in the Sixteenth Century.* 1928.

ANDERSON. *Annals of the English Bible.*

ARBER. *English Reprints,* XLV, 1871. *Rede me and be not wroth.*

The First English N.T. 1870.

ARNOLD. *Customs of London.*

BASKERVILLE. *The English Monks and the Suppression of the Monasteries.* 1937.

See also in *Essays presented to R. L. Poole.*

BATLEY. *On a Reformer's Latin Bible.* 1940.

BARLOW, Sir M. *Barlow Family Records.*

BARLOW, ROGER. *A Brief Summe of Geographie* (ed. E. G. R. Taylor; Hakluyt Soc., 2nd ser., vol. LXIX).

BUGENHAGEN. *A Compendious Letter—to the faithful congregations in England.* 1536.

Briefwechsel (ed. Vogt).

BICKNELL. *The XXXIX Articles.*

BLUNT. *History of the Reformation.* 1896.

BRIGHTMAN. *The English Rite.* 1915.

BUCER. *Scripta Anglicana.* 1577.

BURNET, G. *History of the Reformation* (ed. Pocock). 1865.

Answer to Mr Varillas. 1686.

BURTON. *Three Primers.* 1834.

Archbishop Cranmer's Catechism. 1829.

CALVIN. *Works* (Calvin Trans. Soc.).

Institutes (tr. Norton, 1611).

CAMDEN SOC. *The Grey Friars Chronicle* (ed. Nichols). 1852.

Diary of Henry Machyn (ed. Nichols). 1848.

Narratives of the Reformation (ed. Nichols). 1859.

Troubles connected with the Prayerbook (ed. Pocock). 1884.

Wright. *Letters relative to the Suppression of the Monasteries.*

Wriothesley Chronicle (ed. Hamilton). 1875, 1877.

CARDWELL. *Documentary Annals,* vol. I. 1844.

The Reformatio Legum.

CARLYLE, A. J. and J. W. *Mediaeval Political Theory.*

CLARKE and HARRIS. *Liturgy and Worship.* 1932.

CLODE.	*Early History of the Merchant Taylors.*
Communion	*Order of* (ed. Wilson). Henry Bradshaw Soc. 1908.
COCHLAEUS, J.	*De Actis et Scriptis Martini Lutheri.* Paris, 1565.
CONSTANT, G.	*The Reformation in England*, vols. I and II.
	Le Schisme Anglican. 1930.
	La Réforme en Angleterre. 1939.
	See also *Rev. d'Hist. Eccl.* 1911.
COOPER, C. H.	*Athenae Cantabrigienses.* 1858.
	Annals of Cambridge. 1842.
CRANMER.	*Works* (ed. Strype, Jenkyns and Parker Soc.).
	Cranmer's Liturgical Projects (ed. Legg; H.B.S.). 1915.
DANIÉLS.	*Liturgica.*
DEANESLY.	*The Lollard Bible.* 1920.
DEMAUS, R.	*William Tyndale.*
DENIFLE.	*Luther und Luthertum.* 1904.
DENZINGER-BANNWART.	*Enchiridion Symbolorum.* 1928.
DIXON.	*History of the Church of England.* 1892.
DUGDALE.	*Monasticon.*
EELLS, H.	*Martin Bucer.*
ELLIS, H.	*Original Letters.*
ERASMUS.	*Epistolae* (ed. Allen).
	Erasmus and Luther. R. H. Murray.
FISH, S.	*Supplication of Beggars.* E.E.T.S.
FISHER, J.	*English Works.* E.E.T.S.
FOXE, E.	*De Vera Differentia.* London, 1534.
FOXE, J.	*Acts and Monuments.* 1684.
	Acts and Monuments (ed. Pratt). 1877.
	Works of Tyndale, Frith and Barnes. 1573.
FROUDE, J. A.	*The Reign of Henry VIII.*
FROUDE, H.	*Remains.* 1838.
FRY.	*Description of the first English N.T.*
FULLER.	*Church History* (ed. Nichols). 1868.
	History of Cambridge. 1840.
FURNIVALL.	*Political, Religious and Love Poems.* 1866.
GAIRDNER, J.	*Lollardy and the Reformation.* 1908.
	The English Church in the Sixteenth Century.
GARRETT, C. H.	*The Marian Exiles.* 1938.
	See also *C.Q.R.* 1944.
GASQUET and BISHOP.	*Edward VI and the Book of Common Prayer.* 1890.
GRISAR, H.	*Luther.* 1913.
GRUNDMANN.	*Religiöse Bewegungen im Mittelalter.* 1935.

212   BIBLIOGRAPHY

HAGENBACH.   *History of Doctrine.* 1847.
                       Leben u. ausgew. Schriften der deutschen Väter.
HALLE, E.   *Chronicle.*
HARDWICK.   *History of the XXXIX Articles.*
HEFNER, J.   *Entstehungsgeschichte des Trienter Rechtfertigungs-*
                          dekrets. 1909.
HENRY VIII.   *Assertio Septem Sacramentorum.*
HERFORD, C. H.   *Literary Relations between England and Germany in*
                          the Sixteenth Century. 1886.
HOLL, K.   *Gesammelte Aufsätze,* vol. II. *Luther.* 1927.
Homilies   *Book of.*
HUIZINGA.   *Erasmus.* 1928.
                       The Waning of the Middle Ages. 1924.
HOOKER, R.   *Learnèd Discourse of Justification.*

JACOBS, H. E.   *The Lutheran Movement in England.* 1890.
JANELLE, P.   *Angleterre catholique à la veille du schisme.*
                       Obedience in Church and State. 1930.
                       Rev. d'hist. et de phil. rel. 1928.
JOYE, G.   *An Apology made by George Joye.*
KIDD, B. J.   *Documents of the Continental Reformation.* 1911.

LAGARDE.   *Naissance de l'esprit laïque.*
LATIMER, H.   *Remains* (ed. P.S.).
                       Sermons. 1824.
LAURENCE.   *Bampton Lectures.* 1805.
LENZ.   *Briefwechsel. Phil. v. Hessen mit Bucer.* 1880.
LIETZMANN.   *Kleine Texte u. Studien.*
LOOFS.   *Leitfaden zum Dogmengeschichte.* 1906.
LLOYD.   *Formularies of Faith.* 1856.
LEVER, THOS.   *Sermons.*
LUTHER, M.   *Works* (W.E.).
                       Primary Works. ed. Wace and Bucheim.
                       Reformation Writings. Woolf.

MARITAIN, J.   *Three Reformers.* 1941.
MACKINNON, J.   *Luther and the Reformation in Germany.*
                       Calvin.
MARTYR, P. M.   *Loci Communes.* 1624.
                       Commentary on Romans.
                          Also art. by Benrath in *Schaff-Herzog Encyclo-*
                          paedia.
MAITLAND, S. R.   *Essays on the Reformation in England.* 1849.
MELANCHTHON, P.   *Works.* In C.R. Series.
MENTZ, G.   *Die Wittenberger Artickel.* 1905.
MESSENGER, E. C.   *Reformation Mass and Priesthood.* 1936.

MORE, THOS.	*Works* (ed. Rastell), 1557; (ed. Campbell).
	Life. R. W. Chambers.
MORRISON, S.	*English Prayer Books*. 1944.
MOZLEY, J. F.	*William Tyndale*. 1937.
	John Foxe and his Book. 1940.
MULLER, J. A.	*Stephen Gardiner and the Tudor Reaction*. 1926.
	Letters of Stephen Gardiner. 1933.
MULLINGER, J. B.	*History of the University of Cambridge*.
NEWCOURT.	*Repertorium*.
PARKER SOC.	Ed. of the works of the Reformers.
PECOCK, R.	*Repressor...of the clergy* (Rolls Series).
PICKTHORNE.	*Early Tudor Govt. Henry VIII*.
POLLARD, A. F.	*Cranmer*.
	Henry VIII.
	Wolsey, and *C.Mod.H*.
POLLARD, A. W.	*Records of the English Bible*. 1911.
POTE.	*Reg. Eton*.
PREVITÉ ORTON.	*The Defensor Pacis of Marsilius of Padua*. 1928.
PROCTOR and FRERE.	*Hist. of the Book of Common Prayer* (rev. ed.)
PRUSER, S.	*England und die Schmalkaldener*, 1535–40. 1929.
RANKE, V.	*Geschichte der Reformation*.
ROYE, W.	*Dialogue between Father and Son* (ed. Wolf). Vienna, 1874.
ROWSE, A. L.	*Tudor Cornwall*.
SCHAFF.	*Creeds of Christendom*.
SCHOLES, P.	*Puritanism and Music*.
SEEBOHM.	*The Oxford Reformers*.
SMITH, M.	*Pre-Reformation England*. 1938.
SMYTH, C. H.	*Abp. Cranmer and the Reformation*. 1926.
SOHM, R.	*Kirchenrecht Deutschlands* 1.
STAEHELIN, E.	*Oecolampadius*. 1939.
STOKES.	*The Augustinian Friary in Cambridge*. 1917.
	Mediaeval hostels in Cambridge. 1924.
STROHL, H.	*Substance de l'évangile selon Luther*.
	Epanouissement de la pensée de Luther. 1924.
	Rev. de l'hist. et de phil. rel. 1933.
STRYPE.	*Ecclesiastical Memorials*.
	Annals.
	Cranmer.
SUMMERS, W. H.	*The Lollards in the Chiltern Hills*. 1906.
SYKES, N.	*Crisis of the Reformation*. 1946.
SYMONDS, J. A.	*Renaissance in Italy*.

TAYLOR, V.   *Forgiveness and Reconciliation.*
TOMLINSON, J. T.   *The Prayer Book, Articles and Homilies* 1897.
TOUR, I. DE LA.   *Origines de la Réforme.*
TROELTSCH, E.   *Social Teaching of the Christian Churches* (Eng. ed.).
                      1931.
TYNDALE, W.   *Works* (ed. Parker Soc.).
                      Works. London, 1831.
                      Works (ed. Foxe). 1573.
                      New Testament (ed. Wallis). 1938.

VENN, J. A.   *Alumni Cantabrigienses.*

WESTCOTT, B. F.   *History of the English Bible.* 1905.
WHITNEY, J. P.   *History of the Reformation* (rev. ed.). 1940.
WILL, R.   *La Liberté Chrétienne.*
WILLIAMS, R. R.   *Religion and the Eng. Vernacular Lit.* 1940.
WILKINS.   *Concilia.*
WOLF, ADOLF.   *William Roye's Dialogue.* 1874.
WOOD, A. à.   *Athenae Oxonienses.*
                      Fasti.
WORKMAN, H. B.   *Dawn of the Reformation.*

INDEX